D0814028

ALL THIS AND MANY A DOG

Memoirs of a Loser / Pessimist

Also by Jim Godbolt

A History of Jazz in Britain 1919–50

A History of Jazz in Britain 1950–70

The World of Jazz in Printed Ephemera and Collectibles

ALL THIS AND MANY A DOG

Memoirs of a Loser / Pessimist

Jim Godbolt

Northway publications

Published by Northway Publications
39 Tytherton Road, London N19 4PZ, UK.
www.northwaybooks.com

The publishers acknowledge with thanks the permission of Quartet Books for the use of the original typesetting. Front cover photo (jitterbugging at the London Jazz Club in the 1940s) by Charles Hewitt, courtesy of Getty Images; photo on frontispiece (author on his balcony in the mid–1980s) by Caroline Jefford; image on page opposite (detail from drawing) by Stephen Nemethy; dog cartoon after index by Roger Cotterrell; cartoon on back cover (author reading meters) by Hedley Picton. The publishers also acknowledge with thanks the kind permission of copyright holders to reprint the photographs and drawings used in this book. Permissions have been sought in all cases where the identity and location of the copyright holders are known.

A CIP record for this book is available from the British Library.

First published 1986. This revised edition published 2007.

ISBN 978-0955090844

Printed and bound in Great Britain by Cromwell Press Ltd, Trowbridge, Wiltshire.

'Godbolt, thin and tense, his head with its pointed features crouching between his shoulders as though emerging from its burrow into a dangerous world, his eyes as cold and watchful as those of a pike in the reeds... Around this thin, heron-like figure a whole comic tradition of disaster has grown up.'

George Melly, *Owning Up*

For Joan

Contents

Preface

In 1972, after over twenty years in the jazz band agency business and in the latter part of the stint primarily booking rock groups, the volume of their music and their general behaviour (making jazz musicians seem almost saint-like in comparison) prompted me to quit the scene and become a writer. I was soon to discover that I was over-optimistic and in 1974, urgently needing regular work, I became a meter reader with the London Electricity Board calling on two hundred addresses a day.

I jotted down my experiences, many of an unpleasant variety encountering dogs. During the four years I was with the LEB my autobiography, *All This and 10%*, was published, but one volume didn't lead to a writing career. There were no invitations to literary lunches nor were publishers pleading with me for further manuscripts.

It was not until 1979 that I was able to escape the unwanted attentions of Rover, Prince, Rex and Popsie. At last I was making a living out of writing, editing *100 Club News* and *Jazz At Ronnie Scott's*, and then my *A History of Jazz in Britain 1919–50* and *1950–70* were published. The same publisher, Quartet, accepted my meter-reading recollections, but it was decided that these should be combined with *All This and 10%* under the title *All This and Many a Dog*.

Both *10%* and this book, its successor, now republished with revisions, are unique documents in that no one had previously, or since, published such memoirs. The uniqueness doesn't make this volume a literary masterpiece but, hopefully, there will be some amusement to be had from the tales I tell from both experiences.

My editor at Quartet, a very nice man, was Julian Bourne. There was much about his features that reminded me of someone I knew, but I couldn't place that person and it worried me until one day he revealed that he was a nephew of Humphrey Lyttelton. If ever the transmission of genes resulted in physical and facial likeness to immediate relatives, Julian is a classic example. I am very grateful to him for the difficult job he had in re-editing and relating the material from two books written at different times.

As in the 1986 edition of this book, I also wish to reiterate my thanks for their help and encouragement to Geoff and Joan Kemp, Campbell Burnap, George Melly, Gordon M. Williams and Wally Fawkes. Particular thanks are due to John Chilton for the initial suggestion that I write *All This and 10%* and for his assistance in its preparation. I also wish to thank Harold Pendleton of the Marquee Organization for allowing me to consult the files of *Jazz News*, and the then editor of *Melody Maker*, Ray Coleman, for the same facility with his paper.

Jim Godbolt
February 2007

PART ONE

1

That Noise Will Drive You Mad

I came into the entertainment business by accident, and stayed in it for twenty-five years, an outcome that was often stimulating, sometimes lucrative, frequently otherwise and constantly exasperating. It also had its very funny moments.

As a thirteen-year-old approaching school-leaving age at an elementary school in 1936, I had no notion whatsoever of what I was going to do to earn a living. I was totally devoid of ambition or sense of direction. I became an office boy in the City of London for fifteen shillings a week and remained in that position with minimal increases in 'salary' until I was eighteen and a half, when I applied for a labourer's job (the wages the inducement) at a local building firm erecting air-raid shelters.

A friendly site foreman looked glumly at my skinny arms and inquired where I had worked previously. He stared despairingly heavenwards when I told him, and gave me the job of time-keeper in the site hut. Booked as a labourer I got the worker's rate – five pounds weekly, then a very good wage. I was in on the beginning of the inflationary spiral. This lasted six months until, in December 1941, two months after my nineteenth birthday, I was conscripted into the Navy.

For the next five years I did nothing more enterprising than holystoning and swabbing the decks, painting ship, keeping look-out and – the most satisfying of my duties – steering. During my 'tricks' at the helm, and peering over the vast expanse of the Indian Ocean from the crow's nest, I pondered on how I, totally unskilled and poorly educated, was going to be employed after demobilization. These thoughts were particularly frequent as I came to the end of what for me was a relatively easy war spent aboard armed trawlers on convoy duty in the Atlantic and Indian Oceans, and based in South Africa with its benevolent climate and total absence of food rationing.

My war was more a 'sociological' than a military experience, despite some hair-raising incidents, like the night when HMT *St Zeno*, one of the ships I served aboard, attempted to ram a surfaced U-Boat which had sunk two freighters in our convoy. We dropped depth charges and picked up survivors. Sometimes I think I dreamt this particular experience, so remote does it seem now.

The Navy fed and clothed me and my pay was squandered in the bars of Cape Town, Port Elizabeth, East London and Durban. Had I suffered a tough war I suppose I would have been more eager to get out of uniform, but in these comparatively benign conditions I faced 'Civvy Street' with some apprehension. Service life had induced a euphoria wholly unrelated to the world 'outside'.

In the event I became manager of a jazz band, then a clerk with a firm of signwriters, then an agricultural labourer, then editor of a picture magazine. After that I was employed as a booker in an entertainment agency before going into business on my own account. Performing my mundane duties on HMT *Indian Star*, the ship I was aboard in the dog-days of my service, I had not envisaged any one of these jobs, and looking back on my convoluted life I see that the only calculated step I ever took was to become a writer, and for a long time precious little good that premeditation did me! But I was a very lucky young man to have become interested in a form of music, jazz, which was to enthrall me for the rest of my life, and to become involved in a business that was also my hobby, nothwithstanding the ups and downs of this association.

From about the mid-thirties, the history of jazz began to be thoroughly researched and interest in this previously abused and emasculated music came to be centred on its origins in New Orleans.

It was the new 'Jazz Age', the term having more significance then than when it was first coined in the twenties. Jazz flowered in that decade but the music associated with the 'Jazz Age' had the most tenuous connection with jazz. It was mostly corny dance music, highly arranged, jerkily syncopated and largely without improvisation.

The interest in New Orleans jazz owed much to the activities of record collectors mostly in England and France. In the thirties they met almost clandestinely in their 'dens' to play treasured records, often in the teeth of intense opposition from their family and friends, who had long been conditioned by the sweet music of the dance bands so much 'a rage' in the twenties and thirties. They thought ethnic jazz a strident, unmusical cacophony, only to be expected of the primitive negro.

By the mid-forties, particularly in England, many young record collectors had become musicians with a passionate and single-minded determination to play in the New Orleans idiom. Until then there had been several excellent British jazzmen, but their models were mostly the 'swing' soloists of the thirties, like clarinettist Benny Goodman and trumpeter Harry James. They played mostly in professional dance bands.

Those professionals were scornfully regarded by the New Orleans purists; in like fashion the purists condemned a potent new jazz development – bebop – a completely new manner of improvising that was challenging the old modes that were being so strenuously revived. Jazz in all its aspects had never enjoyed such public interest, never aroused such controversy before. This was the immediate background of my entry into the business.

The most significant, and for a time, the most famous of the English disciples of New Orleans jazz to play in that idiom were George Webb's Dixielanders. There were a few other bands of similar character active but none had the storming impact of the Webb band. They had the traditional instrumentation of trumpet, trombone, clarinet, drums, piano and banjo. Their repertoire was the tunes of the New Orleans pioneers, their style a combination of solo and collective improvisation in the fashion of their models.

Quite astonishing, then, was the *seeming* authenticity of their music. Of course, it wasn't authentic. This could only be said of the American original, but in those heady days of revivalism the Dixielanders had an authentic *quality*. They were utterly dedicated to absorbing the soul and essence of early jazz, notwithstanding their technical limitations. In our eager acceptance of their sturdy principles, we overlooked their faulty technique. Many regarded these deficiencies as virtues and some of us were given to such overblown phrases as 'contrapuntal interplay' when talking about collective improvisation.

The Webb band deliberately rejected the band uniforms worn by their dance band contemporaries. They had no music stands. They'd have been superfluous. Only one of them could read music.

Despite the emotional impact they made in this completely sincere attempt to absorb the musical language of another social culture of a time past, they were not entirely successful in their aims. They hadn't the musicianship of their inspirations, nor was their environment anything like the Afro-American culture that spawned jazz at the turn of the century.

George Webb's Dixielanders' real significance was in spearheading a movement that was to alter the pattern of the popular music industry in this country, notably during the fifties but with results still perceptible today in the bands of Acker Bilk, Kenny Ball, Chris Barber, Ken Colyer, Alan Elsdon, Monty Sunshine and many more.

The Dixielanders played every Monday evening in the garden basement of a pub called the Red Barn in Barnehurst, Kent, the headquarters of the Bexleyheath and District Rhythm Club founded during the war.

Barnehurst, a typical thirties subtopian development, was half-an-hour's train journey from Charing Cross, and the most unlikely Mecca for the spawning of revivalist jazz, but that basement was packed every week with enthusiastic upholders of the faith listening to this out-of-tune band playing blues, rags, stomps and marches. Rumbustious ensembles and soaring improvisations shook a suburban milieu so many thousands of miles away and so utterly different in character from Lulu White's Mahogany Hall and other New Orleans sporting houses where so much early jazz was played. The pilgrimage to these sessions had a romantic, almost evangelical fervour.

Local dance band musicians, themselves improvisers if the opportunity arose, were very critical. They complained about the old-fashioned conception, the poor intonation, the vocalized tones and some claimed that they, too, could play in that antiquated manner if they so wanted.

Generally, this wasn't true. With all their superior technique they hadn't the feel for the music the Dixielanders were playing.

At the same time there was a group of professional musicians, the Vic Lewis–Jack Parnell Jazzmen, playing in a similar style. They recorded for a major company, broadcast regularly and made a lot of public appearances, but, lacking the Webb band's patent dedication and conviction, they didn't impress, soon disbanded and the personnel returned to the palais' dance bands.

Another revivalist band of the time was led by trumpeter Freddy

Randall. The purists considered his band flashy and it played 'white' jazz in contrast to the Dixielanders' superior 'coloured' style. Randall's band came from Walthamstow, East London, and the Dixielanders from the opposite side of the river. The geographical distance was also an artistic and ideological gap. Dotty days . . .

The Dixielanders were formed in 1943. In 1945 chance nudged me into hearing them. During my naval service I had kept in touch with jazz collectors and writers I'd met before call-up. One of them, Max Jones, was then editing a private monthly magazine called *Jazz Music* (the organ of the Jazz Sociological Society of Great Britain!) and had recently joined the *Melody Maker* staff.

One leave I went to see Max with a story I had written about my discovering a veritable Aladdin's cave of rare 78 rpm records in a Cape Town hardware shop.

Jazz record collectors have long sought rare records in junk shops and this haul must rank as one of the greatest ever. They were almost all rarities on labels that had never been issued in England and were in mint condition. The labels alone sent my blood racing. Paramount, Cameo, Vocalion, Emerson, Harmony, Okeh, Banner, BlueBird, Victor . . . and the artistes . . . Blind Lemon Jefferson, Lil Armstrong, Dixie Syncopators, Louisiana Five, Clarence Williams, John Williams Synco Jazzers, Will Ezell, The Washingtonians, Blind Blake, Lonnie Johnson . . . it was like wandering into a jazz collector's Eden.

I bought about 150 at a shilling apiece and deviously wangled them past an obdurate Afrikaner customs officer in Cape Town harbour and stowed them aboard the *St Zeno* and later the *Indian Star*. Thanks to the devoted thoroughness with which I packed them, they eventually made the journey home in a troop ship without a single breakage. Nowadays the financial value of this incredible find would run into thousands of pounds, rare jazz records fetching as much as a hundred pounds each. That's a sobering thought for one who has sold virtually all this treasure haul to counter successive financial crises – one of the many actions I deeply regret.

After I had given this story to Max, he sadly told me he *had* to go and listen to some so-called 'New Orleans' band called George Webb's Dixielanders. We exchanged knowing looks but both of us were due for a shock. He at the Feldman Swing Club in Oxford Street and I, weeks later, at the Red Barn.

When I first heard the Dixielanders, I was utterly overwhelmed by their sound and what I thought it signified. It was like a divine revelation. I vaguely remember gushing my appreciation to George and he gave me a typically quizzical look. I was undoubtedly over-rapturous in my admiration, my rapture probably inflamed by several glasses of mild and bitter at one shilling a pint.

I was surprised to find that I knew the band's clarinettist, Wally Fawkes, and equally surprised to find he had become a musician. In 1940 Wally and I had been members of the 161 Rhythm Club, so-called because it was 160th in formation after the founding of the No 1 Rhythm Club in 1933, under the sponsorship of the *Melody Maker.* Jazz being synonymous with nameless depravity, I entered into this Bacchanalian abandonment of moral values every Monday evening at the Station Hotel, Sidcup, Kent, where the club – maximum attendance of nine – met and listened to records played on a portable turntable plugged into the electric light socket.

The club room, above the saloon bar, was rented to us for five shillings a session and the strains of hot jazz filtered through blacked-out windows to mingle with the more sinister noises of aeroplane drone, bombs falling and bursts of ack-ack fire. We drank very little but, when we did, mild and bitter was sevenpence a pint, Scotch eightpence a nip (old pence, of course).

Some of the pub's regulars, particularly the residents of 'old' Sidcup (the Victorian, as opposed to the newly developed 'subtopian' part), regarded the sounds from our gramophone with almost as much apprehension as the battle noises outside.

Our sessions were solemn affairs. Jazz was a serious matter that called for avid listening and profound comment. We would take it in turns to give 'recitals' followed by fierce and asinine debates, with me heavy on the asinine. No mock self-denigration here. It's an unfortunate characteristic of my middle-age that I am acutely embarrassed by crystal-clear recollections of my adolescent behaviour and attitudes.

During my term as 'timekeeper' on the building site the undreamed-of sum of £5 a week enabled me to venture from Swinging Sidcup to the dimmed lights of the West End to attend meetings of the No 1 Rhythm Club. I was star-struck at meeting famous jazz 'experts' whose names appeared in the feature pages and the correspondence columns in the *Melody Maker* each week. I dared not talk to musicians. That would have been too much of a presumption.

A great honour was accorded me by the club's secretary and founder, Bill Elliott, a most affable man. He asked me to act as one of the stewards at the first ever recorded 'Public Jam Session' to be held at EMI Studios in St John's Wood in November 1941. I was flattered beyond belief and lorded it over my fellow members of the 161 Rhythm Club, especially as the *Melody Maker* carried the story that the stewards had been chosen from various rhythm clubs. The 161 was mentioned but, to my intense disappointment, my name wasn't, though it was included in the programme notes. I was thrilled until I looked more closely and noticed that I was given as Jimmie Codbolt. Still, I thought, those present would know who I was. Hadn't my name appeared as secretary of the 161 Club in our weekly notice in the *Melody Maker*? And what of the 'controversial' article called 'Jazz Jeremiahs' in which I roundly attacked those who asserted that jazz was dead, in the *Melody Maker* of June that year? (It was now November but surely they would remember?)

The *Melody Maker* did not acknowledge receipt of this article but more important, printed it. As usual I bought the paper one Friday morning on my way to work and was thrilled to see my first ever article in print. I read it and re-read it on the No 44 tram to Southwark Bridge, fourpence return, workman's ticket.

The *Melody Maker* in those days was totally different from what it is now. It was primarily the journal of the dance band musician but jazz was given good coverage. Its phraseology, now quaintly archaic, included references to 'Ace Saxophonist' Art Christmas, 'Keyboard Wizard' (or 'Ivory Tickler') Gerry Moore, 'Nimble-fingered Claryist' Nat Temple and 'Swing Canary' vocalist Gwen Jones. They were fond of the headline, 'Bombshell Hits The Profession', alluding to nothing more explosive than, say, violinist and orchestra leader Sydney Simone, not exactly a household name, leaving a West End restaurant after a long residency. The paper cost tuppence and although reduced in size because of paper rationing, it proudly carried on as 'spokesman for the profession' and was up in arms over slurs in the national press that dance band musicians were evading call-up.

One night there was a flutter of excitement at the 161 Rhythm Club. A local palais bandleader dropped in, accompanied by a girl. She looked glamorous, as befitted a bandleader's lady. She sat in a corner, bored and aloof. A record, 'Shim-Me-Sha-Wobble' by a band called Miff Mole and His Molers was played and during an agitated solo by clarinettist Frank Teschemacher she emitted a shriek of horror and fled the room. Teschemacher's playing was indeed shrill and dissonant, but this wasn't the reason for her screaming departure. She had idly looked up to see a large spider crawling down the wall. As secretary of the club I bought her a glass of port to steady her nerves when she returned, weepily, to the club room. I charged the cost, fivepence, to club expenses.

Wally Fawkes and I lived in the subtopian part of Sidcup, and walked home together. He was a quiet young man and I, a very garrulous young man, did all the talking. If an air raid was in progress, we would back against the nearest wall, but only when injury seemed imminent did we raise our precious discs of shellac above our heads as protection from shrapnel hissing down from the skies. When I got home I'd maybe play a record I had borrowed that night, or a 'find' discovered in a pile of 78s in a junk shop and purchased for a few coppers. My father loathed jazz and his features would contort with pain as it assailed his ears. He warned me, 'That noise will drive you mad.' He couldn't understand my liking for something that 'hadn't got a tune to it'.

In the last days of my naval service, I artfully contrived to get myself on a gunnery course at Whale Island, Portsmouth, and constantly travelled up to London to listen to the Dixielanders, even at rehearsals. I didn't learn a thing about gunnery. My thoughts were on getting up to Barnehurst to hear the band that, to me, was Messianic in its propagation of the gospel of New Orleans jazz.

Shortly after demobilization I became the Dixielanders' manager. Correction – George Webb jibbed at the term 'manager': I became the band's general factotum, for three pounds a week, with the title of 'secretary'. I was also the whipping boy for two members of the band.

I mention this animosity as my first experience of the attitude of many musicians towards non-playing functionaries. The banjo player, Buddy Vallis, had a particularly long nose for my faults, but was extremely obsequious to George. He wore a perpetual smile (except when addressing me) to display overtly a fine set of teeth (which he managed to expose even when smoking a pipe), making me forever wary of individuals with a constant beam.

George was a chirpy, forceful character and quite ferocious when aroused. He had considerable strength of character, and kept the band together for five years. He received very little financial reward for his pioneering endeavours and many who made large sums out of the trad jazz boom of the fifties owe much to his push and determination in the trail-blazing forties.

It was very difficult to obtain engagements for the band. Concert and dance promoters were wary of a band so uncompromising. 'Jazz and Only Jazz' was their slogan and they meant it. Some promoters realized their intransigence only when their customers demanded 'something they could dance to'. They didn't repeat the booking. It was a standing joke in the band that they had played every hall in the area – once.

But they did play monthly concerts at the Congregationalist Memorial Hall in Farringdon Street, near St Paul's. It was a cold and forbidding barn of a place, not really suitable as a jazz venue. The concerts were sponsored by *Challenge*, the organ of the Young Communist League who backed jazz as a proletarian art form and presented it as the language of the oppressed.

This party line had little relevance to the young men from London's suburbia, but the YCL were indeed good friends of the band. Their concerts gave them badly needed exposure in Central London. The programme comprised a recital of jazz records by a well-known critic, followed by the band's session. Busts of grim-visaged Congregationalist notables long dead looked from high-arched windows on a spectacle their models would surely have abhorred, but in the late forties the music from these scruffily dressed individuals on the stage had an appeal pertinent to the time. Many, not particularly interested in jazz or its ideologies, found the music a happy noise in the grey post-war era of food rationing and general shortage.

The Dixielanders held their first rehearsals in the drawing-room of the Webbs' home in Bexleyheath, near Barnehurst, much to the chagrin of George Webb Senior who described the noise as 'filthy jizz' – among stronger epithets. George's mother, a lady of exceptional grace and dignity, took the events in her stride and supplied refreshments for the young revolutionaries. Sadie Webb, possessing a rare warmth and generosity of spirit, was one of the most ladylike women I have ever met. I stayed with the Webbs for a while and she was like a mother to me.

Most of the band worked in the Vickers Armstrong factory in nearby Crayford but Wally Fawkes, who initially tuned his clarinet by dropping pieces of string into the mouthpiece, was drawing 'column-breakers' for the *Daily Mail* under the pseudonym of 'Trog'.

First jokily billed as Spider Webb and his Cobs, the band made their debut at the Red Barn. They soon became the resident band, adding another trumpet and, later, a sousaphone.

Youthfully enthusiastic, they played on buses and trains on the way to engagements, delighting in the astonished reaction. I travelled with the band to Derby where they made records for 'Jazz', Britain's first independent record label, run by James Asman and Bill 'Fu' Kinnell. In the scramble for seats in an overcrowded train, the band piled into a first-class carriage and were soon playing. The bell of Eddie Harvey's trombone was within inches of a full colonel seated, ramrod fashion, in a reserved corner seat. The colonel took this unexpected entertainment stoically, didn't say a word or raise an eyebrow, but alighted at the next stop obviously to find another seat, it being certain he was no jazz fan. The ticket collector, overwhelmed by the novelty – especially the sousaphone – forgot to make the excess charge.

At the recording session I held Roy Wykes' bass drum to prevent it from 'creeping' and gave an enthusiastic yell at the end of the recording. Kinnell severely admonished me and George gave me one of his crushing scowls. My exultant cry was cut.

The band played an engagement at a local town hall, sharing the bill with a local dance-cum-swing band dressed in formal wear known as monkey-suits. The Dixielanders were dressed in whatever had taken their fancy and some of them didn't have much of a wardrobe to choose from. George Webb had taken off his jacket, displaying his braces.

During a lively stomp from the Dixielanders one of the dance band waggled a glove puppet from behind the back-drop curtain. Only George, playing piano side-on, noticed this. A small stocky man, with little fear in his make-up and not one to argue the rights and wrongs of a matter where more direct methods would suffice, he arose from the piano stool, strode over and landed a hefty blow on the outline of the puppet-waggler while the band played on. The puppet disappeared from sight and the curtain puckered wildly as the joker grabbed it to save himself from falling. George returned to the piano stool and recommenced playing. The mocker had acted unprofessionally and was summarily punished. George's words on the matter, growled in a strong cockney accent, were brief. ' 'E was a bleedin' liberty-taker, won'e?'

Apart from the ebullient George there were other rare characters in the band. Owen Bryce, second trumpet and founder member, was a strict vegetarian who walked sockless ou -of-doors in the coldest of weather. He wore a pair of brown corduroy trousers that came almost up to his nipples. He had a large upturned nose and was dubbed, among other things, Cyrano. He came in for a lot of ribbing. It bounced off him. His ego, largely deprived of praise, fed on antipathy. He had a fine conceit of himself and was severely astringent in his criticism of others. He made few exceptions in this blanket criticism of the human race. It was he who stood alone.

He worked extremely hard to make his record and radio shop a deserved success and although an avowed socialist, he sanctimoniously preached honest endeavour and self-reliance with the fervour of a Samuel Smiles. Owen was a very Smilesian man. He had a withering contempt for our 'incorrect' diet and a missionary zeal to convert us all to vegetarianism. Every morning, winter and summer, he would go for a swim in the local baths, emerge, have a hot shower and plunge straight back into the pool. The band vehemently refused his insistent invitations to join him in this health-giving exercise, nor were they enthusiastic about the nut cutlets, raw vegetables and dandelion coffee so much a part of his diet. They were in stupefied awe when he fasted for up to three days. Like most fervent missionaries, his terminology rationalized his beliefs. If I had a boil on my neck, I was eating the wrong foods. If he had a boil on his neck, it was the poisons coming out thanks to a correct diet. Against such sophistry it was hard to win.

I admired and liked Owen and was considerably influenced by him. Despite his massive egotism he was a staunch, honest individual, although my faith in his vegetarianism was considerably strained when he became a pig breeder.

Despite occasional upsets I got on well with trombonist Eddie Harvey. He developed tastes and aspirations outside the limited style of the Dixielanders. He played in local dance bands to gain experience and this shocking, almost traitorous deviationism showed in his playing. A meeting, ostensibly to discuss band matters, was called, but it was really an inquisitorial council to pass judgement on Eddie for straying from the paths of righteousness. Such was the parochial rigidity of our thinking in those days, we demanded that this nefarious practice of playing with dance bands cease forthwith.

Eddie was shortly to be called up and was replaced by Harry

Brown, whose style was more in keeping with the band's funda-
mentalist policy. He, too, soon received his calling-up papers. In
both cases I engaged in lengthy correspondence with the Ministry of
Labour, pleading that they were highly specialized musicians and
quite irreplaceable. The authorities were oddly unimpressed.

Wally Fawkes was the star of the band. His warm tone and free
flowing line inspired by the great New Orleans clarinettists earned
much praise. Tall, lantern-jawed and laconic, he was considerably
more sophisticated than the rest of us. Working for a national
newspaper and much admired for his clarinet playing, his personality
had matured considerably from the time I had known him as the
quiet sixteen-year-old at the 161 Rhythm Club. Success had given
him a relaxed confidence. He had the air of a young man who knew
he was going to make his mark in life.

After disagreements with the Young Communist League, we
started promoting our own concerts once a month under the name of
the Hot Club of London, first at the Victoria Hall, Bloomsbury, and
later at King George's Hall, headquarters of the YMCA in Great
Russell Street.

Both had proper stage amenities and if I deserve praise for
anything during my stint as the band's factotum it was for finding
these venues in war-damaged London and talking the managers into
letting us use them. I had to be wary of mentioning jazz. It was still a
dirty word, partly due to Fleet Street's unremitting misreporting of
jazz events and jazz people. I claimed we were a music club and was
careful not to say what sort of music.

George Webb Snr, now using slightly less scurrilous epithets to
describe 'filthy jizz', used to drive us and our equipment to and from
King George's Hall in an ancient Ford. One night as we stopped at a
traffic light not far from the West End, a long, low, glistening coupé
drew up alongside. At the wheel was Noël Coward, presumably on
his way to his country house at Godstone after finishing a show.
Elegant young men with fluffy poodles on their knees lounged in the
passenger seats. Webb Snr, a barrel-chested man with strong,
gnarled features, put his head out of the window, slapped the side of
his battered vehicle and addressed Coward in a rich cockney accent,
'Swop yer?' Coward roared with laughter. It was an unexpected and
highly comic confrontation between two entirely different people –
from every possible point of view – and the cameo is etched in my
memory.

George Webb with his Dixielanders and singer Beryl Bryden, c.1946, in the garden of the Red Barn at Barnehurst, Kent. *Left to right*: pianist and leader Webb, trumpeter Owen Bryce, drummer Roy Wykes, trombonist Eddie Harvey, banjoist Buddy Vallis, clarinettist Wally Fawkes, Bryden, the author (manager of the Dixielanders), trumpeter Reg Rigden. (Courtesy Beryl Bryden)

The young Humphrey Lyttelton at the Red Barn, Barnehurst, 1947.

Humphrey Lyttelton's band. *Left to right*: John Picard, Bruce Turner, Johnny Parker (foreground), Eddie Taylor, Jim Bray, Lyttelton. From the concert programme for *Jazz Saturday*, presented by BBC Radio at the Royal Albert Hall, February 1957.

In January 1947 we heard of a trumpeter of exceptional ability playing every Sunday at a pub called the Orange Tree at Friern Barnet, North London. It was reported, almost in hushed tones, that this trumpeter, Humphrey Lyttelton, was an Old Etonian and ex-Brigade of Guards Officer, an unlikely and hardly credible combination of parts. All spoke very highly of his playing and George despatched me to the Orange Tree one Sunday morning to book Lyttelton for a guest spot at the Hot Club, but he wasn't playing the morning I arrived.

A journalist we knew claimed a close acquaintance with Lyttelton (considering our subsequent knowledge of Lyttelton this was as false a claim as was ever made) and guaranteed his appearance at the Hot Club. We assembled a band to play with him and Humph, a tall, stooping figure with heavy lips and hooded eyes and wearing a dyed battle-dress, made his first concert appearance in London at King George's Hall on 18 January 1947. On arrival he swore that his first knowledge of the engagement was from reading a fly-poster. He added that his name had been misspelt.

His session was wild and unco-ordinated. It had some of the extreme purists in a rage. Wasn't this the jam session free-for-all the Dixielanders and Hot Club opposed? But Lyttelton stood out as a player with a conception and ability no other British jazz trumpeter had displayed. He was a sensation.

He played an engagement with the Dixielanders at Hawick, in the Scottish lowlands. It was a mystery that the band should have been engaged to play in a place so far remote from any jazz activity, especially as we quoted £75, no small sum for an unknown band in those days. Reg Rigden, the Dixielanders' first trumpet, was unable to take time off from work and again George sent me to seek out Lyttelton. I went to the Camberwell School of Art where he was studying, waited for him to come out of class and asked him to play the engagement. He didn't appear surprised that it was 332 miles from London, nor did we engage in any ungentlemanly haggling about fees, although I vaguely recall that the princely sum of £7 was agreed on.

Rigden subsequently announced that he was available, but George directed that the Lyttelton booking should stand. This led to Lyttelton joining the band and Rigden – we had not got on well – accused me of conspiring to row him out. It was an absurd accusation – George would never have tolerated any interference in the band's affairs.

Humph rehearsed with the band the Sunday morning following our meeting. It was painfully cold. We were in that long, bitter winter of 1946-7 when the fuel crisis was at its worst. My contribution to jazz history that morning was to gather twigs and leaves from the garden to make some sort of fire.

The journey to Hawick was in the aftermath of a snowstorm and took about fourteen hours. On arrival Wally found he had left his clarinet on the train and I spent a couple of sweaty hours tracking it down. It was returned to Hawick and I rushed into the dressing-room five minutes before the show was due to begin dramatically brandishing the clarinet. Attendance was sparse. The locals were disappointed although not particularly on musical grounds. One gentleman was quite huffy. 'We thought you were going to be darkies,' he said with a strong Scottish burr, and that possibly explained how the band had obtained the engagement.

Lyttelton was not only a marvellous trumpeter but an excellent clarinettist. He was a musical 'natural' who also had a commanding personality and a sharp wit. The appearance of this physically and musically towering figure from an aristocratic background in a fundamentally proletarian stir of activity received considerable publicity. Why not? Neither Humph nor George sought this kind of attention, but in a class-divided society such interest was inevitable and the publicity it received welcome. It gave the central figure a certain wry amusement. It was a unique situation. Old Etonian ex-Guards Officers blowing hot jazz trumpet were not thick on the ground and this one understandably enjoyed being pursued by a wondrous press. It's certain that there would have been a 'revival' in Britain without Webb or Lyttelton, but this strange flowering of an alien culture in a drear-dull London suburb, led by an upper-crust gent and a band of factory workers, spearheaded a movement that spread throughout the country with quite sensational results.

Lyttelton left to form his own band in November 1947. Somewhat peremptorily, he addressed me at the Red Barn one Monday evening: 'This is my swan song, Jim.' I had already received some intimation of this and tried not to show my concern. Shortly afterwards Wally Fawkes and trombonist Harry Brown joined Lyttelton. The Dixielanders broke up.

This had been my first taste of the entertainment business. I felt a certain pride in having played a small part in a unique crusade, despite the occasional unpleasantness with my adversaries, and despite the fact that our musical hopes were never fully realized. In those heady days some of us imagined that British jazz, after clearing the first hurdles of apprenticeship, would run in harness with the American original and fuse with its history and romance. Considering the social, racial and musical factors it's no surprise that these aspirations were never fulfilled. They were no more than the illusions of ardent young romantics. Truthfully, I can claim that I wasn't concerned with financial gain. It just didn't occur to me. Had it done, I might have had my eyes open for the prospects that lay around the corner.

I got a job with a local signwriting firm, first selling signs to local shopkeepers and subsequently organizing the various departments. I was the one unskilled employee among a dozen or so craftsmen and critically regarded as the guv'nor's man. Not liking this invidious position I left to go and work on the land.

2

A Fateful Step

In November 1949 I returned from my agricultural labours and moved into a bedsitter in Gloucester Place, off Baker Street, sharing with Ian and Keith Christie. Clarinettist Ian was short, hunched and waspish; trombonist Keith taller, gangly, indolent. Both were natural musicians: although only in their teens, they were playing in Lyttelton's band. They were from Blackpool and I first met them when they 'sat-in' with the Dixielanders. Would jazz historians, I wondered, mention this significant co-habitation – the influence I had on them, etc. etc. – along with my steadying Roy Wykes' bass drum in that historic first private label recording with the Dixielanders at Derby, my stoking the fire at Lyttelton's first rehearsal with the band at the Red Barn, and my rushing into the dressing-room at Hawick with Wally Fawkes' clarinet when all seemed lost?

Such stories would surely rank with the anecdote about American bandleader Eddie Condon's brother Pat leaving a rehearsal to buy some whisky and reappearing some fifteen years later, and the many recollections of American jazz musicians who roomed with the legendary cornettist Bix Beiderbecke and shared his socks. Not that I shared Keith Christie's socks. These were indisputably his. Stiff with malodorous perspiration (he was in the RAF at the time and doing a lot of square-bashing), they were propped up at the end of his bed when he retired.

It was a small room and had only two beds. I contributed a third – a collapsible camp bed. Keith, pathologically lazy, could never muster the strength or will to circumvent or step over it. If it was in his path, he trod on it and it soon disintegrated. Our rota of two weeks in proper beds and one in the camp bed also collapsed and we moved into a larger room on the ground floor.

Keith resolutely kept expenditure of energy to the barest minimum. If Ian left a wet towel on the back of the only armchair Keith would sit in the chair in an acutely uncomfortable position so as not to rest his back on the towel. Removing it to its proper place would have been an unthinkably tiring exercise. Both frequently used the sink as a lavatory bowl and on one occasion this imparted a particular tang to a lettuce I had left soaking.

In the next room lived guitarist Nevil Skrimshire, also with Lyttelton, and saxophonist Bruce Turner, playing with Freddy Randall's band. The latter, always raffishly attired in a silk dressing-gown, had assignations with a variety of ladies that often resulted in harsh words, for which we avidly listened.

The rest of the occupants loathed us, and we fought a running battle with a haughty female on the first floor who abhorred jazz and claimed she was a classical impresario, her business apparently conducted from the coin-box telephone in the hallway just outside of our room.

We had an archetypal Irish landlady, Mrs Mitchell, who frequently castigated us. Rightly so, for we used to play records at full volume well after the permitted hour and were often noisily drunk, but she was a good-hearted lady and her outbursts of fury would dissolve into throaty chuckles.

Exasperated by the Christies' incredible untidiness and the sock-befouled atmosphere, I jumped at the chance of occupying a small room that had become vacant at the end of the hall. When Mrs Mitchell was doing her chores and muttering critically about 'them Christies', I would wholeheartedly agree with her. 'A dreadful pair, Mrs Mitchell,' I would say and if I played records late at night I blamed it on Keith or Ian. But my assiduous cultivation of the landlady's goodwill was shattered one embarrassing morning.

All the 'guests' were supposed to leave by eleven o'clock at night, a regulation consistently if surreptitiously ignored. I was in bed with my girlfriend and had left the door unlocked. Hearing the latch turn I leapt up to push the door back. By the time I had sprung to the bottom of the bed, Mrs Mitchell had opened the door and stood transfixed at the spectacle of me naked and erect, in both senses, in a stance not unlike that of Eros but without the bow and wings and with an expression more strained than seraphic.

Shortly after I returned to London I became, by freakish chance, editor of a jazz magazine. Bert and Stan Wilcox owned a radio and television shop in St John's Wood High Street and also ran the London Jazz Club, first at Mac's Rehearsal Rooms and then at 100 Oxford Street. I earned myself a few pounds packing 78 rpm records into parcels for customers on their mailing list. The brothers had also started publishing *Jazz Illustrated*, although they knew nothing about magazine production or journalism, an amateurism consistent with jazz magazine publication in those days.

I also knew nothing about the mechanics of producing a magazine, but under the pseudonym of 'Odbot' I had contributed a few articles to the Wilcoxes' weekly *Puffo*, a duplicated news-sheet with some gossip and a 'humorous' feature. My payment was free admission to the London Jazz Club. On the strength of this somewhat tenuous link with journalism I was handed the job of editor of *Jazz Illustrated* at eight pounds a week, two pounds or so above the average national wage.

Jazz Illustrated was a lush publication compared with most of the home-produced jazz magazines of the period, although I produced my first issue from a corner of a small desk in the tiny packing room of the Wilcoxes' shop, standing up. There was no room for an editor's desk and chair.

The magazine defied a few conventions primarily because its editor was ignorant of them. Mistakes, I'm sorry to say, were thick between the covers. In one issue I apologized for this and claimed that 'we' had been through the current issue with a fine toothcomb to eliminate every mistake. I jocularly invited pedants to get cracking and prove me wrong. A super-pedant obliged. He sent me a detailed list of mistakes divided into six columns: for the page, the column, the paragraph, the line, the error and the correction. Fifty-two in all: split infinitives, misspellings, typographical inconsistencies, omitted hyphens, inversions and many more in a shattering compilation. I checked to see if he was right. Not quite: there were two blunders he had overlooked. I wrote thanking him for his scrutiny and congratulating him on his scholarship but, apropos the errors he had missed, I suggested he be more careful next time. It was a feeble riposte and there was no next time. The paper had lasted for eight issues, five of them under my editorship.

While preparing this book I braced myself to look through some copies of *Jazz Illustrated*. I shuddered a bit, but withal, it was not too bad an attempt at something new in jazz journalism, and

Humphrey Lyttelton's cartoons of famous jazzmen are gems.

The Wilcoxes had also started a band agency, run by Les Perrin. Perrin had a mass of exploding ideas and was constantly flying off at different tangents, sometimes, it seemed, simultaneously. He also handled publicity for the Wilcoxes' artistes and promotions. After the collapse of *Jazz Illustrated* the Wilcoxes decided that Perrin's mercurial temperament was better suited to publicity than the slog of getting work for bands. This chore was passed on to me.

I cannot recall one single scrap of conversation which led to this fateful step. Why I do not know; I have acutely detailed recollections going back to my childhood. In the light of some of my experiences as an agent/booker, I sometimes suspect that the memory blank is Freudian. Nor can I recall how much I was paid. I think it was the same salary as I received during my short-lived grandeur as editor of a glossy magazine. I was soon to discover that there was no grandeur in being an agent.

Up to the time I became one I had only a vague idea of how an agent functioned and this was culled from pre-war British films seen from the ninepenny seats of the local Odeon. These films featured stars from a then thriving variety business and the stories were based on real-life situations. The agent was portrayed as a somewhat excitable character, perhaps rather shady, always corpulent, often Jewish, and the casting couch was conveniently situated near his enormous desk.

This rather unsavoury image of a hustling, cigar-smoking middle man exploiting honest troupers continued after the war when the music halls went into unhappy decline, and jazz bands became the troupers, touring clubs and palais up and down the country.

My first booking responsibilities were two 'modern' jazz bands – the Johnny Dankworth Seven and Kenny Graham's Afro-Cubists, the leaders both brilliant arrangers and fine musicians, Johnny on clarinet and alto saxophone and Kenny on tenor saxophone. Their music was inspired by the then new bebop school of American jazzmen, trumpeter Dizzy Gillespie, alto saxophonist Charlie Parker and pianist Thelonious Monk. Both bands had only a limited appeal, and the struggle to find them work quickly gave me an insight into the mechanics and harsh realities of band-booking. It is, in any case, a job that can only be picked up by day-to-day experience.

Graham's band was particularly difficult to sell. Kenny would put his head round my office door (the Wilcoxes had moved to Earlham Street, off Cambridge Circus) and dolefully enquire if there was any work. Les Perrin (who has since become the most famous and respected of PROs, with a dazzling list of famous clients) worked hard on publicity ('Don't Be A Square, Be An Afro-Cubist') but I quickly discovered that publicity alone never sold bands.

Dankworth's band was easier to book. It had a more 'commercial' sound and Johnny had been top of the *Melody Maker* polls as arranger, alto saxophonist and musician of 1950. Kenny, a gruff, genuine person, was slightly resentful that he wasn't getting as much work as Johnny and thought favouritism the reason. This wasn't the case. An agent/booker would sooner earn commission from two bands than from just one, let alone saving himself the embarrassment of facing the workless bandleader day by day.

Kenny's band was musically excellent but its lack of drawing power taught me that the public are not wholly interested in good musicianship. The rapport between artiste and audience is often an intangible magnetism or an element of showmanship quite separate from musical ability.

Dankworth's Seven, although sincerely dedicated to bebop (and none more than its trombonist, one Eddie Harvey, whose reprehensible deviationism in the Webb days was bearing fruit in this band), compromised by playing current hits. They had a marvellous husky-voiced singer with a remarkable range. Her name was Cleo Laine. Johnny was a nice person but he had a rather annoying penchant for sitting on my desk and cracking peanuts over my date sheets.

In the late forties and early fifties, the schism between the traditionalists and modernists was extremely pronounced. From entrenched positions, the protagonists belted abuse at each other, the traditionalists by far the more bigoted of the two and given to stern moral postures. We knew our watertight artistic compartments in those days! Now that I was acutely involved in the economics of jazz, my private convictions were subjugated, although I was probably certifiably schizoid in my determined pursuit of bookings for modernists while still a passionate traditionalist.

Bert, the elder of the Wilcoxes, was an amiable and self-effacing man, but also the architect of the company's more bizarre schemes. He was out to build an empire in the shortest possible time. While *Jazz Illustrated* was still being published, he signed the Vic Lewis Concert Orchestra for a nation-wide tour, under the heading 'Music

For Moderns'. The grandiose nomenclature of the orchestra and the fancy title of the show had me seeking refuge behind the nearest pile of unsold *Jazz Illustrated*s that lay about the office, but Bert blithely took Lewis on at a large salary and with the additional cost of organizing the concerts. My objections to 'Music For Moderns' were not entirely musical. I didn't see it as a commercial proposition and indeed it proved to be a highly expensive failure, and deservedly so. It was no more than a pretentious farrago of half-baked classicism with bits of solo bebop thrown in, the whole flamboyantly 'conducted' by the leader. It was in direct imitation of American bandleader Stan Kenton who started this kind of confection but with a band that had a lot more verve and talent than Lewis could muster.

Later, when I was running his agency, one of Bert's more inexplicable actions was to sign an Olde Tyme Orchestra, an ensemble quite out of keeping with the image of the office. As a result I had yet another, older, face peering round my office door, its owner, a man called Leon Smallbone, anxiously inquiring if there was any work for his Olde Tyme Orchestra. He would insist on playing me test pressings of waltzes, valetas, glides and two-steps his orchestra had recorded. Mr Smallbone came to see me nearly every day, but I failed to obtain a single engagement for him. There was a date sheet on my desk that required a lot more urgent attention.

Bert had signed Graeme Bell's Australian Jazz Band for a nine months' tour of this country at a guaranteed salary plus fares from Australia and travelling expenses here. The Bell band had appeared at the Hot Club of London in 1947, after barnstorming Czecho-slovakia, a courageous adventure. They stayed in England with great success, pioneering what was then the almost heretical idea of dancing to jazz. Prior to that, audiences had listened to the music with heads nodding metronomically, the males with pipes firmly clenched in hand or teeth. There was a lot of pipe smoking among jazz buffs in those days. The pipe emphasized the seriousness of our concentration on the intricacies of the inner rhythms and the contrapuntal interplay. Happily, the Bell band altered all this. They urged people to dance and promoted a lively and relaxed atmosphere, thereby attracting a larger audience to jazz.

On their return to this country they faced strong competition from British bands which had improved considerably since their first visit, while the Bell band had lost a lot of its sparkle. Booking them sufficiently lucrative engagements to cover costs and perhaps recoup some of the travel expenses was difficult. Profit was a dream which curled from my much-puffed pipe. Not that the Australians admitted any failings. There was more than a touch of normal antipodean cockiness about them and Graeme was given to making patronizing remarks about British bands.

I got on well with their manager, Ernest 'Mel' Langdon, a bluff, resilient character and, happily for me, realistic about the band's earning capacity. He was fond of a drink and spoke an initially bewildering 'strine': 'I'm off to a sneak-go (an obscure bar) to get a taste (a drink) and see this Sheila (girl).' He used such beguiling phrases as 'old as God's dog', 'they've got an impediment in their reach', referring to tight-fisted musicians, and 'I smell a blue duck' for portending disaster.

Mel and I used to have a few drinks after office hours and once, visiting the London Jazz Club, we were watching with mounting amusement the dancing dervish antics of the Guardees and their debutante ladies who attended only when Humphrey Lyttelton's band was appearing. Their movements on the floor were without exception wild and totally unrhythmic and it was physically dangerous to be in proximity when they were in full thrash. A description hit me as we gaped at this spectacle. I had recently read a selection of short stories by Damon Runyon called *Tight Shoes*. In one of these there is a rich layabout named Calvin Colby whom Runyon describes as 'strictly a Hurrah Henry'. Of course! Those gallumphing Guardees were Hurrah Henrys! But the phrase had somehow stuck in my brain as 'Hooray Henrys' and that was how I described them. Mel laughed and from then on 'Hooray Henry' became much used in the jazz world, and as with other terminology from minority groups, it soon passed into general usage in both speech and the media.

My initiation into the rites of booking bands in the Wilcox Organization soon made me realize that the popular conception of an agent as a corpulent shark automatically better off by ten per cent of the negotiated fee every time he picked up the telephone was one big myth, and there were alarming pitfalls.

Les Perrin was a great help to me in this initiation period. He warned me about the agent's bug-bear – barring clauses – stipulations in the contract that preclude an artiste or band appearing in an area within a time and distance of the date of the engagement. His advice didn't always stick and I overlooked many a barring clause, resulting in many disputes.

Les was a likeable, warm-hearted person but he could be extremely infuriating. He had a meandering, interpolative mode of address and it took him an inordinate time to make a simple observation. We had an argument that resulted in a flurry of fists, sheaves of paper billowing into the air and the telephone cord strung round my neck. The difference of opinion was over the release of a news story that the Dankworth band was going to refuse all BBC Jazz Club engagements. They had made the compromise necessary for survival and didn't wish to be typed purely as a jazz band, for fear of deterring ballroom promoters from booking them. This was a classic dilemma that had faced many American bands led and manned by jazzmen, and here it was on my doorstep. I don't recall my objections to the story being released. I think I was about to make a Jazz Club booking when Les intervened. Whatever, a comic scuffle ensued. Undoubtedly,. I was at fault. I was in a state of considerable nervous tension – I had yet to take the hurly-burly nature of a booker's life in my stride – and the office at the time had the appearance of Waterloo station in the rush hour.

Conveniently situated in the West End, it had become a meeting place for a mixed assortment of people, some connected with the business, some not. Mr Smallbone had probably been in to play me a Boston Two-Step; maybe I had overlooked a barring clause; the Bell band was undoubtedly complaining about the kind of engagements I had managed to squeeze from a business coldly indifferent to their talents; Kenny Graham's band was teetering on the breadline.

Conditions at Earlham Street were further complicated by Bert launching out as a theatre impresario. His first, and only, venture in this hazardous area of show business was a production called 'Non-Stop Hollywood' for which Bert had found a backer in bandleader Mick Mulligan. 'Non-Stop Hollywood' came to an abrupt halt after only two weeks and all Mick Mulligan got for his investment of £2,000 was one of the chorus girls on the opening night, surely one of the most expensive nights of passion in the whole history of show-biz.

Prior to the show opening a procession of comedians, jugglers, impersonators and chorus girls were interviewed in my office, there being no other space available. The producer had the girls show him their knees, these joints being well covered when the girls arrived by the voluminous 'New Look' skirts of the time. With this succession of titillating flashes going on before my compulsive gaze, it was difficult to concentrate on the affairs of the Seven, the Afro-Cubists, the Australians and Mr Smallbone.

Les and I went for a drink in the pub next door almost immediately after our scuffle and Dankworth's decision made the headlines in the next issue of the *Melody Maker*. It also made Les's point but, a month or so later, the Dankworth band returned to BBC Jazz Club as if nothing had happened.

Disasters struck the Wilcox office. After the failure of 'Music For Moderns' and 'Non-Stop Hollywood', there were further blows. The Dankworth band signed to another agency and Lyttelton's management, not slow to notice the marked disparity between the money Humph was getting at the packed London Jazz Club, now at 100 Oxford Street, and the money Vic Lewis was receiving for playing to poor houses, claimed an increase. It was refused and the association between the Wilcoxes and Lyttelton ceased.

On the band's final night at the club, Stan Wilcox twice announced that there had been differences between themselves, the employers, and Lyttelton, the employee, and the association was to cease as a result. Lyttelton's expression as he was referred to as an 'employee' the second time was worth seeing. In my mind's eye I can see it still. Rebel he may have been, but his class conditioning was immutable and his impassivity cracked. Not much, but enough to show.

The empire that had flourished suddenly, collapsed with even greater speed. I felt very sorry for Bert, but he had only his delusions of grandeur to blame for the catastrophes. It was a classic example of healthy resources wasted on wild-cat projects. It should have been a salutary lesson to me. It wasn't. Later I made the same sort of mistakes, although not on such a grandiose scale.

I left the Wilcoxes and went into partnership with Mel Langdon, representing the Bell band and Kenny Baker's band. Kenny had consistently been in the popularity polls as Britain's No 1 trumpet player with Britain's top swing band, Ted Heath's. It was another lesson to me. To make a name with a particular band doesn't necessarily ensure success at the box office with your own. Kenny was a nice person and a superbly skilled player but his band was far too 'modern' to be a success.

Mel and I operated from a small room in the Lyttelton office rented to us at a nominal sum. It was difficult to make our venture pay its way. The maximum we could obtain for the Bell band was

£60 and they had to take jobs as low as £30 to make up the weekly gross. If we managed to accrue a weekly total of £200 we were lucky and out of this figure we had to pay the band, ourselves and our overheads.

We got by – just. The band cut their salaries and some of their wives reluctantly found jobs, not without tart references to the inadequacy of the band's booker.

When the band returned to Australia Graeme Bell's parting shot, quoted in the *Melody Maker*, was that 'If British bands stick at it and rehearse they should improve.' The Australians brought a breezy humour, fresh approach and a wide repertoire to jazz presentation, but modesty was not one of their shining attributes, and their leader was patently unaware of the word.

After the Bell band's departure, I joined forces with Lyn Dutton, he managing and booking the Lyttelton band and I booking the Mick Mulligan, Chris Barber and Crane River bands. Representation of Chris was almost a total failure. He was a likeable young man and unlike most revivalists, had studied music – at the Guildhall School of Music – but initially he was a hopeless bandleader. Later, he took over leadership of another band and quickly rocketed to fame although, unfortunately, not signed to me.

In 1950 Lyn Dutton booked the legendary New Orleans blues singer and guitarist Lonnie Johnson for a tour of Britain, to be accompanied by British bands. The booking was made with the National Federation of Jazz Organizations, a non-profit-making body formed by enthusiasts to promote jazz generally. They obtained work permits for Johnson's visit from the Ministry of Labour but the British Musicians Union goose-stepped in and strictly forbade the bands to appear with him, as their permission had not been sought.

Since the mid-thirties, the Musicians Union had been successful in preventing American bands from appearing in the UK on the grounds that their entry would rob British musicians of work. Their claim was feasible with regard to formal *dance* bands but they could not, or would not, accept that jazz musicians were a special case.

From 1933 jazz enthusiasts had been denied the pleasure of hearing in the flesh the players they knew on record and in 1950, in the full surge of revivalism, there were vehement objections to the MU's obduracy. The MU's attitude in the Johnson case was particularly mystifying as British bands had been booked to appear with him and they couldn't have objected to him putting blues singers out of work since we didn't have any.

Moreover, the MU executive was dominated by individuals with a political hatred of America. My belief is that had there been any Russian jazz musicians they would have been over here in droves, with the MU's fervent blessing.

The MU's directive came too late for Johnson's contract to be cancelled and the NFJO had extensively advertised his appearance at the Festival Hall, this apart from their contract with Lyn Dutton. As the bands were forbidden to appear, other arrangements had to be made. Marie Bryant, a well-known Harlem cabaret performer who had appeared in the classic film short *Jammin' the Blues*, was in the country, and was booked to partner Lonnie. The tour was not a great success, partly due to Johnson singing treacly songs instead of the blues, but partly because the traditional style bands didn't appear. This was significant. Owing to the ban on American jazz musicians, the local product was fast becoming accepted over the American original, a situation that was to develop during the ensuing 'trad' boom.

I travelled part of the tour. Johnson, then fifty-two years of age and confused by the politics surrounding his visit, had another unexpected cross to bear – jazz record collectors. He had played guitar on record with Duke Ellington and Louis Armstrong, and he was besieged by ardent discophiles who pummelled him with questions about the past (I was one of them) and plied him with drinks he didn't want (not by me). One of his questioners, a jazz 'authority', forcibly attempted to whisk him away to the suburbs, ply him with more drink and badger him with more questions. As I had to collect Lonnie from his hotel the following morning and board a train to Liverpool I refused to let him go. To Lonnie's distress there was a fierce argument between this 'authority' and myself but I won the day. When I called for Johnson the following morning he was relatively fresh. He most certainly would have been otherwise had he been spirited away and his memory thoroughly, exhaustingly ransacked.

Lena Horne was appearing at the Liverpool Empire and invited Lonnie to visit her after he had finished his show. I honestly can't recall if I was invited – I think I was – but three members of the Merseysippi Jazz Band (who had been booked to appear with Lonnie until the MU decreed otherwise) came along at my invitation and four utter strangers presented themselves at Miss Horne's apartment. It was an awful bit of cheek on my part but we were cordially greeted by her husband and musical director, Lennie Hayton.

Hayton had played on records with cornettist Bix Beiderbecke and he came in for some lengthy questioning about Bix and these recordings. He took the eager questioning in good humour but dryly remarked that as we appeared to know more about the records than he did himself, perhaps we could leave it at that.

Lena Horne entered the room. She had a striking beauty, with eyes of quite hypnotic luminosity. She looked so gorgeous that we were spellbound and practically speechless. We forgot about Bix Beiderbecke. She soon excused herself but not before Lonnie had respectfully addressed her as 'Missie Horne'. Lonnie, a coloured man born in New Orleans before the turn of the century, grew up at a time when race barriers were very marked. Lena Horne was an international star, lighter skinned and, being much younger, had pronounced and well-publicized views on racial inequality. The difference between these two of the same race, although neither pure Negro, was quite striking and crystallized in Lonnie's deferential address.

The unfortunate story of Lonnie's tour had a regrettable finale. The Festival Hall concert was a fiasco because of the enforced changes in the programme and poor planning but, to their credit, a few musicians defied the union and appeared, Lonnie Donegan, George Webb and George Melly among them.

During my time with Lyn Dutton I tried to interest Mecca Ballrooms in employing jazz bands. I was granted an interview with Mr Eric Morley, then Managing Director of Mecca and since famous for his sponsorship of the edifying Miss World contests. I told him about the jazz revival making its impact throughout the country and proposed that our office book jazz bands for his ballrooms. Mr Morley put his feet up on his desk, waved a silver pencil before his nose and said, 'Mr Godbolt, I am a man of taste. I play several musical instruments and consider jazz to be an abomination. As long as I have anything to do with Mecca Ballrooms no jazz will be played in our halls. Good *day*, Mr Godbolt.'

A few years later when the traditional jazz boom was relatively big business, I was baulked in my attempt to book Acker Bilk's band, the country's biggest attraction at the time, to play Edinburgh for a client of mine, Duncan McKinnon. How was I baulked? By a more lucrative offer from another organization with a ballroom in Edinburgh – Mecca Ballrooms, in fact – and Acker's booking came directly through the office administered by that multi-instrumentalist of taste and organizer of the Miss World contests, Mr Eric Morley.

Front page of a 1950 issue of *Jazz Illustrated* edited by the author. The singer is Neva Raphaello.

Humphrey Lyttelton's band and fans greeting the return to Britain of Graeme Bell's Australian Jazz Band, Tilbury, 1951. *Left to right*: the author, a fan, Ian Christie, Stan Wilcox, Beryl Bryden, Humphrey Lyttelton, Keith Christie, unknown banjo player, Mickey Ashman and an intrigued docker. Wally Fawkes is hidden at the rear.

3

Mick Mulligan and Bert Ambrose

By 1952 I was in business on my own account working in a tiny dungeon in a back street off Tottenham Court Road. Financially I was in a bad way. Eddie Harvey offered me a loan and Duncan McKinnon, operating a chain of dance halls in the Scottish lowlands, gave me sole booking of London-based bands into his venues. I was representing Mick Mulligan and his band, featuring singer George Melly. This was a traditional-style jazz band but Mick had dispensed with the plonking banjo then common in similar bands. I was extremely grateful to Eddie for the loan, and to Duncan for his business, but there were times when I had grave misgivings about the association with Mick, although it lasted for twelve years, right up to the time he disbanded.

Our initial meetings were hardly cordial and when he surprisingly asked me to become his agent I mockingly refused. We met again, he repeated the offer, and we shook hands on a verbal agreement that I was to represent his band. It was an odd start to a relationship that was constantly stormy and, for me, frequently bordering on the traumatic.

Mick was a wild man; inconsistent, highly exasperating but, at his best, very funny and extremely likeable. His agent was something of a querulous paranoiac although not, I like to think, without humour. It was a combination of parts alternately harmonious and combustible. Mick had the most winning ways and knew it, but they didn't always mollify me and considering the pitch and frequency of our battles it surprised me that he didn't sign with another agent.

Whether he would have been any better off had he signed elsewhere is now purely conjectural, but he could easily have determined this by dispensing with my services.

Perhaps he didn't change offices out of 'loyalty', an attribute Mick highly praised and demanded in others – although in his case it usually meant his agent and personnel going along with his wildly idiosyncratic behaviour. I didn't and there were fierce rows. He was a good friend ('loyal' he'd say) when at one stage of my career I was without an office and he gave me the use of his flat and telephone. Later, at another crucial stage, I told him I was ceasing business altogether and he was most insistent that I didn't, and helped me financially. Working from his flat in Lisle Street, near Soho, was an inconvenience to him and beset with dangers for me. I accompanied him to nearby pubs more often than was good for my health, my pocket, or, such as it was, my business. Had Mick sacked me, then I might have left the business for good. On the other hand, had I spent less time with Mick and his fellow ravers, I might have taken the matter of being in business more seriously. Not a world-shattering consideration, but I give it the occasional thought.

Intermingled with the arguments there were some hilarious moments. We had a lot of laughter together and although we were utterly diametrical in character we had had a close affinity. The bad moments were quite upsetting, for Mick could be unpleasantly abusive when drunk, and something of a bully if he thought anyone beholden to him. When I retaliated, he would often adopt a hurt-surprised expression, protest that I had misunderstood him and suggest, 'You had better come and have a drink, cock,' an invitation which, if accepted, inevitably resulted in my collapsing in a drunken heap several hours later, often with his ferocious, evil-smelling bull terrier, Twist, as a bed-mate. 'Just *one* then, cock!' was his cry should the invitation be refused, an entreaty I learned to regard with apprehension. There was no such thing as 'just one' with Mick. I can't possibly recall the number of times I got drunk with him and the effect these marathons had on my health in general and my liver in particular, I dare not contemplate.

Mick was very much the man's man and his persuasive charm quickly allayed anger, but we often came near to blows. I'm not one for physical violence but one night at an engagement he incensed me so much I invited him to come outside and fight. I was so furious that I was inclined to thump him on the spot, but as I was the booker for this particular function, a college dance, precipitating fights with the bandleader I also represented would hardly be good for business. At least, that was my rationale for holding back. Mick affected his hurt-surprised look, demurred, but indicated that if I persisted in this hostility he might well take me up on the invitation. It wasn't fear of me that restrained him. It was a late finishing dance and the bar was still open. That was a consideration to be put before and above all else.

He wasn't only a man's man. I've never known anyone who could attract and win the girls like Mick. With an urgent dedication somewhat lacking in his professional and business conduct he diligently applied an animal magnetism not to be gained from correspondence courses. Not that he was a smoothie of the hand-kissing variety, nor did flattery play much part in his astounding tally of successes. 'Oh, I do love Mickie,' gushed one young lady. 'He's so delightfully grubby and you know exactly where you stand with him.'

Indeed this was true on both counts. An extremely handsome buck, he was nevertheless excessively careless about his appearance. He rarely cleaned his teeth. 'I'm the last of the Emerald Green Brigade,' he informed a lady reporter from an evening newspaper, who quoted this admission.

Amorous gentlemen who would bathe regularly, clean their teeth and fingernails, anoint themselves with various deodorants and eschew bad language in the presence of the desired one, would gape in disbelief that this drunken, hard-swearing figure should charm the girls so effortlessly.

The direct approach was half his success. Attractive (and some not so attractive) girls would be left in no doubt about Mick's intentions. His invitation to fornicate – not that he employed such formal phraseology – was a successful shock tactic and Mick confirmed my long-held belief that women, all women, of all ages, are fascinated by rakes.

The band played an engagement at the Royal Festival Hall for a famous charity organization. It was a 'class' engagement that could have resulted in similar bookings had the band made a good impression. That afternoon I urged Mick not to get drunk. That entreaty was a mistake. He would probably have got drunk anyway but a request of this nature, particularly from me, would mean that he'd do precisely the contrary.

He arrived at the Festival Hall with eyes glazed. Although he had paced his drinking throughout the afternoon and was well practised in concealing his intoxication he couldn't accurately judge when it was too late to feign sobriety. This evening the alcohol was well in control. We had a row. When I get angry, I mispronounce and in this heated exchange 'lackadaisical' popped out as 'lacksadiacal' and Mick gleefully seized upon the error. I spluttered with rage and Mick imitated my stutter. Just then he came extremely close to being thumped without any formal invitation to step outside, despite the physical consequences to myself, and regardless of how a fracas would affect the engagement; but, within minutes, the boiling anger was replaced with utter incredulity.

Christopher Chataway, then known as a world-famous athlete, was present with an extremely attractive, well-cleavaged girl. Chataway was handsome, smart, undoubtedly well-scrubbed and looked the picture of an assured, successful man escorting a lovely girl. It wasn't long before the girl, who hadn't met Mick before, was running her hands through his matted locks. Mick's eyes gleamed through the beery glaze and the Emerald Greens flashed like those of the pantomime devil when he's just about to embrace the despairing heroine, except that the lady here looked anything but despairing. Chataway was not amused. I had the utmost difficulty in getting Mick to the bandstand. His thoughts were far removed from playing the trumpet yet once the session was under way the band was the success of the evening, the other bandleader, Ken Mackintosh, quite put out by the reception they received.

On an earlier occasion the band had a spot on one of the bandleader Ted Heath's 'Swing Sessions' held every Sunday afternoon at the London Palladium. Mick arrived very drunk but sensibly employed the concealment technique of keeping silent. Had he spoken, it would have been confirmation of what the band and I already knew and what Heath eventually suspected. In his cups Mick's complexion and eyes were his giveaway. The former went a greasy grey, the latter heavily glazed. Mick, not normally one to be easily impressed, was rather in awe of Heath and didn't attempt his usual insinuating ploys to pre-empt any criticism about his condition. The band played their three numbers without any mishap. Mick was in control – just. Afterwards Heath sternly told me that if Mick had been drinking he wasn't to take the customary bow with the rest of the bill. In refuting the suggestion that Mick was drunk I did my best to sound convincing and at the same time appear rather hurt at the very idea, and Mick took the bow. Had he plunged into the orchestra pit below I wouldn't have been the least bit surprised. Certainly it would have made for a more enjoyable finale than all that show-biz beaming and bowing.

Mick Mulligan and George Melly – the terrible twins of British traditional jazz, pictured in 1953. (Photo: David Redfern)

Mick Mulligan and band, from the programme for *Jazz Saturday*, 1957. *Left to right*: Mulligan, Pete Appleby, Ronnie Duff, Ian Christie, Alan Duddington and Frank Parr.

Bert Ambrose leading his Mayfair Hotel orchestra, c.1930

Ambrose, pictured in 1952. The most famous and wealthiest of pre-war British band leaders, down on his luck in the early 1950s.

Heath, a teetotaller and highly successful dance bandleader with sixteen musicians, and Mick, a boozer and struggling jazz bandleader with only five, had at least one thing in common. Both had three vocalists. Mick's penchant for supernumerary personnel was one of his more extraordinary indulgences. In his first band he had two banjos when every other band was content with one, the additional player hired 'because he's a good nut, cock'.

Mick could have been a much better trumpeter than he was. He had an exceptionally strong lip and on his good days he played with considerable power and feeling, but he rarely bothered to practise and had an almost pathological objection to rehearsals. With the most honourable of intentions his clarinettist Archie Semple, George Melly and myself conspired to get Mick round to my office, where we stressed the necessity for rehearsals. Mick was furious. This was 'disloyalty', a heinous crime in his book. Very much in the manner of a Victorian patriarch reprimanding a presumptuous servant, he told me to mind my own business.

In addition to the traditional jazz bands and a few 'modern' small combinations some big dance bands were still touring the country, two of these led by Bert Ambrose and Roy Fox. Both had been household names in the thirties. Both had made and lost vast fortunes. Both were trying to scratch a living playing one-night stands. Both were instrumentalists. Ambrose played violin, Fox the trumpet, but neither were good enough musicians to play in another band, or play 'sessions' in recording and broadcasting studios, even if their pride would have let them. They were having an unhappy time. The jazz bands were taking an increasing bite of the available business and most of the big bands, bowing to current fashion, were employing bebop stars, these often reluctantly making their bread and butter in such employment and allowed only the occasional solo. Although traditional jazz borrowed heavily from the past it was, in a sense, as much a music of the time as bebop. Ambrose and Fox had dated associations, although the former had uncomfortably dabbled with modern-style arrangements.

Agent Harold Davison suggested co-representation of Ambrose and, unwisely, I jumped at the chance, even though 'co-representation' meant a smaller share of the commission. Davison introduced me to this colourful character in his Mayfair flat. 'Ammie' was a legend in his own time, and I was rather in awe of him when the introduction was made. Mock Grecian urns were spread around a somewhat garishly furnished lounge and as he wearily flicked cigarette ash into the nearest urn he candidly admitted that he had squandered a fortune estimated by many at over a million pounds and this at pre-war values. 'It all came too easily,' he said. 'I had no understanding of its value.' Also present was his secretary, Joan Linton. She had the hauteur of a duchess. 'We've not heard of you before, Mr Godbolt,' she said. It was when she made this observation for the third time that I felt constrained to murmur that she, too, had not impinged upon my consciousness until that moment. Ambrose told her to shut up and I liked him for that.

Bert Ambrose had style. Born in the East End of London he played mediocre violin but rose to become an international name employing only the best musicians, some of them recognized jazzmen. While rubbing shoulders with royalty and society at exclusive night clubs, he was also an idol of the masses, his records selling in thousands, his broadcasts occasions on which the nation stayed in. Before the war he took his band to Deauville, Cannes and Monte Carlo, played before the crowned heads of Europe and later gambled with them at the casinos, losing, it was reported, £20,000 in one night. Now, in 1953, he was well over fifty, broke and balding and had to take a band on the road merely to pay his way. I didn't feel sorry for him on that account, but I warmed to him for a frank approach and an undeniable presence.

I didn't warm to Miss Linton, who was put out that a big agent like Davison was delegating the booking of her Ambrose to someone like me, someone – and she said it again – she'd not previously heard of. Nevertheless she wanted to know when I would be coming up with the big money jobs, seemingly unaware that conditions had changed since Ambrose reigned supreme. There were no more residencies in night clubs for him. Although these plush establishments still existed, the budgets were too tight in those days of comparative austerity for the luxury of a baton-waving, old-style bandleader – every man had to be an instrumentalist. The kind of glitter and affluence he had known in the thirties had disappeared. Indeed, some of the sons and daughters of his old 'society' admirers were now hurling themselves around the dance floor at 100 Oxford Street to Humphrey Lyttelton's band for the admission price of a few shillings.

Ambrose loathed one-night stands as much as he loathed the wild men of bebop his fixer sometimes employed, many of them straight from the Club Eleven in Gt Windmill Street, the cradle of the bop movement in this country. He bemoaned their behaviour in the band coach. 'Farting and belching contests,' he murmured, sadly shaking his head. '*Savages*,' he added with acerbic vehemence.

He arrived at one ballroom in the north of England to discover that the 'advertising' of his appearance consisted of his name chalked on a blackboard in the hall foyer. No glittering neon shimmered his name, no respectful uniformed doorman to assist him out of a chauffeured limousine – only this chalk scrawl to greet him after a journey of 250 miles in a trippers' coach hired for the day.

It was the writing on the wall as well as the blackboard for Bert Ambrose. Instead of the West End and Riviera fleshpots, his round was now the King's Hall, Clitheroe, the Drill Hall, Workington, the Casino, Warrington and he wasn't blowing up a storm in any of these dismal halls. Instead of playing to aristocratic swells and their elegant ladies, his audiences were Teddy boys and girls, with the prospect of a farting match on the way home.

Ammie was frequently interviewed by the musical and national press. They were interested in a man who had been as rich as Croesus, but was now being pursued by creditors, including the landlord of that Mayfair flat. In one of the interviews he referred to the days when he tried to make a comeback, explaining how things went badly for him, and that he had for an agent a 'young man equal to the occasion'. I'm not certain he was referring to me, for he had many agents, but it could easily have been me. I didn't exactly steer him back to the golden highway.

Roy Fox, long cocooned in night clubs, waving his baton in front of silver- and gold-plated trumpets and saxophones and a tier of violins, approached me after it became known I was representing Ambrose, but his band was equally difficult to sell. In fact I spent a lot of time and money trying to sell the unsaleable.

Because it was known that I was representing these orchestras I was prevailed upon to represent a newly formed big band. When the leader came to my office he warmly shook my hand, fixed me with big blue eyes and avowed that I was his man. I subsequently discovered that the reason for his approaching a small-time agent like me was that all the bigger offices had turned him down. He claimed an inexhaustible supply of capital from a backer to sustain the venture. This backer soon withdrew his support and without funds other than limited band earnings the band soon ran into financial trouble.

There was a different personnel almost every night, the musicians leaving when they didn't get paid. This bandleader had an appealing earnestness and persuasive manner that were most impressive, but his smooth blandishments would soon change to harsh words, especially under the influence of drink. In one of our heated exchanges he threw out the hoary old saw about agents being 'bloodsuckers'.

'It's people like me,' he roared, 'who keep bastards like you in a living,' rather overlooking the large sum in commission he owed me, not to mention four pounds for a telephone call to Cairo. This charge was the end product of a publicity stunt his road manager had engineered, although the bandleader, a humourless and self-deceiving individual, probably convinced himself that the exercise was for real.

The manager had read that the recently deposed King of Egypt, Farouk, had a sister who was a night-club singer and he hit on the idea of offering her a job with the band. The very notion that an Egyptian princess, albeit one no longer enjoying regal status, would leave her native land to sing in the drill halls, palais and corn exchanges with a bandleader she didn't even know was bizarre enough, but it also revealed how gullible the press and its readers were in regard to the band business. About a dozen representatives of the press packed into my office one phantasmagoric afternoon and a telephone call was put through to a Farid El Atrash in Cairo. Mr Atrash was the link man in this charade and I recall the name so clearly, probably because I was charged four pounds for the call.

My supply of drink was soon consumed by thirsty pressmen waiting for the bandleader who, wanting a full audience for a drama-charged entry, arrived late. He wore an expensive-looking, tight-fitting Crombie overcoat and a Homburg hat – formal wear suitable for an occasion that was to be a landmark in the history of British dance music.

As this stunt was going to result in a stupendous increase in business the bandleader thought the cost of the call should be my contribution to the exercise. I still have a copy of the bill. In my poverty-stricken years when I could have made good use of four pounds I often mused that this was the price of my involvement, albeit tenuous, with the sister of a deposed monarch.

When I told Mick about these misadventures his eyes gleamed. 'Oh, we're not such a bad lot after all, then!' a meaningful observation bearing on my repeated criticisms of his behaviour. Too true! For the next ten years I stuck to jazzmen as business acquaintances and, with one exception, I didn't encounter the sort of difficulties, trickery and chicanery which I had unhappily experienced with the has-beens and would-bes.

4

Cheap and Cheerful

After parting from the Wilcoxes, Humphrey Lyttelton continued to play at 100 Oxford Street on Wednesday nights, under the name of the Humphrey Lyttelton Club. By the end of 1952 his office was promoting at these premises seven nights a week.

Only soft drinks were available in the club room, a dowdy, oblong basement with faded reproduction murals of sylvan scenes on the walls – it was a restaurant by day – and alcoholic refreshment was sought at the Blue Posts, a pub (since renamed the Rose and Crown) at the corner of Newman and Eastcastle Streets, about two hundred yards away.

The 'Posts' was the fraternity's meeting-place before entering the club, although once a heavy drinking session started there were many who frequently didn't manage to hear a note. Some, flush with William Younger's Scotch Ale, would scurry to make the last number or, hopefully, one of the club's beauties.

The Blue Posts–100 Oxford Street nexus was a *scene* with a distinctive atmosphere. A new camaraderie had emerged. Many young record collectors had become instrumentalists, some on a full-time basis and playing as they pleased. The odd waltz and a very brief version of the National Anthem were the only concessions to palais requirements.

A phrase used by those newly emergent professionals was, 'It's better than working' – even though they were travelling hundreds of miles a week. However, they remained essentially amateur in character. To play traditional jazz was still something of a crusade, although it had become accepted by the entertainment business generally. Agents and promoters, hitherto uninterested, were asking for jazz bands. 'It's traditional I want,' said one agent to me, 'something cheap and cheerful.' The abbreviation 'trad' later became the accepted label, although it was much disliked by many revivalists for its associations with a stereotyped formula.

The instrumentation was invariably trumpet, trombone, clarinet, piano, bass, drums and banjo, the latter instrument a prominent insignia of the style. The routines were one or two choruses of the theme collectively improvised, a sequence of solos and more collective choruses for a rousing finish. The tunes were almost always those recorded by the New Orleans giants and, in some cases, the routines and solos were directly copied from records.

The standards of musicianship had improved considerably but there are some quite hilarious records of bands who rushed into recording studios all too prematurely.

'Dixieland' was also a term disliked by the revivalists. This suggested 'white' jazz (such as the Original Dixieland Jazz Band, the first jazz band to be recorded, all of whose musicians were from New Orleans but all of whom were white). Furthermore, many British pre-war dance-band musicians like Sid Phillips and Harry Gold had jumped on the bandwaggon and formed bands playing 'dixieland'. The term was derisively used by bebop musicians (some of them able, if unwilling, members of conventional dance bands) to describe the music of the revivalists, who preferred the appellation 'New Orleans', this being suggestive of the coloured style (although all the revivalists were white). The revivalists in turn continued to employ the word bebop, knowing how much its practitioners hated it, preferring their music to be known as 'modern jazz'. The modernists retaliated by referring to revivalists as 'mouldye fygges'.

Modernists were sharp dressers – sartorial identification with a music a lot more complex than trad. Trad musicians rarely took drugs, apart from socially and legally acceptable alcohol and nicotine. Some bebop musicians took illegal drugs, with a few tragic consequences.

There was yet another school of thought and action well to the left of the average revivalist. It was comprised of critics, fans and musicians who had a zealous allegiance to the primitives of American jazz.

The primitives' unexpected rise to fame in their late years is one of the most romantic stories in jazz history. In the 1920s most of the New Orleans musicians migrated north. They made their classic 'New Orleans' recordings and achieved international fame in Chicago and New York. Among those who stayed in New Orleans were trumpeter Bunk Johnson and clarinettist George Lewis. After an extraordinary series of events, resulting from a letter addressed to Bunk Johnson 'c/o Post Office, New Iberia' from two American jazz critics in 1937, he was first recorded in 1942 at the age of fifty-three. George Lewis was then forty-two. Both were working in humble jobs during the day and Johnson was so impoverished that he couldn't afford false teeth and, allegedly, he had to refuse his first offer to record on this account.

Johnson's first records made a sensational impact. The music, technically crude and often out of tune, had a rough power, a pristine innocence and a naïve charm that was almost pre-jazz by accepted standards.

In the Blue Posts, Newman Street, London W1, a far cry from New Orleans, the sincerity and *purity* of the Johnson–Lewis bands were fiercely declaimed, especially after a few pints of Younger's Scotch Ale. They were favourably compared with their more successful New Orleans kinsfolk like Louis Armstrong and Sidney Bechet who had achieved fame earlier. The poor were exalted, the successful – especially the white musicians – were derided. The hungry background of the primitives – particularly appealing to well-fed critics – imbued them with a rare saintliness. There were racial factors: Johnson's not being able to afford teeth was a symbol of white oppression.

The purists hated the saxophone. The three-part polyphony of 'true' jazz, performed by trumpet (tenor), clarinet (soprano) and trombone (bass), best exemplified by the Johnson–Lewis bands, was the holiest of jazz verities and if a saxophone squirmed, serpent-like, into this ensemble to sully its purity, it had to be cast out. There was an Old Testament fervour about these proclamations.

The Johnson–Lewis style, seemingly so antiquated, was devoutly emulated by many young white musicians halfway through the century. The foremost disciple and exponent of this style in this country (and elsewhere, including the United States) was the London-born trumpeter, Ken Colyer. The 'Guv'nor', as Ken was affectionately called, was utterly, almost fanatically devoted to the jazz of his choice. His burning passion for his heroes was exemplified in a way quite untypical of a bandleader. An admirer approached him and unwisely expressed the opinion that his, Colyer's, band was better than George Lewis's. Ken looked incredulously at his flatterer and promptly thumped him for such unforgiveable heresy.

In the early fifties Ken signed as deckhand aboard a merchant ship, but only with the motive of paying homage at the shrine, New Orleans. Once there he jumped ship. He was eventually jailed and deported but not before he had played with George Lewis and others, defying the rigid colour bar that still existed in a city whose most famous sons were its black jazz musicians.

Ken's suffering imprisonment to play with the gods elevated him to the pantheon. So revered, he made a triumphant return to lead a band formed in his absence. Chris Barber was on trombone. Ken, the fervent purist, had differences over musical policy with the band and soon departed. Chris Barber became leader. With some changes of personnel and modification of the purist policy the band became an international attraction earning a lot of money.

Had anyone forecast to me a year or so earlier that Chris was going to be the leader of a highly successful band I would have fallen about with maniacal laughter. When Chris broke as a big name I may have allowed the odd rueful smile to pucker my normally taut lips, but I didn't fall about laughing, not with all that commission going to another agent.

In 1951 representatives of all styles appeared in a concert at the Royal Festival Hall staged by the National Federation of Jazz Organizations in the presence of HRH Princess Elizabeth. Those responsible for Her Highness's surprising patronage were an Irish peer, the Marquis of Donegal, and the Honourable Gerald Lascelles, a cousin of the Princess.

A jazz concert attended by the next in line to the throne at the invitation of two blue-bloods, and with an ex-Etonian bandleader on the bill caused a flurry of excitement in Fleet Street. The press was jolted by this seal of royal approval. Jazz became news. The fraternity were treated to many priceless gems in 'society' columns which impart to the poor the junketings of the rich.

In the *Evening Standard* we read of a coming-out ball in Kensington where the guests included a Lady Jane Wallop, a Lady Chetwynd-Talbot, a Mr Richard Tatham and a Mr Jeremy Grafftey-Smith. These two latter 'sent a row of flower pots bordering the bandstand over like skittles as they joined the band for a jive number'. This entertainment was followed by 'Mr Grafftey-Smith giving an imitation of Louis Armstrong singing'. We were entranced by the report that the eighteen-year-old Duke of Kent had 'tried his hand at the drums' on one of these sprauncy occasions, and that Princess Alexandra did the same. Other guests followed suit and 'soon there was a queue of volunteers to play "hot" jazz numbers'.

Hoorays 'having a go on the drums' were quite commonplace. The drums and the string bass were instruments apparently playable without any tuition. You never heard of the odd Honourable or Duke 'trying his hand' at the saxophone.

On a less elevated level, Riverboat Shuffles were annual events in the late forties and throughout the fifties. These emulated, in spirit at least, a former Mississippi institution, the giant riverboats that once steamed up and down that mighty river from New Orleans to towns as far north as Davenport, 942 miles as the crow flies, many of them employing jazz bands. The British successors to these Mississippi steamboats were Thames pleasure boats plying from Richmond, Surrey, to Chertsey, Surrey, some six miles, and back again, with British trad bands performing. If the sun shone, and with the bars being open all day, these events were great fun.

The papers usually sent a reporter and cameraman along. With the constant jiving aboard and on the river banks, with much billowing of skirts and some of the girls dancing in their bikinis, it was enough, in those days, to have the reporters agog with the 'lasciviousness' of it all. One young lady reporter from the magazine *Illustrated* got quite carried away. Under the heading 'Old Jiver Thames' she wrote, 'The boat contained 250 of the London Jazz Club's wildest members ... the bands tom-tommed all the way from Richmond to Chertsey . . . Bob Barclay's ragtime tuba almost drowned the ship's siren calling enthusiastic bebop dancers from the river banks ... they had left the ship to cut a couple of rugs ... this is where the fans forget their Iron Curtain blues and dance. . . .' We used to enjoy the wild and immoral associations the press consistently engendered. When introduced to us as 'jazz fiends', young ladies would back away, children hide behind mum's skirts. At least that's what we hopefully looked for. There was no point in being a 'fiend' if there wasn't a frightened reaction.

We were conscious of our separateness, and very happy about it. It was a pleasure to be separated from the fans of Ted Heath, Edmundo Ros, Harry Secombe and Liberace. Like other minorities we developed an argot of our own. It was a mixture of American jazz and cockney rhyming slang and some Australianese left behind by the expressive Mel Langdon. My introduction of 'Hooray Henry' was developed: Henry's female counterpart became a 'Henrietta', often abbreviated to 'Hetty'. Henry's working-class opposite was an

A Riverboat shuffle c.1950. Author (*foreground*). Riverboat Shuffles with jazz bands started in the 1930s when they were run by the Number 1 Rhythm Club. They took place regularly in the late 1940s and 1950s and the boats were not subject to the usual licensing laws. The author took full advantage of this fact.

Jitterbugging at the London Jazz Club, 100 Oxford Street. The photo illustrated an article in *Picture Post*, November 1949. The author's head is circled,
right of centre. To his left is Ron McKay, later drummer with Acker Bilk's
Paramount Jazz Band. Another photograph featured in the article carried the
graphic caption: 'dancers work themselves into an ecstasy to the rhythm of
New Orleans Jazz'. (Photo: Charles Hewitt, courtesy Getty Images)

'Erbert', his lady an 'Emma'. 'Hooray' soon applied to cars, areas, certain sports, clothes, speech and, most of all, social and political attitudes. It was a handy class label. A 'cheer' of Hoorays and their Hettys were immediately identifiable on the dance floor at 100 Oxford Street. Their extraordinary antics were the comic spectacle of the jazz scene. Conversely, it was an odd sociological fact that the 'Erberts' and 'Emmas' were almost all rhythmic and disciplined in their movements. A sense of timing, a feel for rhythm were necessary for jive dancing. What looked uncontrolled was, like the music that inspired it, highly disciplined.

The Hoorays were congenitally incapable of realizing this. Humphrey Lyttelton in his book *Second Chorus* mentioned one in particular. He would leave his partner and charge around the floor like a rogue elephant. Hetty would remain stationary but swaying, mouth agape and eyes fixed on the ceiling as if in a trance. Returning to her after his solo charge around the floor, Henry would grab her arm as if to remove it from its socket and they'd resume their elephantine cavortings.

In the Blue Posts during the interval their strident honks pierced the buzz of ordinary conversation. We got to know their real names.

'Arabella! What would you like to drink?' Arabella was bedrag' .ed and perspiring, having been roughly hurled about by her escor These Hoorays treated their women with quite ungentlemanly brutality.

'Oh, Gideon, I'm so FRIGHTFULLY thirsty. A H-UGE orangeade would be SOO-PAH!'

After a while the Hoorays and Hettys stopped coming to the club. They must have found another 'craze'.

The Hoorays and Hettys were the upper-crust representatives of the social spectrum. Mingling happily with these were sober-suited office workers and professional men, bearded, sandalled and duffel-coated students and factory workers. The girls were mostly office workers and art students, with the occasional heiress consorting with jazz musicians in the same spirit in which some of them thought it 'super' to associate with criminals.

The Blue Posts, a nondescript pub redeemed only by some superb Victorian engraved and gilded mirrors, had hitherto been a quiet place in the evening, its clientele a sprinkling of porters and caretakers from nearby hotels and flats. When the jazz invasion hit them they gaped and wondered at the antics and the language of the more free-spoken of the fraternity.

One of the characters used to parade and caper in the distance between club and pub. Outside the pub doors he would play the trumpet to the intense annoyance of the landlady, a formidably shrewish woman. We used to know him as Martin Feldman and his antics were extremely unfunny. He subsequently rose to tremendous popularity, although not as a trumpeter. That Martin Feldman was Marty Feldman, one of the great comics of our time. None of us would have believed this possible in the 1950s.

Another character was drummer Lennie 'Herr' Hastings. His speciality was to climb on to a table and do a splendid imitation of the fruity Austrian tenor, Richard Tauber. With his trouser legs rolled up and a monocle stuck in his eye he'd render 'You are My Heart's Delight' to rapturous applause. Trumpeter Spike Mackintosh, after a Scotch or two, would interlard his ecstatic praise of Louis Armstrong with vocal imitations of the great man's solos; Laurie Ridley, known as 'Jewish Laurie', parodied his own intense Jewishness after a few 'sherberts'; Mulligan, outrageously, successfully, invited the 'birds' to fornicate.

There were some I knew only by nickname. Les the Bohemium, Charlie the Pointer, Johnny the Conductor, Soppy Sid, Ray the Bopper, Bacon and Eggs, the Royal Oaf, the Pocket Romeo and the Singing Potato.

And the ladies . . . Trixie, Susie, Katie, Pauline, Ro, Little Beryl and Big Beryl – Beryl Bryden, the singer, whom I first met at the Public Jam Session in St John's Wood as far back as 1941. There were other girls who had rather unflattering nicknames: Miss Uplift, the Horse, Ox-Eye Daisy (also known, allusively, as the Bicycle), Cow Pat, the Two Duckys, and two girls always together, one very large, the other diminutive, called the Whale and the Pilot Fish.

Behind the bar there was an old-style 'living-in' spinster barmaid whose Red Indian cast of features earned her the sobriquet, the Squaw. She stood no nonsense from the Mulligan clique and silenced them with a freezing glance.

One of the many ex-public schoolboys on the scene was Jim Bray, sometime bassist with Lyttelton and Barber. Jim had been to St Paul's. We used to fence about class attitudes and conditioning. 'Look at Godbolt,' he would say, 'he's managed to pull himself up by his boot strings.' Jim was notoriously scruffy, extremely well read, and owned a large Rolls-Royce which he had bought for £30. It once belonged to King Zog of Albania, whose royal arms were displayed on the front doors. I used to go for trips with Jim in this status-symbol vehicle and enjoyed the deferential attitude shown to the scruffy Bray by other drivers and policemen. As he had all the external appearances of a tramp they must have thought Jim an eccentric millionaire, surely convinced that no poor person would dare dress as badly as that . . .

The average age of the clan moving from club to pub and back again was mid-twenties but it wasn't unusual or thought out of place to see middle-aged men genuinely interested in the music and mixing with the younger people.

There was glamour at the club. Joan Collins, then a starlet, looking utterly delectable in tartan trews and a tight-fitting sweater, was invariably surrounded by eager young bloods, one of them clarinettist Cy Laurie, who thought of himself as the reincarnation of New Orleanian clarinettist Johnny Dodds. Laurie was one of the few Jewish people ever to become prominent in trad jazz.

One night I danced with Diane Cilento. This was before she achieved fame as a film star. I asked for her telephone number. 'Oh, you don't want my number,' was the way she phrased her refusal. Her type, I discovered later, was more in the James Bond class. She married Sean Connery. I remember all my dancing partners on that crowded, steaming floor at 100 Oxford Street. The Dulcies, the Renes, the Junes, the Pats, the Muriels, the Bettys, the Sandys, the Joans . . . There were some truly lovely girls at the club . . . or maybe distance lends enchantment to the memories of my youth. No matter, I'll stick with them. Now that I'm wretchedly middle-aged by God I'll stick to them!

Parties were always being hatched at the Blue Posts. Addresses would be given, whispered or demanded. I gate-crashed one in a South Kensington mansion and danced with a coloured girl whose movements were a joy. She refused a second invitation, perhaps because I reeked of Scotch Ale or because of something I said. Whatever, the refusal was emphatic. This marvellous dancer, I discovered years later, was Shirley Bassey.

Much later I visited a flat in Portman Street that spawned a national scandal. The occasion was a wedding reception for one of my clients, given in the one-time residence of the late Stephen Ward, one of the central figures in the Profumo case. I noticed that the parquet flooring in the lounge was pitted from end to end with the indentations of stiletto heels, indicating that a very large number of young ladies had been present at those purple parties that led to a Cabinet Minister's downfall.

The three most successful bands spawned in the trad boom were the three B's – Chris Barber, Kenny Ball and Acker Bilk. Lyn Dutton, my one-time partner, was the most successful of the trad agents. His clients included Acker Bilk, Humphrey Lyttelton, Chris Barber, Alex Welsh, Monty Sunshine, and many more. Understandably, bands queued up to be represented by such a successful agent. He was nicknamed 'the Emperor'.

I owe a lot to Lyn and always found him to be a very fair and reasonable person, even if we did have a few differences. At one stage he was royally inaccessible. If I did manage to reach him by telephone or physically penetrate the fiercely protective cordon of receptionists and secretaries, inquiries for Acker engagements would have him, enviably, yawning in boredom.

The trad phenomenon was truly quite extraordinary; the music of another era and a distant environment exhaustively researched, analysed, emulated and, to a considerable degree, assimilated. It was the first ever example of a musical culture to be absorbed from gramophone records, and it was very exciting to be involved in it.

In the late fifties there was a reaction against trad. It fell into critical disrepute. The banjo, initially favoured by the revivalists for its 'cutting edge' over the 'effete' guitar, dominated the entire rhythm section, inducing staccato phrasing throughout. It was, without doubt, a very popular instrument. 'Show me a banjo and you show me a profit' was the cry of one promoter and he spoke from the bottom of his heart. The banjo's relentless chig-chug was only one unlovely feature of the stereotype that was being prettified in the recording studios to make 'traddy-pop' records aimed for the 'hit parade', and brutalized in the clubs by rip-roaring tempos for maximum excitement.

From the rejection of the worst of trad came the style known as mainstream.

5

Carefree Mulligan and True-Blue Melly

'MULLY–MELLIGAN–TERRIFIC DIXIELAND MUSIC AND SUPERB DANCE ENTERTAINMENT' with the sub-heading 'CAREFREE MULLIGAN and TRUE-BLUE MELLY' was the wording on a poster that faced Mick Mulligan and his band in the foyer of a Scottish dance hall on their arrival. There was also a leaflet covering the entire tour with photographs of the alleged Carefree and True-Blue. It read: 'Mick Mulligan, Debonair, Handsome and Hail-Fellow-Well-Met and George Melly, Artistic and Emotional singer of the Blues. Mick and George occupy and retain a place of their very own in the fantastic, unorthodox and altogether fascinating world of jazz.'

It was, partly unintentionally, the most accurate of blurbs with 'unorthodox' the operative word. They didn't come any more unorthodox than Peter Sidney Mulligan, educated Merchant Taylors, ex-Lt Oxford and Bucks Light Infantry, one-time director of a long-established City firm of wine merchants and now jazz bandleader, and George Melly, educated Stowe, ex-Royal Navy Ordinary Seaman, art salesman and authority on Surrealism, now blues singer.

They were the terrible twins of jazz, both highly amusing, each the perfect foil for the other, although not always in accord. In disagreement theirs was verbal jousting of a high order that had me, for one, helpless with laughter. Regrettably I find it impossible to convey any of these exchanges in print even if censorship and ordinary propriety would allow.

Mick was soft-spoken (officers don't shout), generally self-effacing and mostly friendly to everyone, although capable of caustic thrusts and unwarranted abuse. He was utterly without remorse.

George was loudly spoken, extrovert, generally friendly to everyone, but often patronizing and, in attack or defence, skilfully employed the lifemanship at which the middle class are so adept. Both were from ordinarily respectable middle-class homes, both were completely amoral in their sexual behaviour. Mick was extremely right-wing in his politics and invariably unreliable; George was the apolitical anarchist and thoroughly dependable. Like two lovable knockabout comedians, Carefree and True-Blue were on the road for twelve years, a unique liaison between two uniquely memorable characters.

The upsets between Mick and myself persisted. In 1954 he became George's personal manager and he fancied himself more in this line than as a bandleader. He disbanded and entered into an agreement to become 'business manager' with another agent, but having contracts to fulfil he 'fronted' another band – led by Alex Welsh. Alex conveniently played trumpet and Mick, relieved for the most part of this tiresome chore, was able to leave the stand and engage in what he called 'soash-biz' (phonetic spelling, as near as I can get). This meant being sociable in the pursuit of business and usually involved a sharp movement towards the bar with the hall manager or owner.

It was a situation that produced many complications. One week Mick would appear at a venue with Alex's band and a week or so later the same band, without Mick but sometimes with George, would appear at the same venue under Alex's name. When Alex wasn't available, a pick-up band under Mick's name appeared.

While Mick was 'business manager' for another agency (I never discovered if he actually conducted any business) I was nominally Mick's agent, a confusing situation. This arrangement soon folded and Mick was back on the road with his own band with George as vocalist and me as the agent, but Mick could still allow himself a word about the larger aspects of the business side.

His role, he told me in the Star Tavern in Charing Cross Road one night, was to fashion the grand design, and my job, as a functionary, was to implement the details. I asked him to elaborate. I was curious as to how the term 'grand design' applied to booking a jazz band in palais and corn exchanges. At that moment someone he knew walked in and Mick greeted him with his usual mock-cockney, 'Watcha gonna 'ave, then?' It soon developed into a heavy drinking session and Mick became too incoherent to impart details of his grand design. He never got around to it, despite my further queries. I suspect it was no more than a transient wisp of a notion born of too many light ales.

Drink, the stimulant, the lubricant, the buttress, the catalyst. It was an integral part of Mick's activities. It was inconceivable that we entered a tea-shop when the pubs were open. Had this ever been suggested to Mick, assuredly his jaw would have dropped in sheer disbelief.

Mick and George were interviewed for the *Melody Maker* by Maurice Burman, drummer and critic, at his flat. Burman quipped, 'I hear you're a drinking duo.'

'Not for the past fifteen minutes,' was Mick's snappy rejoinder and Burman apologetically produced a bottle of gin kept for Christmas and special occasions. The guests soon polished off the contents.

The Mulligan band were *the* top drinking band. No other band of topers could lay claim to this dubious title. Despite the effect alcohol had on their playing, despite its often fragmenting the handsome, debonair, hail-fellow-well-met demeanour of the leader, their renowned intake was undoubtedly part of their appeal. When Mick and George were about things happened. Outrageous they may have been, but never dull, and they had around them a band noted for their idiosyncrasies. Indeed, they were a rare assortment.

In George Melly's book *Owning Up*, it appears that Mick thought I had my share of idiosyncrasies, not that I had to read this very funny chronicle of a jazz band on the road to be aware of Mick's sentiments. George asked my permission to use the stories about myself. I can't say I was overwhelmed with pleasure when I read the original draft but there were one or two fairly complimentary references which slightly mollified me. However, Diana Melly, who was editing the book, cut out these references before my very eyes, leaving me like the film actor agonizingly watching his best scenes fall in celluloid curls to the cutting-room floor.

When the book was published all manner of people from far and wide, some totally unconnected with the business, eagerly, gleefully declared to me: 'I've been reading about you,' as if I had been on trial for some awful offence. A variant to this approach, referring to one story, was: 'Had any good nightmares lately?' I was even invited to parties on the strength of my oddities being mentioned in *Owning Up*, a claim to fame I could well have done without.

I first saw George at the London Jazz Club cavòrting about the dance floor in the wild Hooray fashion and, without giving myself any credit for being particularly observant, I knew we had a posturing exhibitionist in our midst. In the Blue Posts during the band's interval I could hear his declamatory bellowing above the hum of normal conversation. It was plain that we were to be his audience, like it or not.

I also observed a considerable vanity hardly in keeping with an appearance that was never Byronic, a self-esteem that showed no signs of abating as the girth and jowls increased. 'He thinks he's the last red bus home,' tartly observed a barmaid at a drinking club after George had tried to chat her up, but I soon discovered a very likeable, kind and highly intelligent man behind this flamboyant exterior, and we became good friends. I was vastly entertained by his fertile imagery and brutally accurate mimicry and invited him to write for *Jazz Illustrated.* One contribution of his was a brilliant parody of 'Jabberwocky' from *Through the Looking Glass.* Entitled 'Jazza-wocky' it summed up the difference in attitudes and dress between the traditionalist and the modernist.

I may not have foreseen Chris Barber's success as a bandleader, but I did recognize George Melly's potential as a writer. The title of George's book is the jazzman's term for self-honesty and very much a part of his ethos, but it took a long time for George to own up. There was a time when he would have accepted that barmaid's tart observation that he was indeed the 'last red bus home' although I fancy he would have preferred a more exotic metaphor.

For thirteen years George wrote the script for Wally Fawkes's strip cartoon, 'Flook', in the *Daily Mail* and there were occasions when he tended, perhaps unconsciously, to overlook Wally's contribution. Wally was in a Chelsea pub when he was asked what he did for a living. Wally's reply naturally mentioned Flook. The questioner's eyes narrowed. He looked hard and long at Wally and said, menacingly, 'Now look here chum, whoever you are, I'd be more careful if I were you. I happen to be rather a close friend of George Melly's.' Mick and the band quickly spotted this quirk of George's and would pointedly ask how *his* illustrator was behaving, inquire if the fellow was toeing the line, etc., etc., and affect not to remember his name.

And he could be most patronizing. We met in the King's Road, Chelsea, one Saturday, the day the 'Beautiful People' make a ritual of parading this fashionable highway, heads constantly jerking from side to side to see and be seen. George was with a little clique of preening Chelseaites. He wore a wide-brimmed hat, a black cape and carried a silver-topped walking stick. He stared at me. 'What on earth are *you* doing here?' he exclaimed, as though I hadn't the right sort of credentials to use what, after all, is a public pavement.

Indeed he loved being among these 'Beautiful People'. He frequently joined them for what I mockingly described as 'George's Little Dinners' – really quite prolonged and expensive affairs in chic Soho and Kensington restaurants with obsequious waiters encircling candle-lit tables and the rest of the flim-flams of 'good eating', a striking contrast to the roadside greasehouses he was forced to patronize on tour.

Although passionate about the blues which he sang with the utmost sincerity, I don't think George managed to assimilate the blues feeling. Other British singers, notably Sandy Brown and Long John Baldry, have been infinitely more successful in projecting a blues sound. It was as a showman that George excelled. His act, exhibitionistic and flamboyant, included exaggerated hand and body movements with much facial distortion and rolling of the eyes. In essaying the female role he stuck beer mugs up his sweater to simulate breasts and sang in a squeaky falsetto.

In his *tour de force*, 'Frankie and Johnny', he fell about and off the stage with quite alarming realism to lend emphasis to the line when Frankie shot her faithless lover down. It was a unique act; there was nothing like it anywhere. The voice and the movements were the camp Melly imbued with *bravura*, the theatricalism of the congenital show-off, but his pronouncements revealed a razor-sharp wit, his conversation and writing showing considerable erudition. He was an intriguing combination of ham and intellectual. Understandably, he revelled in the surprise at the apparent contradiction.

George has long professed a hedonist's philosophy. In the austerity of the late forties and early fifties, coming after the relative puritanism of the thirties, his bisexual promiscuity, heavy drinking and bad language were seemingly quite outrageous and much of it was deliberately intended to shock. He can look back on himself as a pioneer of permissive behaviour, or 'raving' as it was called in the jazz world. It was an infectious philosophy. A lot of people happily embraced it, although few were able to extend themselves with the panache of Melly.

During the fifties I got my girlfriend Joan Biggs, a potter, to strike special ravers' badges, to be awarded to top ravers. I was in my early thirties at the time and I go hot and cold at this recollection of an unduly protracted adolescence – somewhere about are ravers' badges as unfortunate proof of this. I assigned these badges and not seeing much of George at the time he wasn't awarded one. He was quite put out, until I explained I hadn't seen him as he was moving in more select social circles. 'True', he said with a chuckle. 'My parties are now more Sloane Square than Stoke Newington.'

While I have derived much pleasure from watching George's act over the years, I still feel a twinge of embarrassment at the spectacle of an English, white, affluent, middle-class man singing the songs of the oppressed and poverty-stricken Negro. I admit it's an illogical objection. I have no complaint about English, white, affluent middle- (or upper-) class men playing the blues through factory-manufactured instruments.

I didn't travel much with the band that by 1954 included my old room-mate the witty, waspish Ian Christie. I pleaded that I couldn't stay up half the night *and* be at the office fresh and early to battle on their behalf. In truth I hadn't the moral fibre to face them too often.

They were not known for their exchange of sweet pleasantries. As a change from savaging each other, who better than their agent? They used to go for me like wolves round a sheep pen. One of the agent/band myths is the trip from Land's End to John O'Groats, or a similarly lengthy distance, covered in one day. This was allegedly arranged by the agent blindly stabbing pins into the map and fixing the engagements accordingly – or deliberately contriving this mammoth journey.

Against Mick I could sometimes retaliate with effect. Against seven of them, I stood no chance. I was a trafficker in human souls. Ensconced in my warm, cosy office these troubadours, travelling hundreds of miles a week cramped in a badly ventilated tin box, were my victims. That's how they assiduously propagated the myth of the relationship.

On the occasions I entered the bandwaggon I saw, apart from the happy troubadours, every kind of detritus. It was never cleaned out and Melly's fussy and querulous attempts to keep it tidy were deliberately sabotaged by those determined that it should remain a mobile dustbin. After one trip I left some large envelopes in the waggon. They were addressed to promoters and contained photos and write-ups of the band. It was obvious from the names and addresses what the envelopes contained and it might have been expected that one of the band, Mick particularly, would have picked them up and posted them. A week later I myself retrieved the envelopes, the addresses muddied beyond recognition.

But I had one or two memorable moments on tour. In one of Mick's first bands there was an Irish-Scots bass player called Pat Malloy. Pat, constantly beset with problems, frequently approached Mick with the dreaded words, 'Perhaps we can have a little chat' and Mick would sit and suffer while Pat poured out his heart. For even Mick wouldn't rubbish the kind and inoffensive Pat. On one trip he presented me with a classically Irish poser. He had tax problems and for the purposes of his calculations would I, as I had access to diaries, let him have the date of every Friday for the previous five years . . . ?

I accompanied the band to a party given by Lord Montagu at his ancestral pile at Beaulieu. I admit I liked the idea of seeing the inside of a stately home without having to queue up on Sundays with the rest of the proles. On the journey to Bournemouth where the band played a concert before the party, I sat next to Pete Appleby, the band's drummer and driver. 'You were in the Navy, weren't you, Bolt? So was I. What were you then? Oh! Ordinary seaman, eh?! I was an 'onorary officer. Mind you, the loot wasn't much. Only about twelves, but I 'ad me own batman.' This intelligence was imparted with a characteristic shaking of the shoulders. I recalled that honorary officers and batmen didn't figure in naval administration but remained silent. I enjoyed Pete's make-believe and inquired what his duties were as an honorary officer. He had the answer. 'Ow! Just deciphering Russian code messages, things like that. Piece of cake, really.' I was stunned by the fertility of his imagination. On this occasion he made no mention of his close friendship with 'Phil', otherwise Lt Philip Mountbatten, RN, later Duke of Edinburgh, with whom, Pete claimed, he was 'like that' during his naval career. I liked Pete very much and admired the way he, a teetotaller, adjusted to the alcohol-induced changes of personality around him.

It was a dull party at Beaulieu, enlivened by Ian Christie's rightly taking umbrage at the band being offered only that sickly beverage, brown ale, known for its proletarian associations and, presumably, ordered especially for the occasion. However, the band, and their agent, helped themselves to the more exotic drinks, and at Mick's urging – in contrast to his spirited defence of Montagu in the bandwaggon on the journey back to London.

Theatre critic Kenneth Tynan, one of the guests, had squeezed in for a lift and we got talking about cornettist Bix Beiderbecke. We both knew a superb solo of his on a record, 'Sweet Sue', by Paul Whiteman's band. As a change from the furious argument about the noble Lord's gaffe, we sang – or rather, in jazzman's fashion, burped – Bix's solo, only to be howled down by Christie, himself no admirer of Beiderbecke and still highly incensed at his Lordship's cheek in giving us brown ale. George defended Montagu and the class war waged heavily in this cramped bandwaggon. Tynan was quite taken aback by the ferocity of the struggle.

'Why didn't you help yourself to the other drinks like the rest of us?' inquired George Melly.

'I can tell you why, George,' Ian rasped sarcastically. 'It's because I'm too humble.'

'Don't be humble, dear boy,' said Tynan. 'You must stick up for your class.'

In 1956 the band played a charity show in Wormwood Scrubs prison. Apart from a few nights in naval cells after drunken episodes, this was my first experience of being inside a jail proper. I vividly recall the all-pervasive sickly-sweet odour of sweat on the rough serge worn by the inmates in cramped and badly ventilated conditions. I remember being awed by the bleakness of the prison approaches and the endless corridors once through the massive gates, and realizing, above all, what incarceration here entailed. That visit was in itself a deterrent for me ever to consider committing a crime punishable by imprisonment.

Before the band played, I chatted to a 'trusty' who was serving a life sentence for murder and it was his considered opinion, expressed with some glee, that another currently on trial for the same offence was due for a fate he indicated by going through the motions of a rope being tightly drawn around his neck. He made a deft grab at the fag-ends the band stubbed out as they mounted the improvised stage. This 'trusty' was also a 'baccy baron'. The band was a sensational success. Mick, with impish delight, had chosen a programme appropriate to the engagement. 'I'm Beginning to See the Light', 'Who's Sorry Now?', 'After You've Gone' and 'Keeping Out of Mischief Now', were a few of the titles and George, camping madly, sprang on to the stage wearing an old-style convict's striped shirt to sing 'Send Me to the Electric Chair' and other numbers with titles bearing on the current predicament of the audience.

The inmates roared their delight, especially at George's garb,

Wally Fawkes' impression of himself and fellow character-assassinator, George Melly who collaborated with him in producing the *Daily Mail*'s *Flook* cartoon strip. (Courtesy Wally Fawkes)

The Ravers: the only cricket eleven initially made up entirely of jazz musicians and others active in the jazz world, c.1963. *Left to right, rear*: Cliff Wren, Denis Povey, John Robinson, Jim Godbolt, Mick Mulligan, Glyn Morgan, Bob Dawbarn. *Front, seated*: David Miller, Wally Fawkes, Frank Parr, Robin Rathborne, Ray Smith.

excepting one youth with the coarse-grained features of a psycho-path who sat utterly expressionless throughout, but I'm sure even he would have been won over had Mick chatted him up. Mick could charm blood out of a stone, or humour out of a psychopath.

Three members of the Mulligan band – Mick, trombonist Frank Parr, a brilliant wicket-keeper, former Lancashire CCC professional, and once tipped for an England cap, and Pete Appleby – formed a jazzmen's cricket eleven called, appropriately enough, the Ravers. Although I had barely held a bat before, I turned out for a giggle one afternoon and, at the age of thirty-three, became hooked. I stayed in the team for twenty years.

Other members of the Ravers CC were Wally Fawkes, George Webb, Max Jones, Lyn Dutton, Jim Bray and Bruce Turner. It wasn't a joke side. Our cricket was played seriously, although not solemnly. In fact we soon gave up fixtures with show-biz elevens. The comics, singers and disc-jockeys in these sides thought the contests an opportunity to parade their chat, most of it abysmally unfunny and highly irritating on a cricket field.

Mick, myopic and frequently hung-over, was a superb close fielder, as quick with his catching and picking-up as he was with his wit. Pete, a good bowler, had an inordinately lengthy run-up quite superfluous for his medium pace, and when he took a catch he would dramatically roll over half a dozen times to ornament his feat. He lived his dream-world even on the cricket field.

Melly and Christie were contemptuous of our involvement in this healthy exercise. Both were occupied with more cerebral matters that culminated in the former becoming film critic for the *Observer* and the latter for the *Daily Express*.

Ian was first with Les Perrin's office, then joined the *Daily Telegraph* and subsequently, the *Express*. Like photography and playing the clarinet, writing was something he seemed to take up with enviable ease.

He was always pressing for rehearsals and Mick hadn't lost his strong aversion to them. He eventually bowed to Ian's shrike-like (his nickname was Bird) pecking away at the issue and called a surprised band for rehearsal at the Metro Club in New Compton Street, off Charing Cross Road. The persistent campaigner for more rehearsals arrived late and, rather drunk, wasn't in good shape to remember routines, both derelictions inwardly noted by an intensely watchful, testily sober Mulligan.

Halfway through a scratchy rehearsal author John Braine arrived at Ian's invitation and in a broad Yorkshire accent yelled, 'Play "Georgia" in memory of deal old Nat,' (Nat Gonella, the British jazz trumpeter famous in the thirties, whose signature tune was 'Georgia'). Nat was (and still is) alive, but Braine obviously thought he'd passed on. Mick, eventually incensed by Braine's repeated cries for 'Georgia', jumped off the bandstand, strode up to Braine and said, 'Look here, cock, we don't tell you how to write fucking *Ulysses*, stop telling us what to play!'

In putting this unwanted audience of one at an unwanted rehearsal in his place, Mick also implied the superiority of James Joyce over John Braine. When Mick plunged the knife in he never failed to give it a wristy twist.

'Play "Georgia",' gurgled Braine.

Mick said nothing to Ian at the time. The incident was an entry in Mulligan's mental ledger, to come in handy at a later date; which, of course, it did. Some time after the abortive rehearsal Ian, hopeful that the incident had been forgotten, a vain hope considering the bandleader in question, again pressed for rehearsal. 'Oh, I'd like to, cock,' blandly replied Mick. 'But the chances are you'll get drunk' (Mick could be most censorious about drunkenness in others) 'and maybe invite some literary giant yelling for tunes we don't play . . . Sorry, cock, I'd like to have a rehearsal, but it's the rest of the fellows, y'know, wasting their time . . .'

On the night of the rehearsal I was at the Six Bells, in King's Road, Chelsea, where I ran a jazz club in the upstairs room. I was standing at the top of the stairs hopefully peering down for the sight of paying customers when Ian and a man with a vaguely familiar face came unsteadily up the stairs. No paying customers here, but I was rewarded in kind when Ian proudly introduced John Braine, paused, and perhaps feeling that I hadn't reacted as I should to the introduction, added, *'Room at the Top.'*

The Mulligan band had an ardent fan in a toper with the nickname of Fallabout Fred. Fred was attracted to the band's famed heavy drinking and fell, sometimes literally, into their company when they were in town. A none too tidy person, he had a particular fondness for gin, successive glasses of which he sank in one gulp and with frantic rapidity if he were bent on reducing himself to a shambling absurdity, which was often.

There are hundreds of stories about Fred under the influence but I recall him, quite sober but bleary-eyed after the previous night's excesses, in a Soho pub waiting to take a young lady to the theatre. Fred didn't normally go in for 'fancy' pastimes like theatre-going but the show, *Black Nativity*, was one most jazz people went to see. His drinking that evening had been moderate, moderate for him, that is, and the girl arrived pert and pretty. She leaned forward.

'Do you like my perfume?' she asked. Fred sniffed suspiciously at anything as 'fancy' as perfume. 'It's OK I suppose,' was his unenthusiastic reply.

'It should be, it cost me two pounds.'

'How much!' cried Fred. 'Two bloody pounds! What for, a pint?'

'No, silly, a phial. Perfume's expensive, you know.'

'You've been bloody done,' replied the gallant escort.

With an approach as unsubtle as this it was no surprise that he was, at one time, having scant success with the ladies. When escorting them he frequently lived up to his sobriquet, leaving them with the impression that he was more preoccupied with gin than themselves.

Unhappy about his lean patch, Fred, given to tears and confessionals in his cups, was lamenting his failures to one of the band's girlfriends.

'It's your own fault, Fred,' she sternly replied. 'You look so untidy and get so drunk. You're a good-looking chap and if you smartened yourself up a bit and cut down on the booze you'd do OK.'

At this sort of compliment Fred not only brightened up but felt encouraged. 'All right then, how about a fuck?'

'Certainly not,' replied the outraged young lady. Fred exclaimed, 'There! See what I mean!' And bursting into tears, he fell down.

The Mulligan band's return to town was the unfailing signal for Fred's appearance. Even this band of ardent topers were embarrassed by his antics and confessionals.

In 1956 a film based on the Mulligan band was mooted and author James Kennaway prepared a script. He travelled with the band and was horrified by their behaviour; nor did they take too kindly to his brash exterior, seemingly at odds with the author of such sensitively constructed novels as *Household Ghosts* and *Tunes of Glory*.

What sort of film would have materialized about the Mulligan band is conjectural as the project was scrapped. Certainly it could not have been an honest picture, simply because if it had been it would never have got past the censor.

Before the film was abandoned several people from the industry were suddenly to be seen round various haunts frequented by the jazz fraternity. One was director Alexander McKendrick. I spotted him one night at the Studio Club in Swallow Street, and fancying I knew a lot about films, mercilessly went for his ear.

A week later I was dancing with Joan Biggs at the same club and saw McKendrick again, plus partner. McKendrick was the most soft-spoken person I have ever known, but as we shuffled towards him he said in a vibrant stage whisper that cleaved me in two, 'Look out, here comes the film fan.' At that moment I could have crawled into one of the hairline cracks on the parquet flooring of the club.

The following year, on holiday in Majorca, I entered a bar and someone called out my name. It was Kennaway with his wife Susan. They invited me to stay at a villa they had rented on a quiet part of the island. On arrival we naturally talked about people we knew and McKendrick's name was mentioned. I told them the 'film fan' story and Kennaway said, 'That's a coincidence. He's coming to stay with us tonight.' I went for a long walk and that evening, while McKendrick and Kennaway discussed a script for a film about Mary Queen of Scots, maintained a prudent silence.

Kennaway, a Scot, later invited me to a New Year's Eve party in Highgate. It lasted all night and in the morning Joan and I were sitting on a sofa when a friend of the Kennaway family offered us coffee. 'I hear you are jazz people,' she said amiably, 'and you seem to be quite intelligent.' On the surface this was an inane and patronizing remark, but it was really no more than a genuine expression of surprise. In those days, jazz was a dog with a bad name – it still is in the eyes of some. But evidently I had still not learned my lesson because during the party, well in my cups, I had again gone for McKendrick's ear about films.

At one stage the band was receiving a fair amount of publicity. *The Sunday Times* carried an article entitled 'A Man Called Mulligan' and the *Melody Maker* a feature entitled 'King of the Ravers'. Both articles hinted at truths that couldn't be printed at the time, but they were honest portraits of this Rabelaisian bandleader. In *The Sunday Times* article I was described as a 'gaunt, bowed hair-spring with haunted eyes'. How true: I had been Mick's agent for six years.

Mick was largely unaffected by the publicity. If he had been as commercially successful as Chris Barber, Acker Bilk and Kenny Ball I'm sure fame wouldn't have changed him much and, as far as I was concerned, he couldn't have been more difficult than he already was. He was a genuinely unaffected person – not one for George's star-laced gatherings in NW1 or the swank restaurants. Gluttony was not a part of his animalism. A pie stall was more in his gastronomic line. It was one of the sights of Soho to see an intoxicated Mulligan accompanied by Twist both dining on meat pies at the coffee stall on the corner of Tottenham Court Road and Oxford Street.

Mick's real vanity was his success with women. In sheer numbers he had an astonishing record. He didn't openly boast of his conquests (although he usually displayed them, some attractive, some a mere notch in the cock), but he did once say to me, apropos a certain young lady, 'Even I haven't had that one.' It was an unguarded moment when he betrayed his pride in sexual conquest. His string of successes commanded the admiration of carnal man. There was a player in the band, a Northerner, who cried out to Mick one night in the bandwaggon, 'Yo full o' bloddy animule mugnetism!' It was a cry of envy more than a statement of fact.

He was quick to pounce if I erred or said a word out of place. Inspired by Louis Armstrong's moving version of the waltz, 'I'll Never Walk Alone' I gauchely suggested that the band record a set of waltzes in jazz fashion. Of course, this was something that only an artiste of Armstrong's talents could attempt and then only occasionally. Mick didn't swoop immediately but as the stupidity of the idea sunk home he didn't let up, not for years afterwards. 'Got any more bright ideas for the band?' he would say, once every six months or so, 'like recording an LP of waltzes, for instance?'

He would jump on all spurious attitudes with tigerish speed and I regarded this critical scrutiny as beneficial if hardly enjoyable. Not that Mick's assaults were selflessly directed for the benefit of his victims. That wasn't uppermost in his mind. Quite the contrary.

Nor was he less scathing about insincere praise. The band occasionally found themselves on the peripheries of show-biz – a short variety tour or a mixed bill Sunday concert, when a singer or comic would bounce up to them with transparently phoney goodwill. 'Great, boy! Just great! Loved it!' It was unlikely that the flatterer liked the band at all, especially if they had received a better ovation, but in back-scratching show-biz such laudatory remarks are part of an obligatory ritual. Mick dealt with these spurious compliments in a manner that was lethally effective. It would be some time before the recipient was wondering what had hit him. He had a quite frightening analytical approach and I learned not to attempt any pretence with him.

We used to spend some time on the telephone (usually fairly early in the morning when he was sober) talking business and gossiping about people in the jazz world. Our observations were usually uncomplimentary. Indeed the pleasure of praising people is over and done with in a sentence or two but criticism can be spread out at length. The former may be a more Christian ethic but where is the fun? I had no doubt that I would be similarly torn apart by Mick if I became the subject of conversation with others and I had only to wait until the same afternoon, after he'd had a few drinks, to hear his views about me direct. Mostly, the expression of these sentiments was garbled, but the meanings were always patently clear.

He had an infuriating and, to me, expensive habit of phoning from the provinces and reversing the charges, usually when he was drunk, and usually to have a go at me.

Early one morning I received one of these reverse-charge calls and immediately reacted in a hostile manner. It was well before the hour that Mick normally stirred and I thought I was in for one of his diatribes after a night on the booze. According to Melly in *Owning Up* I could be heard 'barking' at some distance. I was, until I realized that it was a genuine call telling me the band's coach had been involved in a crash (this was before Appleby's time) and that vocaliste Jo Lennard was seriously ill. I had to cancel the band's engagements for the following week, but one promoter in the North insisted on settlement for the cost of advertising.

Believing, as I do, that the devil looks after his own, I imagine that few of his children could have been more favoured than Mick. It was incredible how, generally speaking, he used to fall on his feet. Opportunities seemed to open up, just for him. Much earlier the band appeared at a concert at the Trocadero, Elephant and Castle, before an audience of what, on that side of the Thames, George Melly would have described as 'transpontines'. Mick, an inveterate joke-teller, was host to a yarn about a certain person who had just been convicted of offences against boy scouts. Mick was wondering how he could slip in the joke, when one of the 'transpontines' shouted out a reference to Mick's relatively long hair, something associated in those days with Wildean immorality, and yelled out the convicted person's name. 'Funny you should mention him,' said

Mick. 'I've just been reading a book of his. It's called *The Last of the Windjammers*.' The hall erupted with combustible laughter and the band couldn't put a foot wrong for the rest of the show.

The devil was always by his side even when it appeared otherwise. He was at a party when an acquaintance introduced his girlfriend. The girl, making polite conversation, said, 'I remember something about you.' Mick, well drunk, pulled out his cock and asked if that organ would refresh her memory. 'Oh, no,' she replied, 'I would have remembered one as small as that.' Typically, it wasn't Mick that got into trouble with the boyfriend. It was the girl. She was berated by the man for knowing more about men's cocks than she ought.

Everyone is unique. Mick was that bit more unique than most. A rake-hell with a high standard of social and financial honesty; the rebel who was the High Tory; a charmer with little conscience; a funny man who could be an intolerable bore if too deep in his cups. He was generosity and meanness in disparate parts and never consistent in either; he could be very cruel to those to whom he was, also, a good friend – there was every contradiction in the make-up of this memorable rascal.

The band's repertoire and performance had a familiar sameness over the years, but they made records showing their potential and their better points. Mick, on form, was a trumpeter with a considerable range. Ian's clarinet I've always admired for its flowing ensemble line and sweet, singing tone. The rhythm section, *sans* banjo, was light and springy, Pete Appleby the pivot. They were not just another trad band.

With Mick's inherent gifts as a trumpeter, George's *bravura* posturings, and more rehearsals, the band could have been a lot more successful. As it was their impact was more social than musical.

One EP they made had the sly title 'Young and Healthy' and very droll indeed was the picture on the sleeve. It was of Mick, clad only in gym shorts and slippers, astride a vaulting horse.

Mick disbanded in 1961. I doubt if the band would have survived the hefty knocks the jazz business was shortly to receive but, in any case, he'd had enough of touring. It's an arduous way of earning a living and it would be difficult to assess how many thousands of miles the band had travelled.

He became, of all things, a grocer, in a Hooray country town in Sussex. He shook up a few of the inhabitants of this sprauncy neighbourhood, but the charm still worked, his particular chemistry still having its devastating effect.

A friend of mine, trombonist Mike Collier, arranged to meet Mick at a pub in this town. Mick was late in arriving, of course, and Mike, surveying the customers, was riveted by the comments of a typical 'county' inhabitant. He was in his early fifties. He was wearing cavalry twill trousers, a blue blazer with a regimental badge resplendent on the breast pocket, a check shirt and spotted silk cravat. He sported a military moustache and had a fine line in Hooray chat. He was against Communists, immigrants, the Labour Party and trade unions. He advocated a strong line with strikers putting the country to ransom and had a few searing comments to make about unwashed, long-haired beatniks.

Mick eventually arrived, unkempt, rather drunk, and in need of a haircut. 'Hello, Mickie, old boy,' said the archetypal Hooray. 'How bloody naice to see you. What are you feckin' well goin' to hev?' Mick had obviously got them at it. I doubt if the Hooray talked in this fashion before Mick descended on the town.

After a spell as the most untypical grocer in Britain he received a large inheritance. The devil had smiled on him again.

I owe him quite a lot. Not for keeping me as his agent but for knocking a lot of affectations out of me, in the purely figurative sense; for miraculously, we never actually came to blows.

6

Renegade Traditionalists

The term 'mainstream' as applied to jazz was first used by critic Stanley Dance who produced many records in the United States under this heading. It applied to 'middle-period' jazz lying chronologically and generically between New Orleans and bebop, and the mainstream cult returned to their proper status many great American musicians who had been rather overlooked in the twin upsurge of revivalism and modern jazz.

When in 1945 George Webb recorded on Asman and Kinnell's label 'Jazz', Dance expressed his mistrust of a 'return to original simplicities', and by the mid-fifties his view was shared by many British musicians who had once passionately embraced those simplicities themselves. These 'renegade traditionalists', as Humphrey Lyttelton described them, were the playing strength of mainstream with Lyttelton the principal renegade. It was ironic that the man largely responsible for the popularity of traditional jazz should have been the pace-setter.

In 1951, he had a big band collaboration with Graeme Bell's band and soon after he dropped the clanking banjo in favour of the guitar and *then* dropped the trombone *and* included the alto saxophone. The last was the ultimate heresy! No banjo, no trombone, and a saxophone! To many hidebound purists he was deserting 'true jazz' and going 'commercial'.

Quite the contrary. He was departing from a policy that could have made him a lot of money in the trad boom that was then gathering momentum. He probably thought his public would go along with him, but when they didn't he stuck to his guns. He played as he pleased.

In his news-letters and writing for the musical press he was in a good position to justify any changes in direction or criteria, although some of us rather got the impression he would go to almost any lengths to prove his infallibility. Indeed, if Humph were to stand on his head in Oxford Street in a rush hour he would surely essay an elaborate case for the exercise.

He could certainly go out on a limb. In his band's early days trombonist Harry Brown wasn't always able to obtain leave from the RAF and Humph elected to appear without a trombonist rather than use someone who didn't match his requirements. The absence of a trombone in Humph's 'purist' days didn't then disturb his followers. For example, he packed the Liverpool Empire, a theatre of over 2,000 capacity, with himself, Wally Fawkes and a rhythm section. In those days, Humph was King.

At the Leicester Square Jazz Club he rebuffed 'sitters-in' (musicians, including trombonists, who wanted to play a number or two with the band) and upset some with his refusals. Aware of this he made an announcement to the effect that even if the great US trombonist Jack Teagarden were to walk through the door of the club he wouldn't wish him to sit in. Maybe this extraordinary announcement was meant to mollify the rejected, but it fell harshly on the ears of many.

When Duke Ellington's band came to this country in 1956, many devout Ellington worshippers, myself included, were grievously disappointed by the choice of programme and expressed our regrets. Lyttelton, writing in the *Melody Maker*, actually threatened physical violence if he personally heard any of these criticisms. I wrote in reply: 'Ellington, who, like Lyttelton, even, is a fallible being and can make mistakes in programme planning, could have listened to suspect advice or not taken any advice at all. All this is sad enough, but even sadder is that the articulate and influential Lyttelton should demand uncomplaining acceptance or he'll thump you one.' The *Melody Maker* jokily added a rider that perhaps boxing promoter Jack Solomons would stage a Lyttelton–Godbolt fight. As Humph was six feet five and weighed about sixteen stone, it would have been an unequal, if hilarious, contest.

This wasn't the only occasion that Lyttelton threatened violence. In his book *Second Chorus* he asserted that 'if anyone complains that I am going "commercial" I shall probably let them have it – right between the eyes'.

Hostility to his critics on this score was quite understandable. It was hard enough to pursue a musical policy out of genuine conviction for less money when he could easily have been riding on a lucrative bandwaggon without having these slurs on his artistic integrity.

In 1958 his departure from the traditional instrumentation reached its furthest point with an eight-piece band comprising himself, trombone, three saxophones and a rhythm team. It was a highly musical and swinging band but very expensive to run. Furthermore, the trad idols, Barber and Ball, had overtaken him in popularity. Humph was no longer King.

British jazz owes much to this untypical character. He is an intelligent, witty and articulate spokesman for the music and not only for the kind he plays. He has been a dignified figure in the British scene. Jazz doesn't need dignifying, but it comes to no harm in having such a spokesman and exponent and although his social background helped to give him publicity, it wasn't only this that made him a significant figure.

'The Autocrat on the Bandstand' was the heading for one early article about him, and I quote from another: 'He has the well-bred Englishman's calm and confidence in his place in the world. Combine this with a healthy egotism and his ability to support it and the result is a young man on whom the petty irritations of life leave little impression.' This was written of him in *News Review*, article unsigned, in 1950. The piece continues: 'His outspokenness is a source of apprehension in jazz circles and for good reason. During a recent BBC Jazz Club quiz broadcast, the interrogator attempted to jog Humphrey's memory by writing a name on a slip of paper. He observed this stratagem and denounced it loud and clear over the air.'

That was very characteristic of Lyttelton, but I wouldn't agree that petty irritations left him unmoved. Quite a number of things, and people, irritated him, particularly critics. There was a delightful occasion when the well-bred Englishman slaughtered a cocky American critic with just one word. The American was Ralph Berton, brother of Vic, a drummer famous in the twenties. Berton was given to purple prose but, on a BBC Jazz Brains Trust with Humph also on the panel, he affected the persona of the intellectual beatnik and jettisoned his usual high-flown verbiage in favour of Runyonesque slang.

Humph made his comment and smart-Alec Berton breezily asked, 'Say, Humphrey, old boy, what kind of language is that?'

Humph fixed him with a characteristic fish-eye and the

peremptory, crushing reply, delivered in his well-bred accent, was, 'English'.

Humph has a marvellous speaking voice with none of the irritating over-articulation of his class. Its resonances were well suited to this devastating riposte.

Although he delighted in trouncing critics, this didn't deter him from becoming one, writing regularly for the musical papers. The 'unstudied confidence and healthy ego' permeated his writing, although whatever the tone or tenor of his sentiments he was never anything less than highly readable. He could easily have made a career out of journalism alone, or as a cartoonist.

Some professional musicians gunned for him. Jack Bentley, one-time dance band trombonist, wrote of Humph in the *Musical Express*, in 1951: 'It is high time that someone exploded the Humphrey Lyttelton myth. Lyttelton starts off with a distinct handicap. His ideas are prolific but a limited technique strangles them from birth.' In another review in the same paper Bentley jibed that 'Humph had a "cracking" good time on a certain broadcast,' referring to Lyttelton's cracked notes. These allegations were not entirely without foundation. Humph often used to try and play outside his range and I certainly don't deny the importance of technique, but in one chorus he could express more jazz truths than most of the dance band musicians-cum-jazzmen would in a lifetime's blowing.

These criticisms were motivated by a degree of envy. Most of the professionals had come up the hard way and objected to the extra-musical publicity Lyttelton had received on account of his upper-crust background. Moreover, the more jazz-minded of them were compelled to spend the best part of their working hours grinding out ordinary dance music. The title of Humph's first book, *I Play As I Please*, crystallized the difference between their respective positions. *I Play As I Please* and *Second Chorus* by Humph should be in every jazz-lover's library. Both are unique documents, and very readable. In the former he is extremely funny about people asking him if his uncle, Capt Oliver Lyttelton, then Colonial Secretary, later Lord Chandos, approved of his atypical activities. 'They never ask me,' he wrote, 'if I approve of his.'

He mentions his social background in the same book, asserting that if it would help him to fulfil a long-cherished ambition to take his band to America, he would gladly go out and buy a monocle. He didn't have to. The band toured America with great success without the help of the single eye-glass, once the mark of a nob.

During my term as an agent and club promoter, I booked Humph and his band scores of times and he never gave less than superb value as an *entertainer* whether playing trumpet or clarinet, singing or announcing, not to mention occasional forays on the drums and the piano, although in the late sixties, he left his customers more perplexed than satisfied when many of his sidemen, young modernists, were seemingly at stylistic variance with the leader. Here his technical limitations were revealed as he attempted to keep pace with the young lions he deliberately gathered around him.

My appreciation of Lyttelton's talents and influence is not written under any obligation to the Old Pals' Act. Despite my knowing him in the George Webb days, being in nominal partnership with him and Lyn Dutton and repeatedly booking him over the years, I can't recall more than half a dozen somewhat one-sided conversations with him. A rather aloof man, he would, I think, have often preferred to be otherwise. But it wasn't in him to unbend. I think his physical height and social conditioning had much to do with this. On the other hand although he enjoyed praise and recognition, he patently took the view that the price of admission to a club or dance hall didn't automatically include command of his ears.

It was easy to tell when Humph was disinclined to converse. You were met with his non-smiling smile. Towards the end of my time as an agent, I met him at 100 Oxford Street. We briefly discussed a pre-war film of bandleader Jack Payne hilariously 'conducting' an even more hilarious arrangement of 'Tiger Rag' at the Paris Olympia. Humph told me that Louis Armstrong, then also in Paris, attempted to join the proceedings but was rebuffed by Payne on racist grounds.

It occurred to me that Jack Teagarden would have suffered likewise on musical grounds had he tried to sit in with Humph's band at the Leicester Square Jazz Club in 1949, but I didn't make the comment. Not that I was given much chance. I was about to make a contribution to the conversation when Humph's head slowly turned to an angle of about ninety degrees. This gesture of his wasn't new to me and I moved off. Looking back, I saw that his head was still turned: he had obviously overestimated the time it would take me to go away. He's a man whom I've admired more than I've liked.

I genuinely welcomed the mainstream phase. Even during my most enthusiastic support for revivalism I hadn't jettisoned those records and tastes I had acquired as a collector years before – records of the big bands with whom most of the American mainstreamers 'paid their dues', as well as white players like Bix Beiderbecke, Jack Teagarden and Pee Wee Russell – not to mention a few less fashionable names cast in the critical ditch during the ideological upheavals of the forties.

I became known as the mainstream agent, representing Bruce Turner and his Jump Band, the Fairweather–Brown All-Stars, Wally Fawkes's Troglodytes, the Tony Coe Quintet and Fat John and his band. As an agent, financial considerations were, of necessity, uppermost in my mind but I enjoyed representing these bands. I had pride in my products . . . and quite a few problems.

Although the mainstreamers had rejected trad, they survived only in trad clubs. Apart from the Six Bells in Chelsea there were no venues devoted to the style – an odd situation, because mainstream wasn't harmonically or rhythmically such a drastic departure from trad. In fact some cynics dubbed it 'trad without the banjo' or 'modern without the technique', but with its wider repertoire, more extensive use of arrangements, inclusion of the saxophone in the instrumentation and banjo-less rhythm sections it was sufficiently non-conformist to make bookings hard to come by – a situation to which I was no stranger.

There were many liberal-minded enthusiasts who saw jazz as a spectrum where one could take one's choice of colour. This was an agreeable ideal but, in the hard realities of band-booking promoters and agents, one had to be acutely aware of stylistic classifications. Bread and butter and sometimes a little jam were involved.

Many promoters had the strongest antipathy towards mainstream. Understandably these played safe with the banjo bands, although I didn't always take such a reasonable view of their attitude. In fact I used to upbraid them for not appreciating the *quality* I was offering. It was an utterly illogical attitude. Those businessmen were not obliged to take bands their customers didn't want. But mainstream attracted a degree of critical acclaim and a vociferous minority support as purist and righteous in their convictions as any revivalist. Slowly, I managed to nudge the bands into clubs and obtain the occasional broadcast. Mainstream jazz obtained a foothold in the business.

Wally Fawkes's band included, at various times, four players who had been active in jazz before the war: Lennie Felix, a pianist of *bravura* in the Fats Waller–Earl Hines tradition; Dave Wilkins, a West Indian trumpeter who had played with Fats Waller and Ted Heath; Russ Allen, bassist with many night-club bands; and trumpeter Ian 'Spike' Mackintosh.

Jazz has been a magnet to an extraordinary variety of people, but few as rare as Spike, timber merchant and part-time jazzman. Short, dapper, urbane, plummy in accent and then in his forties, he was an extremely generous and friendly character but had, nevertheless, the most colossal cheek, imperiously knocking up hotels and garages in the early hours of the morning demanding drinks, food or petrol.

In the nocturnal hours he would descend on friends with an armful of 78 rpm records, mostly by Louis Armstrong, and insist on playing them at the loudest possible volume and singing (*à la* Louis Armstrong) the choruses throughout the records, utterly oblivious of any neighbours' reactions to the sound of Louis and disciple at maximum volume so late at night. If the usually unwilling host acquiesced, Spike would be playing records until the dawn chorus joined in. His night's enjoyment over, he would drive home, freshen up and be at his office sharp at 9.30 a.m. as neat and dapper as any city businessman should look. He maintained a punishing raver's life-style well into his fifties. He had, of necessity, an iron constitution.

Although we were the best of friends we used to have a few sharp exchanges. 'A council schoolboy with a chip on his shoulder' was one of his retorts after I had complained about the behaviour of his city friends, some of whom, I can say quite unequivocally, were the nastiest individuals it has ever been my misfortune to encounter. 'Judge a man by his friends' is the adage, but this didn't apply to the charming and genial Spike. Almost without exception his mates were a remarkable tally of bores, buffoons and bullies.

He once claimed that he was 'broke'. In my characteristic manner I remarked that living in fashionable Cuffley, owning a large car and sending his sons to public school hardly added up to living on the bread-line, or maybe he was broke because of these luxuries. Spike was furious, not, apparently, at the prospect of living in a little semi-detached or using public transport, even, but at the thought of the Mackintosh offspring not attending public school. 'Do you expect me to send my sons to a COUNCIL school?' he spluttered in shocked disbelief. He was genuinely alarmed at the prospect.

I was with Spike at a party given by Wally, a very generous host.

There was a lot of drinking. Spike fell against a bamboo screen bringing down the various *objets d'art* arrayed on the ledges. The noise awakened Wally's eldest daughter, Joanna, then about six years old, and she stood, in tears, at the top of the stairs that led directly into the drawing-room. It was well after midnight. Spike, sprawled at the bottom of the screen, with bits of Italian glassware and sprays of potted creeper trailing from his head, looked up, saw Joanna and inquired, 'I know it's none of my business, Wally, but shouldn't that child be in bed?'

When Spike and Mick Mulligan talked politics they were in complete agreement. Both were rank Tories with the unshakeable belief that their party had the divine right to rule. Neither could pursue a discussion with an opponent of this philosophy, but when the arguments arose such phrases as 'it's the training that matters' and 'some are born to lead' were repetitively paraded while the drinks would go down as if there were no tomorrow.

But there was one occasion when Ian rounded on Mick. It was at the Cottage Club in Litchfield Street, off Charing Cross Road, then a jazzman's meeting place. Ian, Max Jones, Mick and myself were discussing the various trumpeters Duke Ellington had used in his bands and how it was sometimes difficult to establish their identity. Mick was mainly silent, but eventually offered an opinion. Mackintosh scoffed, 'Oh, for God's sake, Mick. Don't talk such rot. It was obviously Cootie Williams on that version. Bloody hell, man, you sound just like a day boy!'

On occasions Spike's trumpet playing was exceptionally good, his lead strong and propulsive with a big round tone, very much in the Armstrong manner, but on his off nights he played so raggedly that the band sagged with him. I was often in a state of fearful suspense as to what form Spike would be in. He had a considerable talent which he never quite fulfilled, mainly because of his fondness for a drop.

After twelve months or so Wally broke up the band. He said, 'I'm a believer in quitting at the bottom.'

Bruce Turner had established a reputation on clarinet and alto saxophone with Freddy Randall and Humphrey Lyttelton. He had considerable prowess on the latter instrument, not always appreciated. Like all saxophones it was an instrument long regarded with hostility on ideological grounds by some factions of the jazz fraternity.

Surprisingly, Bruce formed his own band. Surprising, as Bruce was a vague and diffident individual not, it was thought, suited to the tribulations and hazards of bandleading. Bruce's apparent distance from the realities of life was revealed at Gloucester Place when he bought a second-hand motor car. It soon broke down and he was asked why he didn't take along someone who knew about motor cars when he made the purchase. Bruce replied, 'But, Dad, the guy who sold it to me knew all about motor cars.'

He was an unexpected success as a bandleader. No disciplinarian, he commanded respect for the quality of his playing and he imposed a recognizable stamp on his band's style. A vegetarian, non-smoker and teetotaller, he was, however, a massive, compulsive eater of confectionery. For him to devour several Mars Bars in quick succession wasn't uncommon. He never bought anyone a drink, not even a promoter or dance hall manager who might have been more favourably disposed to the band had Bruce been more forthcoming at the bar. He would reluctantly enter bars but only to survey the availability of girls and he hated what he contemptuously described as the 'false camaraderie of the saloon bar'. He never used swear words. 'Gee', 'Crumbs' and 'Gosh' were his expletives. Anyone he regarded as a gentleman he'd refer to as a 'toff' and anyone whose behaviour he frowned on was a 'bad hat' or a 'bounder'.

He was given to making sweeping proprietorial claims about any attractive young lady in sight. I would be talking to one and Bruce would sidle up and say, very softly, 'That's my mouse, Dad. Wish you wouldn't talk to her, Dad. That's my mouse.'

When he saw Joan, he would creep up in the same furtive manner and whisper, 'Marry me, Dad. Great mouse. Must marry you, Dad.'

He made this invitation so frequently that one night, at the Six Bells, she turned and said, loudly, 'OK Bruce. Love to! When?'

'No, you don't mean that, Dad,' he said. 'It's him isn't it?' jabbing a forefinger in my direction. 'Oh yes, it's him, isn't it?'

In the seven years I represented Bruce he never once called me by my name. As with everyone else I was 'Dad' or 'him'.

I travelled with the band to Oslo, a memorable trip in a rugged country. They appeared at the Big Chief Club, run by trombonist Gerhard Aspheim. After one of the sessions, a party was held in the band's honour. There was the inevitable jam session with musicians, traditional and modern, jostling for solo space. Feelings ran high and the opposing schools lined up on opposite sides of a long table shaking their fists at each other. Happily oblivious of the rising tension Bruce sat at the end of the table munching through a four-layer cream cake specially baked by the hostess. He left a small piece on the plate. 'It would be impolite to eat it all,' he said. Suffused with sugar, he was a picture of contentment.

Bruce's band had a touch of magic and a devoted coterie of followers. At one stage it looked as if the band might become a strong attraction. Evidence of a possible breakthrough was the appearance of other agents sniffing around like truffle hounds on the band's in-town engagements. One of these turned up quite regularly, as if a sudden convert to the band's qualities. The moment he expressed the opinion, 'I don't see what all the fuss is about,' I knew he was surveying possibilities.

Tony Coe, also ex-Lyttelton, was one of the most gifted jazz musicians in this country. He was offered a place in the famous Count Basie band. Jeremy French, one-time trombonist with Wally Fawkes, wrote in *Jazz News*: 'Seemingly a mild and introverted person, put a saxophone in Tony's hands and he displays a surging inventiveness and compulsive energy which make his playing seem almost like a cathartic act.' With another ex-Lytteltonian, John Picard, trombone, they formed an unusual combination of themselves and a three-piece rhythm section and produced dazzling two-part improvisations on themes drawn from all areas of the jazz repertoire. They were a great duet, if not the most commercially successful.

Tony Coe was uncannily like Bruce Turner, vegetarian, equally soft-spoken, vague and meandering. In both cases, I, for one, never discovered if their shy and gentle demeanour was truly indicative of their basic characters, or if it was a sharply calculated front that acted as a buffer between themselves and the harsh realities of existence. If it was the latter, it was a most effective facade. One was always hesitant to be frank or outspoken to individuals apparently so fragile.

One night at the Six Bells, Tony made a querulous complaint. It was the nearest I've ever seen him to anger. He hated having to force his way to the bar during the band's interval. 'There should be a gangway for musicians,' he claimed, his features screwing up as the word 'musicians' was emitted, as though he were talking of the gods. I pictured a team of uniformed commissionaires in two ranks with arms linked as Coe and his fellow gods comfortably made their way to the bar. In respect of nicotine and alcohol Tony differed from Bruce.

John Cox (Fat John) was small and chubby, but hardly a bundle of joy. A modernist, he had, for the money, been a reluctant

Bruce Turner's Jump Band at the Six Bells, Chelsea, c.1960. *Left to right*: Jim Bray, John Armatage, John Mumford, Turner, Collin Bates, John Chilton. The same personnel were featured in the film *Living Jazz* directed by Jack Gold in 1961. (Photo: Russ Allen)

Al Fairweather and Sandy Brown, 1953. Two outstanding revivalists who converted to mainstream.

Al Fairweather's impression of a jazzman's progress, published in *Melody Maker*, December 1956 (courtesy Al Fairweather). Fairweather was one of the many traditionalists who were also excellent cartoonists, along with Wally Fawkes, Humphrey Lyttelton, Barney Bates, Diz Disley and Monty Sunshine.

drummer with Mick Mulligan. He bore playing 'dixieland' with fortitude if not without complaint. John's complaints were unceasing. The day had no pleasure for him unless he found reasons for bitter moans and if he couldn't find any reasons he would invent them.

When Mick's band folded John formed a band of highly talented musicians but it was far too 'modern' for those clubs that were sparingly, grudgingly taking mainstream bands. The band folded and to this day the pianist snarls and grimaces when he sees me. His implacable hostility went on for years. 'You sold the band down the river,' was his emotive accusation.

John, despite his unceasing strictures, had a sharp sense of humour and we got on well. He was funny about the vagaries of bandleading. He told a cautionary tale about members of a band wishing to depose their leader, one of them approaching him with the chilling words, 'Harry, me and the boys have been having a bit of a chat and . . .'

Clarinettist Sandy Brown and trumpeter Al Fairweather first played together in Edinburgh, their band based entirely on the classic Louis Armstrong Hot Five and Hot Seven records. They came to London and under Sandy's leadership were soon established as a significant contribution to the scene. They were no longer stylistically hidebound. Steve Race was wholly enthusiastic about them. In his *Melody Maker* series, 'Great Records of Our Time', he included Sandy's *McJazz*, the first British record to appear in the series.

Humphrey Lyttelton also praised them highly. Rightly so. It was one of the delights of the fifties to hear Al's trumpet lead: trim, spare and dry, the perfect foil for Sandy's often extravagant and dissonant leaps up and down the register of his instrument with a broad and muscular tone.

Sandy left to form his own band and Al asked me to represent him. It wasn't easy selling the new band. Again, it was a case of a former sideman who didn't have the drawing power of his former boss. But Sandy came back and under the name of the Fairweather–Brown All-Stars business picked up. I once remarked to Sandy that had he and Al stuck to trad they could have made a lot of money. Sandy shuddered. 'It wouldn't have been worth it,' he said, and Al, who unlike Sandy, relied on the band for his living, was in full agreement. Here were two examples of 'renegade traditionalists' who knowingly forsook certain profit for their musical principles.

Al, a very good cartoonist, used to send me amusing drawings on

the backs of envelopes when he settled his commission accounts –
which he did with unfailing promptness. An agent will clearly
remember an attribute as rare as this. These drawings were little
cameos about the business. He had a hilarious cartoon published in
the *Melody Maker*. It represented the various phases of a jazz
musician's life commencing as an eager enthusiast listening to
records and ending up as a jaded touring musician. It was a gem that
contained so many truths.

Unfortunately, there were many tensions and disputations
between us. Things would go wrong in a way that almost had me
believing that some unseen and malevolent force was bedevilling our
relationship. This feeling was quite irrational, but nevertheless very
real. It was a pity because I liked Al very much. Apart from being a
fine musician he was a very sincere and genuine person.

I was also very fond of Sandy, but he was a horse of quite a
different colour. Unlike the quiet, self-effacing Al, Sandy was the
loquacious egotist.

When he died in 1975 I felt acute shock and grief. I just couldn't
believe that he had gone. I cried for a week. It was only then that I
realized how much he had entered my psyche, how much I regarded
him. Death had to be the cruel reminder of his rare qualities as man
and musician. Should he have looked down on my sorrow which, I
confess, surprised me as much as it hurt, he would at least have been
amused by my tears, for we never lost the opportunity to cut and
thrust. This verbal duelling, sometimes extended to lengthy correspondence, was very much a part of our relationship. It got a little
heated at times, but was never really unfriendly.

I entertained the famous Negro trumpeter, Red Allen, one evening
and Sandy was another guest. I didn't see or hear much of Red Allen.
I heard and saw a lot of Sandy, though. He took over. He liked a
drink and he liked a word. This was an occasion when the
combination was overwhelming. It was a long time before I forgave
him his behaviour that night.

A few months before his death he gave an imitation of me in an
anti-social mood and although this was over the telephone I laughed
heartily in genuine mirth, so accurate were the tone, the accent, the
inflexions, the phraseology. It was the last time I ever spoke to him.

Sandy had not been so active musically in his last years and
ironically, typically, his death had the fraternity rediscovering on
records the surging vitality and lyrical expressiveness of his playing.
He was undoubtedly one of the most original, if not the most

original of British jazz talents as a player, composer and organizer of fine records that will assuredly stand the test of time.

The mainstreamers had an influence in very unexpected quarters. The most colourful of the trad bandleaders, Acker Bilk, decided on a policy embracing aspects of mainstream. He dropped the banjo and looked around for suitable musicians to further this change of direction.

He instructed a booker in his brother David's office, Frank Parr, to obtain the telephone numbers of Bruce Turner and his trumpeter Ray Crane. Parr rang me and by his casual tone I sensed why he was making these enquiries and thought his approach typically cheeky. In truth there was no reasonable objection to Acker directing his office staff to approach musicians but it was characteristic of Frank's gall to ring the agent of the players concerned. However, I gave the numbers without comment, although not without making an entry in my mental black book, which was by now a tome of considerable bulk. Ray Crane declined the offer, much to Frank's astonishment, but another trumpet player from my camp, Al Fairweather, joined instead.

Some time later David Bilk, an individual with whom I had enjoyed a cut-and-thrust relationship, invited me to attend a party given at one of the Czech embassies in Highgate to launch the English tour of a Czech jazz band. Frank was there, very drunk. He was seated, rigid, on the windowsill staring at a row of empty glasses. There must have been a sudden, dramatic awareness that these were the silent spokesmen of his problems and in one sweep he flung the lot into the garden below.

Quickly, large Slav officials of the embassy with padded shoulders and flared nostrils whisked him into another room. It was like a scene from an anti-Communist B movie as the door slammed behind them. I almost expected to hear him screaming as the villainous Reds tortured him, although they would have been hard-pressed to get any reaction from someone so completely anaesthetized.

I was at the bar with Acker and David, and referring to my 'black book', mentioned Frank's cheek in phoning me for the telephone numbers, and jocularly expressed the opinion that had they been in pursuit of Sandy Brown, and managed to get him into the band as well as Bruce and Al, Acker could buy himself a baton and conduct and there might be the makings of a fair noise in the Bilk band.

Not a bad gag, I thought, considering that Sandy and Acker played the same instrument. Acker roared with laughter and David, forced into an awkward position by his brother's merriment, managed a cracked smile. David's reluctance to laugh was typical of the code that obtained at the Bilk office in Wardour Street, usually known as Mystery House, as its occupants were hardly ever at their desks, despite the number of grandiose schemes trumpeted from that source. All would fiercely take up arms on the others' behalf, often in the face of indisputable evidence and irrespective of private feelings. I often wondered if it was an oath they had to take before they went on the pay-roll.

When Bruce left the Bilk band, quite amicably, a promoter in South London displayed a poster with wording to the effect that without the odious saxophone, the band was back to its normal, true trad character. Not so; the impact of Bruce and Al had a lasting effect.

7

It's Polo at 'Urlingham

Clubs have always been the jazz musician's spawning ground and the social backbone of the movement. From the days of the pre-war rhythm clubs to post-war dancing to jazz, the music has flourished best in pubs and basements.

The globe-trotting Graeme Bell Band introduced jazz for dancing at the Leicester Square Jazz Club in 1948. Later, at the London Jazz Club and in his own club, Humphrey Lyttelton enthusiastically endorsed the policy. In the LJC newsletter he slammed serious-minded purists. 'If we're going to be purists let's emulate New Orleans in just one respect. The dance halls in the red-light Storyville district may have been unsavoury places but they were free from the species of cranky "art form" obsessionists who infest our jazz haunts over here. We have an atmosphere in this club which I believe to be just about perfect for the development of our music. Perfection will be attained when some of our more sedate authorities forget their dignity and get out on the floor. Jim Godbolt managed it, after all . . .'

To this day that rider has me puzzled. I can't recall ever having claimed to be an authority and my contribution in the same newsletter under the name of 'Odbot' was slanted against the pompous and over-serious but, as Humph's rider was almost tantamount to praise, and this didn't fall too easily from his lips, I welcomed the compliment.

From after the war up to 1963 jazz clubs were formed by the hundreds. Some, like the Nottingham, Redcar, Luton, Reading and Wood Green clubs, the Mardi Gras, Liverpool, and the Manchester Sports Guild enjoyed a long life, and the premises with the longest jazz associations of all are 100 Oxford Street, which was first used by the Feldman Swing Club as long ago as 1942.

It is now run by Roger Horton, a man with a positive loathing for the British public. His was the heartfelt cry, 'Show me a banjo and you show me a profit', to which he often added, apropos his pet aversion, 'The British public are a load of twats!'

I was associated with quite a few jazz club adventures with varying success, and have spent a few hundred anxious hours waiting for the bodies to surge in. When they didn't it was a miserable evening for all concerned. I lost money, the band lost heart, and the few customers who had paid to come in wouldn't be doing so the following week.

Sparse attendance is one sort of experience, but there is an even more depressing one – the completely empty hall. Years ago the Duke Ellington saxophonist Johnny Hodges recorded a tune called 'Empty Ballroom Blues'. One night that title had grim application as I stood at the door of a club with the space between me and the bandstand devoid of a living soul.

It was at the Piccadilly Club, Denman Street, off Piccadilly Circus. Initially I was the booking agent on behalf of a promoter who had entered into an agreement with two archetypal Jewish brothers, Elliot and John Gold, who owned the premises. In the thirties it had been a night club called the Vortex, owned by a Lady Torrington and Steve Donoghue, the jockey, he of the once-famous catch phrase, 'Come on Steve!' In those halcyon days it was notorious for bottle parties and catered for monocled toffs who attended for the vicarious pleasure of being present when the police made a raid. There were no monocled toffs and befurred ladies showing up at the Piccadilly Club in 1956, but we did get a raid, of sorts.

After the opening night the *Melody Maker* gave the club a favourable review. The reporter praised the atmosphere and Wally Fawkes's band. He also reported that the 'cadaverous' Jim Godbolt handled awkward situations like putting a ban on the bar at closing time with 'great tact and jazz feeling'. There can't be many people in the entertainment business who have put up the bar with true 'jazz feeling' and that compliment was about the only satisfaction I got from this disastrous venture.

The opening night was a great success. Opening nights usually are. Some come along out of curiosity, the practised free-loaders throng the bar and the bandleaders turn up to get their faces in the photographs. But a successful opening night is no true indication of business to come. The promoter, sensing disaster, quit after the first few nights leaving the brothers morosely listening to a music they didn't like.

I took over the erstwhile promoter's responsibilities with the naïve belief that as we were offering something different we must eventually succeed. The *policy* difference between the Piccadilly Club and every other jazz club in London was that our premises were licensed and served hot meals. The *essential* difference between our club and others soon crystallized. They were doing business and we were not.

Every night the brothers, myself and odd well-wishers would conduct a mournful post-mortem. It became a ritual. One night there was a knock on the door and we quickly put the glasses out of sight. Two scruffy men gained admission on some pretext and I sensed they were policemen. They hinted they were thirsty. 'Like a nice cup of tea, *bhoys?*' asked John, nervously puffing at a cheroot. He, too, had sensed trouble. Vaguely, I thought I had seen one of them in a situation outside the normal policeman's beat, although still not certain they were coppers. 'Haven't we met somewhere before?' I asked, casually. His reply was non-committal, but it gave me the answer. 'Was it in Earl's Court?' he said.

A couple of years before, Mick Mulligan had rung me up one afternoon and asked if I would like 'to go to the flicks' with him. I was taken aback. Mick rarely went to the cinema and I was puzzled why he was asking me to accompany him. He archly explained that this was a special screening at a flat in Earl's Court for a special price of thirty shillings. I still didn't comprehend. 'Of course,' said Mick in mock-pained tones, 'if you don't want to come to the pictures with me, or you're washing your hair . . .'

That special showing was the only blue film session I have ever attended. When Mick, George Melly and myself arrived, Mick pointed to the hall sofa strewn with umbrellas, brief cases and bowler hats. The impresario, a City gent, had no problem finding customers from the panelled sanctums of the banks, insurance companies and stockbrokers in the hallowed square mile.

A group of well-dressed, middle-class men of varying ages stood giggling in a corner of the room. The impresario, eager to induce the right mood for the delights to come, was telling them a naughty joke. A sheet had been rigged up to act as a screen and the cinematograph operators, two gentlemen not long off another sort of duty, arrived. Their Oxford-blue shirts, dark blue ties, dark blue serge trousers and heavy boots indicated a calling where access to films of this nature was easier for them than it was for the rest of us. The senior operator mounted a box and fiddled with apparatus. 'Right, gents. Ready for the show? 'Arry, 'and me the lesbian lot, will yer? Ta. Now this will get you going, gents. There's some right little darlings among this team, I can tell yer.'

A lesbian orgy was the beginning of a string of technically crude, quite hilarious pornographic films. They had been made on extremely cramped budgets. One had a particularly thin story line. It consisted of a gentleman walking through a corn field where he conveniently encountered a nude and obliging female. In another epic the casting director had obviously been hard pushed to fill the roles satisfactorily. The leading man, middle-aged and paunchy, had trouble in maintaining an erection, an unfortunate failing in a production of this kind, and one on which the camera cruelly lingered, perhaps in hope of a revival. Perhaps he had exhausted himself at rehearsals. Whatever, we hooted with laughter when the leading lady seized the organ with both hands and furiously jerked it up and down in the manner of an African woman using a pestle to pound maize in a kraal but, alas, to no avail. There was a merciful 'fade'. In another production the undeniable athleticism of two men and a girl compensated for the aesthetic limitations of the theme and the quite gruesome ugliness of the participants. Again, it appeared that the casting director's lot had been a difficult one.

The interlocutory remarks of the senior operator – he was genuinely enthusiastic about his wares – nearly prompted one of the belly-laughter explosions that Mick and I used to have. It was a struggle to contain ourselves. The impresario, a thoroughly gross individual, was put out that we laughed at all. This was a serious porn show, not an occasion for hilarity. We could have been equally put out that the supply of light ale was limited to one bottle per man. Not that we needed drink. The programme was intoxicating enough.

'Well, gentlemen,' said the chief operator after an hour or so, 'we're now coming to the PC de resistant – isn't that right, 'Arry?' Harry nodded energetically and twisted glottal noises came from Mick's direction.

At this point Mick, George and myself left. Mick had a broadcast. This was one category of engagement for which he was never late or drunk, probably because he knew there would be no more broadcasts if he were either. This strict rule wasn't broken even for the 'PC de resistant' of this extraordinary thirty shillings' worth.

Here, at the Piccadilly Club, was the chief operator of the Earl's Court blue film show and still he had not declared himself as a police officer. I eventually drew him out by complimenting him on his apparent knowledge of licensing laws and enquiring how it was he knew so much. He smirked, looked at his mate and said, 'Shall we tell them?' His mate smirked, and nodded. The chief operator produced his card. I was tempted to enquire of this officer how his sideline was doing, but thought better of it.

'Have a nice cup of tea, *bhoys*,' said John, now puffing at his cheroot more nervously than ever. Perhaps the officers came looking for extra-curricular business. If so, they were unlucky and got no more than a cup of tea.

When things go wrong and business is bad, tempers get frayed. There can't be many people with whom Wally Fawkes has quarrelled but I was one of them and after a brief argument he strode out of the club in high fury.

On another occasion Mick and I had one of our periodic disputes and he gave me the sack. He kept repeating, 'It's all down to swallows then. All right? All down to swallows, then?' After he had repeated this about ten times I wearily assented. The following morning I rang him to enquire when we could meet and clear up outstanding business before he went to another office and Mick could barely remember a word of the altercation. I was immensely relieved. After the losses at this club I needed Mick's commission.

The club carried on for a few months and occasionally Spike Mackintosh brought along some of his City mates. I got to fear these visits, not because of Spike, but because of his quite wretched friends. God in heaven above! They were the ultimate in nastiness and, as it happens, extreme right-wing reactionaries to a man.

The club eventually folded and the brothers went into partnership with two young men who turned the premises into a strip club. I went to the refurbished premises one night to sort out finances with the brothers. The club room had been decorated in garish, pseudo-Moorish fashion – 'Like a Jewish Taj Mahal' was Wally's description when he popped in to see the transformation. At the younger brother's firm insistence I stopped to watch the show. It was fortunate that Mick wasn't present or there might have been an eruption of hysterical laughter at the spectacle of raincoated gentleman scampering to occupy the front seats as they became vacant, and at the finale of the show when a young lady, almost naked, walked down the plinth in the centre aisle with all heads turned for the final divestment. Arriving at the end of the plinth she revealed all, but modesty quickly returned and she closed the act by putting her hand over the orifice only momentarily revealed.

Wally Fawkes discovered the room at the Six Bells in the King's Road, and suggested that I approach the brewers with a view to hiring it for a jazz club. We opened on Monday evenings with his band and for several weeks played to only a handful of people, but one Monday evening an unexpected group of forty people arrived. They were members of the Inter-Varsity Club and their secretary, Clive Chester, was a jazz enthusiast. They transformed the atmosphere and the tenor of business. The old adage that people attract people was never more clearly, pleasurably, demonstrated.

The Six Bells already had an honourable place in British jazz history. The writer and composer, Spike Hughes, led a pioneer recording with a band called the Decca-Dents (on account of their recording for the Decca label and, no doubt, in view of jazz's dubious associations). They recorded at the Chenil Galleries, a few yards from the Six Bells. At the end of the session the Decca-Dents would rush into the pub for refreshment, inspiring Hughes to co-write 'Six Bells Stampede'.

Visiting US jazzmen, Duke Ellington's band, clarinettist Jimmy Dorsey and trumpeter Muggsy Spanier, also recorded at the Chenil Galleries and drank at the Six Bells, and from these jazzmen of an earlier generation it became in the late fifties and throughout the sixties a venue for Humphrey Lyttelton, Al Fairweather, Sandy Brown, Bruce Turner, Fat John, Tony Coe and Wally Fawkes.

Wally, a highly popular person, attracted many people who came along to see and talk to him, even if they were not particularly enthusiastic about the band. Of the rich seam of characters in the jazz world Wally was one of the most engaging. He possessed an insouciant magnetism that drew people into his company. He was someone who seemed to achieve many things without ever seeming to try very hard, and attracting people was one of them.

When Humph joined George Webb's band in 1947 he and Wally became close friends. On the journey to Hawick, Humph got into a carriage, saw that Wally wasn't present and hastily retreated to seek him out. It hadn't taken him long to assess the rest of us. We were not on his wavelength. Fawkes was, and in his quiet, steely way, he was a match for Lyttelton. Humph's respect for Wally was revealed, albeit unintentionally, one night at the Blue Posts. The Lyttelton band were taking a rather lengthy interval and after manager Lyn Dutton's almost tearful pleading that they return to the club, Humph addressed his men. 'Right! Off we go! *Bray! Parker! Hopkinson! Picard! Turner!* Ready, Wal?'

I've known Wally longer than anyone in my association with jazz and for these odd forty years we have had a wary relationship, as though each were wary that the other was going to pull the wrong verbal switch. Wally's geniality was the marshmallow covering the hard centre and he showed more than a hint of steel when aroused. If situations occurred that were not to his liking, he would jut his chin skywards and utter a prolonged *mmmmmm*, like a king stag warning off his rivals in a rutting herd.

He was the master of the offhand barb, the seemingly innocuous thrust, the victim often feeling the pain some time after the lunge. He cured me of telling jokes. 'My favourite joke,' he murmured with a keening blandness, chin a-tilt, after I had completed a lengthy, unfunny and oft-repeated tale. Not that he always won. In the fifties his band was on a broadcast with trumpeter Eddie Calvert, who had a hit parade success with a lachrymal confection entitled 'Oh Mein Papa', played in a sickly, braying style. In the dressing-room Calvert extolled the virtues of the trumpeter Harry James over Louis Armstrong. Wally's rapier thrusts buckled against Calvert's armadillo coating.

The latter once arrived at Humph's club and, without any invitation, appeared from behind the bandstand halfway through a number and dramatically, nay disastrously, joined in the performance. Even Humph, who normally could be relied upon to dismiss such an intruder, was too flabbergasted to give the irrepressible Eddie the brush-off.

Wally based many of his characters in his cartoon strip 'Flook' on people in the jazz world. One of them was Len Bloggs, a snarling anti-social inverted snob with a chip on his shoulder. For some reason I was the inspiration for this disagreeable misanthrope. So accurate was Wally's draughtsmanship that I was recognized by total strangers as the model for Bloggs who, in one story, was a schoolmaster. A man I had never seen before in my life approached me in a pub in Earl's Court and asked me if that was my profession. The question came as no surprise. I explained the connection and the man returned to his friend highly delighted with himself for recognizing me. On another occasion, at a jazz concert in the Festival Hall, I was again hailed by a total stranger, this time by name. The stranger was Steve Voce, a jazz critic, who informed me that he knew who I was from reading 'Flook'. He was inordinately proud of his smart deduction. I was a little icy in acknowledging the recognition.

Running a jazz club gave me an illuminating insight into what is quaintly described as 'human nature'. Most people didn't begrudge paying a mere five or six shillings to listen to the cream of the country's jazz musicians, but there were some to whom getting into a jazz club without paying was a cardinal principle. They wouldn't dream of entering a cinema or leaving a restaurant without paying, but jazz clubs involved a different morality. Why, I don't know, but it was one of the facts of a club promoter's life. Some of them would try any physical manoeuvre and exercise ingenious verbal ploys rather than pay for admission. I discovered that the musicians had an extraordinary number of friends willing to lend support – moral but not financial. My standard rejoinder, which never went down well with these mumpers, was that friendship for individuals on the bandstand was best expressed by paying to see them.

I discovered that there were scores of jazz correspondents from all over the United Kingdom. If one of them came from say, a local paper in Westmorland, I was assured that a write-up in that organ about the club would have them flocking from the lakes into the King's Road the following week.

A hazard peculiar to the Six Bells was the 'Chelsea Set'. The 'Set' is an amorphous term, but it will suffice to describe some of the well-heeled arrogants of the area. These were mumpers of considerable expertise, and very cheeky with it.

'Oh, don't be such a silly little man,' spluttered one outraged Hetty when I politely requested payment. I'm six feet tall, but the appellation was indicative of social attitude rather than a reference to my height. 'I know the band very well,' she cried. 'They've been to *hundreds* of my parties! Now let me pass!' was her most imperious demand.

Her escort was silent until I remarked that she was very unpleasant. His contribution was straight from P. G. Wodehouse. 'Oh, I say, look here. I shall jolly well have to ask you to take that back!' She eventually departed snarling malevolently at 'such a silly little man' and protesting that she could 'buy the place over and over again'. An odd claim to wealth from someone not prepared to pay a few shillings' entrance fee.

Generally we had little real trouble, although I quickly made the discovery that individuals in the more exalted professions don't necessarily have higher standards of behaviour. On the contrary. My problem people were actors, doctors and solicitors.

One actor, particularly. To him the world was a stage (he actually declaimed that line to me one night) where he constantly paraded and tediously so when drunk. There was a solicitor, since struck off, who came along solely to conduct the band. He was ferret-like, middle-aged and slightly demented. He had a rival in Johnny the Conductor and one night the band had the benefit of two maestri, each with his own interpretation of tempi, nuance and rhythm.

Another pestiferous nuisance was a young solicitor from a strait-laced north-eastern town where his behaviour, perforce, was impeccable, but he regarded this jazz club in the soft South as a place where, assisted by copious draughts of bitter (which didn't compare with the brews in his home town, of course) he could shake off the weighty burdens of his legal problems. He was called Legal Pete.

There was a young Scots journalist who, freed from the crimping restraint of life across the Border, consistently got drunk, gate-crashed parties and spewed over his unwilling hosts' carpets. He was dubbed Ewan McSpewan, and he endeared himself to me on our first meeting by proffering, as a statement of fact, that all managers and agents are crooks.

In 1960 a film, *Living Jazz*, was produced by Alan Lovell and Paddy Whannel, of the British Film Institute. The film was directed by Jack Gold and featured Bruce Turner's band, and several scenes were shot at the Six Bells.

I was supposed to have a few lines of dialogue but a backer insisted that if this was to be the case, he too wanted to be in a scene at his club in Hertfordshire. My one and only chance of speaking on the silver screen was snatched away from me. I did appear for a second or two, silently addressing drummer John Armatage, but neither of us was launched into a glittering screen career as a result of this telling scene. Far from it; we were to meet later in a very unglamorous sphere of activity.

Humphrey Lyttelton liked playing at the Six Bells and one of the last sessions there was, happily and appropriately, a broadcast on the BBC's Jazz Club celebrating Humph's twentieth anniversary as a bandleader. It was heart-warming to see all the old faces on the bandstand. There were Keith Christie, Wally Fawkes, pianist Johnny Parker and, on a visit, Graeme Bell, as breezy and patronizing as ever. A night for nostalgia and I hope the BBC have retained the tape. It's a slice of British jazz history encapsulated in one evening's performance and commemorating the achievements and ability of Britain's leading jazzman.

Humph made a gracious and witty speech telling, quite in-accurately, how I first approached him at Friern Barnet to play with the Webb Band, how pleased he was to be celebrating his twentieth anniversary as a bandleader at a club in which I was the promoter, and adding that if he asked me to come up and say a few words I would run a mile. He was right about this, but wrong about our first meeting. The evening's programme was comprised of a warming-up session, followed by a taped broadcast. I had to muster the musicians from the bar for the earlier session and started this harangue twenty minutes before the start. The following scene was as traditional and recognizable in character as a Punch and Judy show with every facial response, line of dialogue and bodily movement totally predictable. It took all of fifteen minutes for the message to scratch the surface of their consciousness, and another five minutes before a reluctant move was made, with hardly an acknowledgement of the individual urging them to return to the club room. In fact they barely seemed aware of my presence. When jazz musicians are in full verbal flight, entrepreneurs are neither seen nor heard. As the deadline approached, I became increasingly peremptory. I had a strong precedent on which to base my handling of the matter. I knew with whom I should be firm, who should be treated otherwise. 'Right!' I cried. 'Off we go! *Parker! Christie! Green! Taylor! Lyttelton!* Ready, Wal?'

The Six Bells Jazz Club started in March 1959. It lasted for ten years, surviving, though only just, the rock and roll explosion of the early sixties that closed so many other jazz clubs. It could perhaps have remained as a jazz club to this day, but the owner-brewers thought the pub's situation in swinging Chelsea ideal for a new-style discotheque drinking house – it could hardly be described as a pub, not within my definition of the term.

The interior was completely transformed and there was a resident, all-smiling, all-gagging disc jockey with a transatlantic accent ploughing through a pile of pop records while stroboscopic lights fell

Wally Fawkes' Troglodytes at the Six Bells, Chelsea, c.1963. *Left to right*: Jeremy French, Ray Smith, Dave Wilkins, Jeff Kemp, Wally Fawkes and Colin Purbrook.

Unflattering caricature of the author as leader of a skiffle group ('Len Bloggs') in Wally 'Trog' Fawkes' strip cartoon, *Flook*. (Courtesy Wally Fawkes)

on couples 'dancing' in the strangely asexual manner of the time.

'Ring Out Jazz' was the title of the club's obituary notice in the *Sunday Telegraph*, written by Peter Clayton, when the club closed in 1969.

As an agent I was continually dealing with club promoters, some of them quite memorable. There was a kindly couple who ran a very successful club in north London. They were generosity itself – and very good club promoters – but had strong racialist beliefs, summed up in the following dialogue when someone asked them about their policy.

The man said, 'It's New Orleans here, but we don't have any niggers. Isn't that right, Daisie?'

'Quite right, Ned. New Orleans, but no niggers.'

Some promoters had extraordinary excuses for poor business. 'It's Lent', or 'It's before/after Christmas' or 'It's the weather', be it ice, snow, fog, or sunshine. In fact if an attraction is strong enough it will draw crowds at any time of the year whatever the climatic conditions, or the competition.

The most unlikely, and hilarious, excuse I ever heard came from a promoter running a small club in a dingy hall in Putney, south-west London. One night business was particularly bad. 'Of course,' he said, surveying his meagre crowd, 'it's the polo at 'Urlingham that does it. Once the season starts you've 'ad it.' His premises were indeed near the highly exclusive Hurlingham Polo Club – a bastion of the rich where the sport of consorts and counts is played on a piece of turf worth several million pounds, but it was hard to believe that the game played on this hallowed pasture was rival to solid British trad being pounded out at a church hall every Thursday night.

8

Don and the Visiting Firemen

As business improved, I made an unwise move in engaging a young man with the high-sounding title of 'General Manager'. He proved to be a rogue, if a most likeable one. We parted company in a few weeks but not before I had acted as guarantor in an HP agreement on a car he had bought and I eventually received a bill for £110 in lieu of payments he hadn't made. I was compelled to settle, with costs.

This ex-manager hailed me in the Earl's Court Road one morning. He wore a sharp mohair suit, was his usual affable self and enquired after my health. I replied that my financial health would be better off by £110, plus costs, had he met his obligations to the finance company. He looked intently at me through dark glasses. 'And you paid up?' he asked incredulously. 'You want to get yourself a good lawyer, that's all I can say.' I didn't reply. It's difficult to speak when you're choking.

But I was generally fortunate in my choice of associates. John Chilton, who had played trumpet with Bruce Turner's band, joined me for a while. Highly efficient, he was a great help at a busy time of my life. John Cox later came in on a part-time basis. I enjoyed his persistent moan about the quality of life in general, people in particular and, especially, me. In his undulating West Country accent he would declaim 'Oi 'ates people, they brings Oi roight down!', a sentiment with which I was often in hearty accord.

Eventually, in 1963, I was in the same office with three marvellous people: John Chilton, working as press officer for the Swinging Blue Jeans, a Liverpool 'beat' group; a girl from Grimsby, Ann Moss, a charming and capable secretary; and Don Kingswell.

Don Kingswell was another of those rare birds that seem drawn, as if by some migratory instinct, to the entertainment business. He had been around for some time, notably as Cy Laurie's manager. I first got to know him properly in 1962 when he was working for another agent. He was then in his early forties, plump, broad-shouldered and round-faced with hooded eyes. He spoke with a slightly cockney accent and smoked incessantly. His salty observations had us all convulsed with laughter, although Ann affected to be horrified by his comments on sex and marriage. 'Ooooooo, you are naughty!' she would say, in her soft Lincolnshire accent.

Don was also unconsciously funny, an odd contradiction as most funny people have an acute awareness of their own failings, giving them a sharper appreciation of human lunacies generally. Don was totally unaware that he had any faults although with John, Ann and myself in constant proximity he was frequently informed of them. Congenitally incapable of owning up, it was information that he consistently rebutted.

His unconscious humour sprang from an extraordinarily limited vision of existence. To Don it was the immediacy of things that mattered. He didn't relate the parts of life, had no historical or social perspective, often used to say the first thing that came into his head, sometimes tactlessly, and frequently mispronounced.

I frequently mispronounce. For years my specialities were 'halycon' for 'halcyon' and 'public' for 'pubic' hair. Mick Mulligan and Jim Bray were unstinting in their corrections. With Don, the mispronunciations were a daily occurrence. Not that he would accept the corrections any more than he would take other criticisms. Like a plump seal caught in a net, he would wriggle furiously and employ the most ingenious terminology to prove he was right, getting increasingly involved and contradictory as he struggled. It would have been so much simpler for him to own up, but that would have been contrary to one of his cardinal principles. It was in the spirit of banter for which we were known that I would jump on his mispronunciations.

'The word, Don, is specific, not pacific.'

'*Oh*? You *sure*?'

'*Quite* sure.'

'I don't think so.'

'Will the *Oxford Dictionary* be acceptable to you as a reasonable arbiter?'

He would sense defeat. 'If you say so, then' – a grudging acceptance, but only momentary. He was always determined to have the last word, an infuriating characteristic. I attributed this to his being an only child and, typically, spoilt. 'True, I *was* spoilt, but worth spoiling. I was the apple in my mother's eye.'

Some weeks later he returned to the argument. 'I was listening to the news this morning and the announcer definitely said "pacific" and you'll grant that a BBC announcer knows something about the Queen's English.'

'He certainly does but he was probably referring to an ocean of that name, or even someone of that nature, and it's more than likely that you heard what you wanted to hear, very much a characteristic of yours.'

'*Oh, no!* He definitely said it was a pacific case – what was it? – I *know* – a pacific case of foot and mouth disease.'

'Want a bet on it?'

'Oh, *no!* You're always lucky!'

If Don and I had a bet and I won (and then only by offering the most overwhelming evidence) I was 'lucky', never right.

Don was indeed plump ('Not for my size I'm not') and vain ('Reckoned handsome – ask anyone'). I was in a pub with him when an old film starring the matinee idol of the thirties, Ray Milland, was on the television.

'Bloody *hell*,' said Don. 'He *does* look like me.' Some, comparing Mr Milland's fame with Mr Kingswell's, might have put this observation the other way round, even were it true. Not Don. He didn't believe in hiding his light under a bushel. He repeatedly asserted, 'People like me are hard to come by,' a sentiment with which I was in total accord, although not necessarily for the reasons he gave.

At one stage in my see-saw career as an agent, I was working from my flat and if there was any summer sun streaming through the window I would take off my shirt. One hot day Don pounced. 'A lot of spots on your back for someone who is supposed to be on a health food diet.'

'True,' I replied. 'A bit of acne. Haven't had enough sun and air on my skin.'

'That's not acne. They're bloody spots. My skin doesn't get any sun and air, but it's like *velvet*.'

Don thought my vegetarianism, never really very strict, highly amusing. It provoked him to loud and prolonged guffaws. He claimed that all vegetarians looked ill and cited Bruce Turner, Cy Laurie, Tony Coe, Owen Bryce and myself. 'Must be something in that funny diet of yours that draws the blood from the skin' was his considered opinion, quite unaware that his own complexion had the light brown sheen known as the night-club tan, well suited to his dark hair, which was slicked down with copious amounts of Brylcreem in the manner of the pre-war dance-band musicians.

He tackled me about organically grown foods, automatically suspicious and hostile about anything beyond his own horizons. I told him they were grown without the aid of artificial fertilizers and chemical sprays.

'What fertilizers are used, then?' he asked, peering suspiciously over the rims of his spectacles. ('Nothing wrong with my eyesight. Can't read small print, that's all.')

'Compost heaps of rotting vegetables, or horse manure. Anything of vegetable origin.'

'What about horses that eat meat, then? What about their shit, eh? Is that used?'

'Horses don't eat meat.'

'What, none of them?'

'It would be a freak horse that did. They're natural vegetarians.'

'You sure?'

'Quite sure.'

'*Oh*, well, it's a lot of bollocks anyway!' As often happened with Don, the association of ideas would prompt one of his little gems. 'I'm quite happy with my stable diet, thank you. You won't find anyone healthier than me.' He was coughing over a cigarette as he spoke.

Natural history wasn't Don's strong point. He was a completely urban person. If he never saw another blade of grass, another tree or a bird in the sky, it wouldn't trouble him. To him, water was something that came out of a tap. I confess to flogging the diet issue, mainly to enjoy his responses.

'OK I'm filled with "arbo-carbodrates" and I drink – what do you call it – Teutonic [tannic] acid when I have a cup of tea, but I *enjoy* a cup of tea.' He would heavily emphasize the word 'enjoy'. Mentioning certain foodstuffs he all but drooled. When he spoke of 'fish' and 'cream', he would quiver as the words left his mouth, and if eating something that made a strong assault on his taste buds, he would emit an orgiastic 'Aaaaaaaaaaaah!'

He wasn't to be persuaded that health reform principles were of any value. 'All right, I'm full of toxins, but you rarely see me in a bad temper and doing moodies. I can't see your diet improves your temper, but then you drink too much.'

Don was very censorious about the effects of alcohol, but was hardly ever without a cigarette in his mouth. This was a constant bone of contention ('discontention' as he put it) between us. 'Most *normal* people smoke' was his counter argument to my bitter, ceaseless complaints that I, a non-smoker, was being slowly poisoned by his cigarette fumes. 'It would be a good thing if a neuratic like you had a smoke. It would calm your nerves.' One of his favourite portmanteau words, derived from 'neurotic' and 'erratic', was 'neuratic'. I find it difficult to use either of these proper words now that I have this rich and expressive hybrid at my disposal.

He would profess concern about my nervous tension. 'I know what would suit you,' he said one morning. 'A spell at a kaput [he meant a kibbutz]. But that probably wouldn't please you either. Too many arbo-carbodrates in the food, I expect. *Difficult* fellow. *Most* difficult,' and he would shake his head as if I was quite beyond comprehension.

Don's firmly expressed idea of 'relaxation' was to get home as soon as possible ('No hanging around filthy pubs,' he'd say, meaningfully), change into his pyjamas, slippers and dressing-gown and watch TV without pause, food being served and consumed during his intense gaze; cigarettes, lighter, *TV* and *Radio Times* handily placed. Over the weekends his viewing would total some twenty-four hours.

'That's the *sensible* way to behave,' he would proclaim. 'You won't catch me tearing around a cricket field when I should be *relaxing*. You should do the same. All that tearing about at your age can't do you any good. It wouldn't be so bad if you scored any runs. You give yourself a lot of aggro for nothing. *Relax!* Take things easy like I do.'

He mocked my cricketing, well aware that my enthusiasm was considerably in excess of my ability. When I was working from my flat I used to keep a bat handy and essay a few strokes during the lunch break, accompanied by the cry 'WHAM!' when I fancied the ball had made full contact with the meat of the bat. Don would launch into an imaginary conversation with a client.

'Ah come in, Mr Bradley. Do sit down. Nice to see you again. Have a cigarette, Mr Bradley. Sorry about the broken glass. Mr Godbolt was having a few whams. The ball was a bit uppish, he was going to hook it for four when he made contact with the light bulb. He won't be long, Mr Bradley. Just popped over to the pub for a livener. He likes a drink, Mr Bradley. Keen cricketer, though, not that he scores any runs. Pity, things might be a bit cosier on a Monday morning if he did.

'No, Mr Bradley, I don't play myself. Not on your life. I *relax* on Sundays. Too old to be charging round a cricket field. So is he, Mr Bradley, but he won't own up. Do you play, Mr Bradley? No? I expect you're like me. Like to get your feet up over the weekend. You've got to *relax* Mr Bradley, haven't you?'

Don had no hesitation in telling me what others thought about me. Invariably the comments were critical. It appeared from these readily imparted reports that not a single person had a good word to say for me.

'I went to the Chinese Fish Shop in Berwick Street for lunch. Wouldn't suit *you*, of course. Too much clatter. Too many arbo-carbodrates. I got a good whack of stodge down me. Large piece of cod, double portion of chips, a gherkin and white bread and butter. Finished off with a nice cup of Teutonic acid. It was *lovely*! Real food. Not like your cranky nutmeat cutlets. Saw John Cox there. He asked me if I was still with you and I told him. "*Bloody hell*," he said, "don't know how you stand it." '

Only once did he impart a favourable opinion, but he hedged on this, even. 'You can't tell with him, though. He's such a two-faced bastard.'

Don had a wide command of verbal images: 'shooting gallery' for lavatories (where people 'urianated'), 'the Enemy' for Mrs Kingswell, 'nannygoat shitting on tin' for a vocalist who didn't meet with his approval, 'come before the milkman' for premature ejaculation, 'nonsense' for the penis, and 'knocking a round off' for the male contribution to coitus.

There were many others: 'haven't got a pot to piss in' to describe his impecunity, 'a short session of death' for an afternoon nap, 'the downstairs department' for the genitals, and when pontificating about moderation in all things he would proclaim, 'There's a difference between shitting and tearing your arse.'

And, daily, the picturesque mispronunciations: 'Yes, thank you, I'm in fine fetter', 'Aniahalation of affection', 'They charged exuberant prices', 'I'll reincarnate that enquiry for you, Mr Bradley', 'Look here, son, I want a complicit answer from you' and 'phantasglorium' for phantasmagoria were gems that helped to pass the day enjoyably.

He was a convinced monarchist and extremely right-wing in his politics. If John or myself expressed anti-monarchist or left-wing views, he had a familiar automatic response. 'You people,' (his favourite phrase for those whose opinions were not in accord with his own) 'should go and live in Russia.' He strongly disapproved of public entertainers expressing political opinions, although only if they were left-wing sentiments.

His behaviour, he would have us believe, was *the* criterion. One morning I put some memos on his desk before he arrived. As I heard him puffing up the stairs, I motioned to Ann to remain silent and I hid behind the door. He picked up the notes. 'What's all this? More silly bits of paper? Huh! Bloody nonsense! What does he think he's doing? Must be off his head! This is no good! Pity I'm not running this business.' After he had maligned me further, I suddenly appeared from behind the door. His jowls dropped and out came the classic criterion, so often repeated: '*I* don't do things like that!'

In our early days together he had a strange compulsion automatically to take an opposite point of view to mine and if I suggested that an agency be approached to take a certain band or group he would instantly rebut the idea claiming that the party I had suggested wouldn't be the least interested. After pressure, he would reluctantly pick up the phone, snorting impatiently at something so patently useless. Once he reached the office concerned, his phraseology would indicate the answer he wanted to vindicate his own view.

'Hello, George. Don't suppose you're interested in X group? No? Thought so. Not in your line, is it? Sorry to have troubled you.' He would replace the phone and triumphantly look up at me with an apposite comment. I would explode in fury, he would retaliate and Ann would flee the office in fright. Later we were in accord, but not without periodic shout-ups.

I was extremely fond of Don. The vanity, boastfulness and reluctance to admit his faults were combined with a considerable charm, a generosity of spirit and a memorable wit. I often saw him keep a roomful of people convulsed with laughter for an entire evening. He could unaffectedly treat with kings and commoners alike, and he excelled at tour management; the best in the business.

In the mid-fifties, after intense campaigning from the musical papers, principally the *Melody Maker*, the Musicians Union relented sufficiently to agree to a limited exchange of bands between America and Britain, operated mainly by impresario Harold Davison. The case that a limited entry of American jazz musicians would *make* work for British jazz musicians was proven during the 1960s when Harold Davison brought over solo musicians to play tours supported by British bands. My office co-promoted these tours and Don looked after the visitors.

To meet and talk with these heroes of mine was a thrill, a dream come true. Don mocked this adulation and threw a few barbs about 'fuddy-duddy fan worship'. I had no retort, except to say that I was grateful for those whose playing had given me such deep and abiding pleasure, whose records had changed my life and, indeed, set its very pattern.

When John Chilton and I used to discuss these musicians and their discographies with obvious, perhaps adolescent-like enthusiasm, the Kingswell jowls wobbled in disbelief. '*You* people! You make me laugh! You and your scratchy old 78s!' He mockingly invented his own 'discogaphal' figure, one Matthews, whose instrument Don changed from week to week but who, according to him, recorded for the Regal-Zonophone label in 1926.

'Great player, Matthews! Really socks out the blues. Can't wait to get home and play his 78s. An evening of Matthews really knocks me and the Enemy right out!' The Regal-Zonophone label didn't exist in 1926, but it had sufficiently antique associations to support Don's barbs.

It was this lack of interest in jazz that, paradoxically, endeared him to the visiting firemen. He didn't bug them with ceaseless questions about their past, and he protected them from those who did. This questioning of veteran jazz musicians is one of their occupational hazards and one player, trombonist Vic Dickenson, actually fled a hall and locked himself in a car to escape his questioners.

Many were amazed at the knowledge displayed by collectors. In 1949 Louis Armstrong set foot in this country en route to play a festival in Nice. Among the host of worshippers who arrived at London Airport was an intrepid journalist and collector determined to discover if Louis had played on an obscure record made in 1930 called 'Blue Yodel No.9', recorded by hill-billy singer Jimmie Rodgers. The journalist was Max Jones, who brought a wind-up gramophone to the VIP's room, sat before an astonished Armstrong and played him the record. It was a unique situation. Here was a major artiste of our time, with an international reputation, confronted by a journalist armed with a portable gramophone and a box of steel needles. Louis declared he was on the record and another entry went firmly into the Armstrong discography. The *Melody Maker* proudly headlined their 'Collector's Corner' column CORNER SCOOPS WORLD ON 1930 ARMSTRONG DISC.

I should have known better but I often ploughed in with references to the past without first sounding out the subject's willingness to talk. Once I was having a drink with tenor saxophonist Bud Freeman before he appeared at the Bull's Head, Barnes. I mentioned I had been listening to records he had made with violinist Joe Venuti in 1933. He froze. '*We* don't discuss those *old* records. They were made *so* long ago. *Now* if you could hear the discs I made with two guitars *last* year . . .' At that moment Sinclair Traill, editor of Britain's longest established jazz magazine, *Jazz Journal*, and a close friend of the Honourable Gerald Lascelles, appeared at the door and Freeman, for all his sixty years, bounded away like a young gazelle, leaving me, and my observations about records made in 1933, for dead – probably to discuss some aspect of the British monarchy, Bud being a devout admirer of the Royal Family.

Another visitor, trumpeter Wingy Manone, was quite forthcoming but didn't have too favourable an impression of England. 'Too many niggers on the sidewalk' was one of his pronouncements, an odd comment from a man who frequently boasted about his friendship with Louis Armstrong. But he was professional in his approach, and played well.

There were other visitors whose behaviour was extremely unprofessional and who often played very badly. My dream of meeting so many legendary figures often became a living nightmare and many of the romantic images nurtured over the years were unhappily destroyed after some hair-raising experiences with idols who had feet of clay, and were in some cases over-fond of strong drink.

The tenor saxophonist Don Byas carried an obscene litany which every young lady fortunate enough to know the joy of his passion was obliged to read first. This selection of odes was but one unsavoury feature of an abrupt, aggressive and unlovely person. Don Kingswell, genial and anxious to please, introduced himself. He told Byas that his job was to look after him throughout the tour and mentioned that a previous tour by saxophonist Ben Webster had been spoilt by Ben's excessive drinking. Byas assured Don that he, unlike Webster, could take his drink. Kingswell, relieved, added that

Webster had carried a big knife. He was further relieved that Byas appeared to respond with incredulous disbelief. He soon discovered why. 'You don't say!' exclaimed Byas. 'A big knife, huh? You call that thing Ben had a big knife? That was nuthin'. Look at this, man. Now *here's* a *big* knife,' and as he spoke he drew a fearsome-looking dagger from his belt. Don backed away in understandable fright.

Ben Webster sober was an engaging person and played marvellously. Drunk, he was aggressive and played badly. One night he surpassed himself by striding, naked and unashamed, through a hotel corridor brandishing his knife and tried to obtain entry into a ladies' toilet where his girlfriend was hiding. He had a penchant for ladies' toilets. He repeated his attempt to gain entry into one at a US serviceman's club in London when his lady friend had again fled to safety.

This was a dramatic finale to a phantasmagoric evening. The accompanying band had a fine piano player who was also a renowned soak. With him and Webster both very drunk, the proceedings soon degenerated into a fiasco. When he wasn't actually playing, Webster was haranguing his girl; the pianist was all but slumped over the keyboard; and the rest of the band, understandably, were hardly playing their best.

Don Kingswell, helpless in the circumstances, was buttonholed by the club's secretary, a beefy master sergeant, who pointed to the pianist's condition. Don assured him that the pianist's demeanour indicated total concentration on his playing. As he spoke, the pianist's head hit the keyboard with a resounding crash, producing a cluster of splintered chords that had no relation to the tune he was attempting to play.

'It was phantasglorium,' said Don the following day. 'Absolute bloody *phantasglorium*!' The club paid only half the contracted fee. I could hardly blame them. They had booked a jazz package and got a 'phantasglorium' instead.

I had an unhappy experience with Ben when he was rehearsing with Bruce Turner's band. Normally I never said a word at rehearsals, but Bruce was seemingly struck dumb and the pianist was struggling with unfamiliar tunes Ben wanted to play. I unwisely stepped in and suggested that Ben play some numbers with the band and give the pianist a chance to study the chords. Webster agreed in a surly fashion and still Bruce remained silent. Having previously discussed the programme with Bruce, I prompted him and Webster savagely turned on me. 'Do you *mind*!' he snarled. 'Let the man speak.'

When Ben Webster was aroused his expression was alarmingly malevolent. I immediately retired to a corner and when a brief and scrappy rehearsal was over Ben, a paunchy, shambling man, lumbered over to me and in a tone supercharged with sarcasm asked if the rehearsal had been OK by me. Now thoroughly chastened I mumbled assent. 'Oh, that's *fine*,' he said. 'As long as it's OK by *you*,' and shambled away to talk to a friend. His voice floated over. 'You're right, man. He was a fool, but there's always a fool about.' He didn't have to look in my direction, nor did I have to be paranoiac to appreciate that I was the person he had in mind.

Later I rang him to apologize for what seemed to be interference. It took him some time to connect me with the person he had rubbished that afternoon. Perhaps he had seen a few more off since. I explained that I only wanted to be of assistance. 'That's OK man. I understand, but you must remember I've been rehearsing musicians for ninety-nine years.'

We had a rough passage with US trombonist Dickie Wells. We had been warned that he was a 'drunky-punky', to use Don's pungent description, but when he arrived at my office he looked fit and spruce for someone in his late fifties and an alleged alcoholic. He was charming and fully co-operative but there was a nudging undercurrent of doubt. No one ever offered him a drink and at a dinner party given in his honour by Max and Betty Jones, Betty, placed in an awkward situation, offered him only Coca-Cola when the rest of us were drinking considerably stronger beverages. In this embarrassing conspiracy of silence no one mentioned his alleged addiction. Perhaps the matter should have been brought out into the open.

He and the band (Alex Welsh's) played their first dates in Switzerland, and in a café with a girl he ordered a Coca-Cola for himself. The girl made scornful reference to a jazzman taking a soft drink. This jab at his ego sparked off a disastrous train of events, and on some nights he was too drunk to play. One evening he was in a restaurant with the band and well drunk. He looked hungrily at a steak one of the band was eating, grabbed it with his hand, took a hefty bite and replaced it.

The manager of the hotel remembered him from a pre-war trip to Europe and asked his distinguished visitor to be the first to sign a brand new visitors' book. The distinguished visitor didn't realize that the pen offered him was a biro and when he failed to make it write, he maniacally plunged it into a bread roll, thinking it was an inkwell.

My first intimation of these disasters was a call from Don Kingswell at London Airport, where he had gone to meet Wells. I thought he was kidding, having received a reassuring postcard at the beginning of the tour, but his grave tone and description of Wells covered in blood from a drunken fall soon convinced me otherwise.

Later a representative of the Davison office and myself called on Wells in his hotel room, a functional box, sparsely furnished for minimum requirements. His head was bandaged. The light was dim. Playing the alcoholic's deception game, he warmly greeted us, quickly told us how much he had enjoyed the tour, and what a great bunch of guys the band were. The Davison representative threatened to send him home. Wells pleaded that the tour be continued and promised to abstain from drink. Angry and depressed as I was, I felt sick for him. He had been a giant of jazz in his time. Now he was a pathetic wreck alone in that hotel room.

The Alex Welsh band, themselves renowned drinkers, were understandably fearful of their reputation and pressed for the tour to be cancelled. They were persuaded to continue and my mind darted in many directions to seek a solution, even thinking, with the optimism of the desperate, that Wells could be cured of his addiction.

I phoned the local office of Alcoholics Anonymous and spoke to an official. He thought the man whose condition I described was myself and that I was hiding the fact. He urged me to confess my addiction. 'After all, old boy, we're all in this boat together you know. It's best to come clean and we'll see what we can do to help.' I had to admit that I was conceivably in need of help but my problems were not so pressing. Only partially convinced, the AA man gave me the address of a clinic in West London. As though in a mad dream, I spoke to someone with a thick Viennese accent urging me to send Wells along for a deterrent pill. He asserted that if he were foolish enough to drink alcohol after taking this pill the effects would be dire. He said, ' 'E will turn green, I promise you.' A mental picture of Wells, a light-skinned Negro, turning green on taking a drink was a bizarre touch that had me reeling.

It was a tough three weeks. Wells and the band had been booked to appear on a BBC show called 'Jazz 625'. The rehearsal, at the Shepherds Bush studio, was called at 11 a.m. At 11.30 I got an urgent call from a Alex Welsh advising me to make haste to the studio. He could see our that Wells had been drinking. I rushed to the studio and was relieved to find that he was anything but drunk (having had long experience of discerning that condition), but I was frightened that a few more snorts would put paid to the day's proceedings. I made no reference to his drinking. I tell myself to this day that I remained silent because I wanted no upsets on a show that was one of a series with all the other US visitors lined up to appear in it, but it was undoubtedly moral cowardice combined with the last vestige of hero worship that held my tongue.

When Wells left the dressing-room to rehearse with the band, I discovered a half-bottle of whisky in his instrument case. Some of it had been drunk. I was in an agonizing dilemma. If I left the whisky for him to finish, it might render him incapable. If I poured it away his prop would be taken from underneath him. I temporized, and emptied half the contents down the sink, resisting the temptation to pour the lot down my gullet. I replaced the bottle on its side so that the contents might not appear to have diminished.

It was the longest day. From the time I discovered the whisky I watched Wells like a cat tensed over a mousehole. I reckoned that he would see the day through as long as he *thought* he could get at that bottle. Time and time again he went to his instrument case to withdraw his trombone and give it an unnecessary polish.

It was the appearance of a veteran collector and his wife that could have proved our undoing. The dressing-room had two centre sliding doors. When they met the room was divided into two. The half partition nearer to me was extended and Alex Welsh, changing his trousers, closed the partition nearer to him to shield the lady from the spectacle. This was Wells's opportunity. In a matter of seconds he was away, with instrument case and its precious liquid contents. I searched for him in vain, and next saw him walking down a flight of stairs with a triumphant gleam in his eyes. He'd had his taste; enough to set him up for the show.

As it happened, the show went well, but I wasn't to know this when I first discovered the drink, nor was I to know if this whisky was merely starters; he might have had other bottles hidden away. I rushed to the nearest pub and, putting drinks down me with unseemly haste, muttered curses on all alcoholic jazzmen.

At the end of the show our troublesome visitor came into the dressing-room, sighed and said, 'Must get some sleep. Sure has been a hard day.' I was silently echoing these sentiments when he looked intently at me and said, 'Think you should do the same. You kinda look all-in,' and coolly, deliberately, he added, 'Guess all that liquor you been drinking won't do you much good, either.'

I was rendered dumb. Had I not stood over him all day, there's no knowing what sort of shambles would have ensued.

The shambles came a few nights later at a club on the south coast. He swayed on to the stage, dropped his instrument, couldn't retrieve it, and had to be led off. There were only a few more days of the tour and the band philosophically resigned themselves to the worst.

One of the last engagements was at a West Country university. The home rugby team had won a game for the first time that season and almost all the audience, celebrating victory, were drunk. So was the guest star, but the patron saint of soaks was by his side that night. The social secretary was emphatic that he couldn't possibly allow an artiste of Wells's calibre to appear before an audience so thoroughly boozed. He paid the band off with further apologies.

Propped up in a chair in the corner of the dressing-room, staring rigidly ahead with glazed, non-seeing eyes, was the artiste to whom the condition of the audience would have been an affront. He was sent home. A month or so later he wrote me an allusively apologetic letter and enclosed a weird selection of good luck trinkets for Don, John Chilton, the band and myself. There was also a gift for the Davison representative. It was a particularly evil-looking glass eye, as though Wells had put the Harlem curse on him.

Pianist Earl Hines, confrère of Louis Armstrong in the late twenties, and later with Louis's All-Stars, toured this country in 1965 with Alex Welsh's band. We had met when he toured this country with Jack Teagarden in 1957 but, understandably, he showed no sign of recognition. Touring musicians meet thousands of people and can hardly be expected to remember every face and name, but I imagine that one unfortunate night in his 1965 tour remained etched on his memory long afterwards. It happened at the Hideaway club in Hampstead, at which I used to run sessions.

I had booked him with Alex Welsh's excellent rhythm section, but asked if he would play a spot with some of my favourite musicians, Bruce Turner, John Picard and Sandy Brown. Hines demurred. 'Why do I need other musicians – I've got ten musicians here,' he said, splaying both hands to illustrate his meaning. But, reluctantly, he agreed.

The session was a disaster, and for what reason I'll never know. Bruce Turner, a fine saxophonist, but low on moral fibre, was the first to leave the stand and Picard soon followed, leaving Sandy to

struggle bravely, or obdurately, or both, with a quite unco-operative
Hines. Sandy didn't give up. If Hines had wanted these men off the
stage, he reckoned without the fortitude of Alexander Brown,
FRIBA, clarinettist, composer, blues singer, writer, pianist, painter
and raconteur. It was an utterly dismaying turn of events. When the
number eventually came to a painful close, Hines stormed up to me.
'Don't you ever dare put me on with those guys again,' he yelled,
adding a few steaming epithets about me. For years I had revered
Hines, and at that moment I felt like departing to nearby
Hampstead Heath and seeking the deepest pond.

There were other occasions, too, when I often wished that contact
with my heroes had been limited to gramophone records, but I had
extremely happy experiences with some of our visitors. I cherish
memories of meetings with great Negro jazzmen – clarinettists
Albert Nicholas and Edmond Hall, trombonist Vic Dickenson and
trumpeters Red Allen, Rex Stewart and Bill Coleman among them.

The worst experience in my entire business career was with a
visiting artiste, although not a jazzman. He and his bodyguard, both
Negro, and his manager, Jewish, were blatantly and viciously racial
in their antipathy towards Don and myself. It was a strange
experience to suffer what is the daily lot of millions. Here it had
disastrous effects on a tour that was supposed to be profitable and
prestigious. The component parts of six horrendous weeks turned
out to be deception, blackmail, violence and bloody-mindedness.

I was contractually obliged to various parties to continue with the
agony, but it was only thanks to Don's courage and patience that the
tour went the full course.

A lawsuit followed and my solicitor was enthusiastic about the
outcome. 'I enjoy a good fight, Mr Godbolt,' he said. The case never
came to court (my adversary was prevailed upon to make settlement)
and I received a letter from my doughty solicitor, the relevant
paragraph of which read as follows:

Mr X has agreed to pay £185 from the joint account. In view of
the fact that this matter is now closed I hereby enclose my firm's
bill. In fact the total costs and disbursements listed herewith
amount to £189, but as you are not personally recovering any sum
from the settlement the costs have been deliberately rounded off
to the sum received.

Such generosity overwhelmed me! I swore I would never go into court again merely for the benefit of lawyers. This letter was an appropriate postscript to a tour that was a nightmare. At the end of it the graphic Kingswell remarked, 'I tell you, boy, those three shithouses are rotten all through. I wouldn't piss on them if they were burning!'

Don was a good friend. A good man to have at one's side. Our improbable relationship lasted for seven years and he came into my business at a time when the entire shape and colour of the business generally was about to be drastically transformed.

9

Bombshell Hits the Profession

During the fifties the popular music scene had been extremely varied with big dance bands, trad and modern jazz bands, solo singers like Dickie Valentine, Frankie Vaughan, Alma Cogan and – let us not forget – Eddie 'Golden Trumpet' Calvert. Newly emerging were the rock and roll stars – Tommy Steele, Vince Eager, Duffy Power and Cliff Richard. These were a portent of things to come.

On ITV there was a show called 'Hoots Mon' featuring Lord Rockingham's Eleven, a unit of highly competent dance band musicians cynically, lucratively, playing rock and roll.

Humphrey Lyttelton wrote of rock and roll: 'The rhythmic essence of jazz, extracted, simplified, exaggerated . . . a formula of the heavy off-beat on the drums and honking saxophones . . . suggestive lyrics . . .' He lashed into 'Hoots Mon'. The show's producer, Jack Good, retaliated by averring that the musicians concerned were better than Humph. Hùmph replied, 'I've no doubt these musicians can read music better than I can. No one denies the pro her technique . . .'

Steve Race wrote in the *Melody Maker*, 'Viewed as a social phenomenon the current craze for rock and roll is one of the most terrifying things ever to have happened in popular music. And, of course, we follow the lead of the American music industry. When Father turns, we all turn.'

Many believed rock and roll to be a passing phase. Agent Harold Davison, quoted in the *Melody Maker*, said, 'My bands will be featuring it while the demand lasts, like they featured bebop and the mamba. But any band that ties its destiny to rock and roll is likely to die when the craze burns out.'

The rock and roll craze of the fifties was but a mere tremor presaging the explosion to come. It was not until 1962 that the volcano erupted with a cataclysmic fury when the *Melody Maker* could have used their favourite war-time heading 'Bombshell Hits the Profession' with every justification. Two British groups, the Beatles and the Rolling Stones, were the catalysts of the upheaval.

Not one of the previous developments in popular music this century – Edwardian ballads, twenties dance and jazz music, thirties swing, forties bebop and revivalism – had anything like the shattering impact made by these two groups dramatically rising from obscurity in the early sixties. This transformation of the popular music scene was sociologically highly significant. It was largely created by newly affluent teenagers buying vast numbers of records by performers whose music and life-style were in accord with their own youthful thinking and aspirations. The teenagers' choice of idols affected a mass audience. There could hardly have been a soul in the land who didn't know the name and face of every Beatle and Mick Jagger of the Rolling Stones. This couldn't be said of any other combination of singers and instrumentalists in any other area of popular music at any time.

The revolution wasn't engineered by businessmen. In fact many entrepreneurs in all parts of the business had initially rejected those artists so much a part of the change, but soon the record industry was athrob with frantic activity. Thousands of records were made in an attempt to cash in on the rock and roll bonanza. A mass of hitherto unknown young faces became news; the Beatles were to become millionaires. The 'professional' musician turned rock and roller faded from sight. Jazz reeled from the blast; the touring large dance band all but disappeared; there was much less emphasis on the solo singer; Eddie Calvert emigrated to South Africa.

These shattering changes were to alter the pattern of many agents' activities, mine included. Jazz clubs, and the bands who relied on them for the best part of their income, folded. At the height of the trad boom there were forty bands on the road. The number quickly dwindled to a mere half dozen. Understandably, rock and roll groups proliferated. If two groups of working-class boys could achieve fame and fortune with voice and guitar, the example was there for thousands to follow.

From the mid-fifties I had been booking jazz bands into the Mardi Gras, Liverpool, owned by Jim Ireland. Jim managed the Swinging Blue Jeans, whom I represented. They had a minor chart success with a song called 'Too Late Now', and followed up with a smash hit,

'Hippy Hippy Shake'. It raced to No 2 in the hit parade charts of most papers and to No 1 in one publication.

I take no credit for the Blue Jeans' record success but some praise, perhaps, for the manner in which my office handled the situation. We did the job in which we were experienced and the mechanics of booking are the same for a hit parade group as for one utterly unknown. The financial outcome of the former happens to be considerably more rewarding. That hit record changed everything. It was the same group, with the same act and the same material but with an important difference. They were in the Top Ten, the pop metamorphosis. Before 'Too Late Now' £30 an engagement was the norm; after 'Too Late Now' £75; after 'Hippy Hippy Shake' between £250 and £300 a night.

With this increased income I wasn't unwilling to adapt to the new scene. It was no longer possible to live by jazz bands alone, and I wasn't the only jazz agent, getting on a bit, to be found sitting among screaming adolescents in concert halls wondering what it was all about. It was imperative we found out. Or go under.

Our daily contacts broadened. They were no longer just the friendly coterie of like-minded people that made up the business side of jazz. That familiar camaraderie remained, if somewhat shaken, but the daily round now included people previously unknown to us. I continued to book jazz bands where the demand continued and on Saturday nights I was among people I really knew at the Six Bells, but our daily preoccupation was booking the emergent groups, particularly the Swinging Blue Jeans.

'Hippy Hippy Shake' temporarily changed my status as an agent. It was relatively short-lived glory that I found not only profitable but highly illuminating. Agents to whom I had never spoken before would ring and solicitously enquire after my health. Prior to this they hadn't been too concerned with my well-being, probably because they had never heard of me. Nor had I heard of them.

After receiving assurances that my health was sound, their delight in this knowing no bounds, the agents would invite me to lunch. This concern for my health and appetite was typical of the business ethic. Success, or associated success, was the yardstick by which each individual was measured.

Another agent then new to me rang. 'Hello, Jim *bhoy*. Did you have a nice Christmas?' The enquiry surprised me a little, as the calendar read 7 February.

My new status had its moments, especially when dealing with

certain hard-headed promoters. One of them was eager to place the
Blue Jeans in an extended concert tour. I went to see him with more
than bookings for the Blue Jeans in my sights. I had another group of
Jim Ireland's that badly needed exposure and a nationwide tour with
big names was just the opportunity. I made it an implicit condition
that one wouldn't be booked without the other. I didn't have to
make the stipulation in so many words. My meaning was perfectly
clear. 'This is blackmail,' spluttered the promoter, a ruthless
operator who wouldn't have hesitated one second to apply the same
methods if it suited him. I walked out of his office with a bit of a
power complex, just for once.

Robert Stigwood, a highly successful impresario, then promoting
pop concerts, wanted to speak to me about booking the Blue Jeans.
He was apologetic about being unable to come and see me owing to
pressure of business but if he sent a car around to pick me up, would I
be prepared to come along and discuss a deal?

An enormous shiny limousine, driven by a uniformed chauffeur,
appeared outside my office in Wardour Street to collect me. As I
stepped into this elegant motor, I casually looked around to see if
any of my contemporaries were about. They would have had no
trouble in seeing me. Ostentatiously, I sat in full view, there and
back. The negotiation for £300 a night was plain sailing. The Blue
Jeans were in the Top Ten. I'd expended a lot more time and nervous
energy trying to get a fifty-pound engagement for Mick Mulligan
that morning.

About four years later I was in Stigwood's office haggling with
one of his minions about an inter-office commission dispute when
the impresario walked in, looked straight through me and walked
out without a word. I was lucky to get any commission out of this
wrangle and I caught the 73 bus back to my office.

The Swinging Blue Jeans were a good, musicianly group with a
highly professional approach to their work but, initially, the success
of 'Hippy Hippy Shake' went to their heads a little. Like so many
other young men they were unable fully to adjust to sudden success.
Ray Ennis, the leader, was given to bawling us out on patent
trivialities, and another of the group, who left it shortly afterwards,
felt his position to be so exalted that he would imperiously summon
the road manager into his presence and make peremptory commands.

'Bert! Hand me my guitar!'

The instrument was literally under his nose, but he saw himself as
a big star and the road manager a lackey to obey as commanded. In

fact this particular road manager basked in reflected glory and by his arrogant and high-handed attitude to people in the business generally, it was obvious that he flicked some of the stardust on to himself.

Later, when economic truths faced the group, we all became the best of friends and I remained their agent for seven years, without a contract, right up to the time I left the business.

We quickly discovered that a group's fees for their public appearances were strictly related to their chart successes, irrespective of any intrinsic value. Much depended on good material, and only a small proportion of the mass of material offered was suitable. Few had hit potential, but publishers were a pushing species. During the success of 'Hippy Hippy Shake' my phone was hot with calls from them. Speaking from the bottom of their hearts they would fervently assure me they had 'the very number for the bhoys, *bhoy*. Must be No 1, *bhoy*.'

The Blue Jeans didn't repeat their 'Hippy Hippy Shake' success but occasionally appeared in the charts over two or three years. Their last hit was a version of a tune called 'Don't Make Me Over'. I sent the record to the producer of the TV show 'Sunday Night at the London Palladium', fully aware that it could easily be overlooked among dozens of other recordings. Later I made the usual follow-up calls. The producer had mislaid the record, but his secretary had praised it. He asked for another copy on the strength of her recommendation. On such apparently slender threads are reputations made! I virtually sprinted round to his office with the record and the Blue Jeans got a booking on the show.

The day of the performance was of great moment to Don. To him the Palladium was holy ground. To tread those hallowed boards meant you had truly arrived. He had enjoyed an association with the theatre in his affluent days, before he was reduced, as he often implied, to working for me. He would hire a box every Sunday afternoon for the Ted Heath Swing Sessions, load it with drinks and cigarettes and act as host for the cast of the show. Don always referred lovingly to 'the Green', an abbreviation of 'Greengage', rhyming slang for stage, and his association with show-biz went back to the late thirties when he used to escort Vera Walsh, later known as Vera Lynn, to her first professional engagement with Charlie Kunz's band at the Club Casani, Regent Street.

The Swinging Blue Jeans: chart-toppers from Liverpool who had the author as their agent for seven years without a contract. *Left to right*: Ralph Ellis, Norman Kuhlke, Ray Ennis, Les Braid.

Don Kingswell, 'master of the malapropism', was in the author's employment for ten years. A former publican, he had managed Cy Laurie's jazz club in London's Soho.

Brian Epstein, the manager of the then-unknown Beatles, asked Kingswell to get them jobs in London but he advised them to stay where they were – a reply he later regretted. (Photo courtesy Marquee Organization)

On the day of the Swinging Blue Jeans' appearance at the
Palladium, he shook hands with all the musicians in Jack Parnell's
resident orchestra, puffed with pride that 'his' boys were appearing
on this show of shows. It was an atmosphere that made an
unfavourable impression on me. I have never been prey to show-biz
mystique. It always struck me as the gold that never really glistered,
and I hated all that spurious and vomitory hand-shaking and back-
slapping that is a mandatory exercise among the beaming performers. Don found my attitude utterly incomprehensible.

Not that I was unhappy about the Blue Jeans' appearance at this
shrine of admass entertainment and had there been any bowing or
scraping to be done before the producer and his staff I would have
genuflected without a moment's hesitation, an agent's pride being
entirely expendable.

The show was a boost for the Blue Jeans (and their agent) who
had been out of the limelight for some time, and they performed
extremely well, Ray Ennis particularly. After they had finished their
spot, I made for the nearest pub with a happy but exhausted Don. He
had been at the theatre since ten that morning.

There were a few wives and girlfriends of the group in the pub and
I hesitantly introduced myself to one of the girlfriends, adding that I
was not quite certain who she was. She introduced her mother and
father, and mum, misunderstanding what I had said, looked at her
extremely attractive daughter and replied, 'Oh, yes, we're often
mistaken for each other.' At that moment Don joined the company
and was completely thrown by a claim that can only be described as
exaggerated. His jaw dropped as he took an involuntary, comparing
glance. As it happened it was the sort of flattering comparison he
would have made, had he thought of it. Don could lay the smooch-
treacle on with a trowel if he reckoned it would enhance his image or
further his ends in any way. I had to look away from the flummoxed
Kingswell in case I erupted with laughter. Mum also knew a lot
about the business. Looking intently at me she expressed the opinion
that the group should be doing much better than they were.

At the time, as now, there were searing allegations that the charts
were being rigged by unscrupulous agents, managers and record
producers and the *Melody Maker* rightly came out heavily against
this skulduggery and changed its method of compiling retailers'
returns. It was undoubtedly a sincere attempt to stop any machinations that could affect the paper's long-standing reputation, but
the business was too diversified and involved too many people on a

nationwide scale for there to be a completely effective prevention of these abuses.

I confess I would have had no compunction in trying to fiddle a chart entry had I known how, rationalizing that if records were being engineered into the charts the chances of my groups' records making an entry were reduced – not that I convinced myself, even, of this argument's validity.

Another aspect of the new scene was the number of groups who insisted that the agent should travel vast distances to hear them. Proud fathers would appear at the office with demonstration records of their sons' talents, others with only paternal affirmation of vocal and instrumental ability. 'My boy's got a fine new group' was a claim I heard a few times. I listened to as many as possible. The dread fear that a segment of the Beatles' history might be repeated haunted us all.

Despite the riotous acclaim they received in Liverpool, no one in London – agents, promoters, recording and publishing companies – had been interested in the Beatles. They were just another beat group from the provinces. When they achieved unprecedented global fame in an astonishingly short time, there was much hand-wringing and many sleepless nights from those who had had the opportunity to earn fortunes from this bonanza but had been blind to their chances.

Don Kingswell was one of the first to be approached by Brian Epstein, the Beatles' manager. Don was road manager of a package that featured the American rock and roll star, Little Richard. Before the tour began the organizer gave Don firm instructions that when the show played Liverpool, on no account was a group called the Beatles to play more than two numbers, further advising him that the promoter of the show also managed the Beatles and would insist on more, a delicate situation in which Don was cautioned to 'use his loaf'. Don used his loaf, the Beatles played only two numbers and a possible fortune slipped through his fingers. Epstein asked him to represent the group in London and Don replied, 'Mr Epstein, there are five thousand groups like that in London all looking for work. They wouldn't stand a chance. You keep them working round here where they are known.'

Later, when Don proclaimed that he 'hadn't got a pot to piss in' he ruefully meditated on what might have been.

He was by no means the only one.

Most people in the jazz world congratulated me on my good fortune in representing a hit parade group, but there were exceptions. I was in a pub prior to attending a concert featuring the great US trumpeter Red Allen, when jazz record-shop owner Doug Dobell lurched up to me and venomously hissed, '*Godbolt! Traitor to Jazz!*'

On another occasion I walked into Acker Bilk's office and received a touch of the ideologicals from Frank Parr. He had been a fervent, if expatriate, Liverpudlian but bewailed he'd lost pride in his home-town since its new claim to fame as the spawning ground of 'Merseybeat'. As he was handling Acker Bilk's date sheet, he could earn a living and retain his ideologicals; but he was hardly in a position to adopt such a stern moral posture. He and his office were actively concerned (as I pointedly remarked) in the promotion of All-in Wrestling, surely (as I pointedly remarked) the least edifying of spectacles with the possible exception of the Miss World contests.

David Bilk, not normally one to lose an opportunity to score a point, hastily put a clamp on any further observations about my fall from grace, probably because if the opportunity had arisen for his office to represent any of these emergent attractions he wouldn't have been too bothered about Frank's ideological objections.

Generously, I forgave Frank for his strictures. Most jazzers, including myself, had long adopted moral postures about our beloved music, a habit ingrained after long membership of a minority group and, indeed, I was strenuously protesting the value of jazz over the music that was now making me some real money.

In 1963 the *Melody Maker* carried a five-column spread entitled, 'Dr Godbolt or – How I Learned to Stop Worrying and Love the Boom'. It comprised an interview with myself, approached from the angle of a long-time jazz booker/enthusiast now representing a successful rock and roll group, but still speaking up for jazz.

I answered the questions fairly objectively, but rationalized about the quality of rock and roll. The sentiments I expressed were more than a slight bending of my true beliefs, but professionally I could hardly do otherwise. A plum had fallen into my lap and it would have been ungracious and uneconomic to knock it. I knew well that my luck might not last, and indeed it wasn't long before I was back to the familiar struggle of keeping office and staff together.

The pursuit of profit makes for odd bedfellows. After the Blue Jeans' short-lived glory I found myself dealing with an agent whose bullying, hectoring persona and neighing laugh I couldn't stomach, but the prospect of making money triumphed over my personal objections.

We went to Amsterdam to negotiate a contract. My presence was quite unnecessary. He was the dominant partner in the arrangement and did all the talking, but he wanted company, an essential continually eluding him, and I wanted money, an essential continually eluding me.

The business over, we had several drinks and stumbled into a dubious night club on the town's outskirts, near a canal. We were joined by two young ladies. At least, they looked reasonably young in the club's dim lighting. Drink lent enchantment to the view nearer me and we went to her room in a 'hotel', arrived at after a round trip of the city by taxi, a con arrangement with the driver, I suspected.

After a lot to drink and a lengthy taxi ride there was a considerable build-up in my bladder and on arriving at the foyer I was bursting for a pee. There was a further hold-up as the girl insisted that the proprietor saw that we were signed in, presumably to present the appearance of respectability to this establishment. In the not-so-dim lighting of the 'hotel' foyer, and having sobered up a bit, the view was infinitely less enchanting and I hardly looked my romantic best writhing about, my bladder protesting for relief.

The upshot of these factors was carnal failure. I made what I thought to be a generous settlement, bearing in mind the circuitous taxi ride, and tumbled into the street, narrowly avoiding falling into the canal, with my ego, funds and mid member much depressed.

I walked what seemed for miles before I got a cab and was lucky to have just enough to pay the driver. Back at the hotel I thankfully slumped into bed, but (just my luck) my associate made his return a minute or two afterwards.

I feigned sleep, but he shook me and boomed, 'Well, how did you get on then?'

'Brewer's Droop,' I replied and pulled the bedclothes over my head.

'Hard luck,' he chortled. 'Mine was a cracker! Marvellous shag. She said I was the best she'd ever had and gave me my money back.'

I groaned in sheer disbelief. An Amsterdam whore returning her fee to *him* . . . the mind boggled. But he wasn't finished.

'On the way back here a car drew up with two marvellous dollies in the back. The guy asked me to jump in. "We'll go back to my flat and have a session," he said. "Which do you prefer? The wife or her sister?" I had the wife. What a grind! Hell, I'm shagged out, must get some sleep.'

Which is more than I got. His snoring, at first a quivering whisper, gradually developed in a wall-shuddering crescendo. After an hour of this thunderous din I couldn't bear it any longer and I made for the door, taking my mattress with me. I squeezed through a constricted passage, aiming for the furthermost point, the bathroom, but couldn't negotiate the mattress through its narrow doorway. I settled for the corridor and was at least separated from this heaving beast by the thickness of the door, but throughout the night I was frequently awakened, despite a bellyful of drink, by the monstrous volume rising and falling from within.

When morning came he opened the door to get to the bathroom and stepped over me without a single word of inquiry or expression of surprise as to why I should have picked up my bed and walked. Obviously it was no new experience to him.

He had a good business brain, the manners of a hog and an utter contempt for human values. He later screwed me up without mercy, but I had only myself to blame. I had truckled to his dominant personality, one of his succession of dogs, but I didn't always come to heel. I had held a candle to the devil for the sake of profit. I'm not the only sinner in this regard, and that's some sort of consolation.

10

Musty Smell of 78s

In 1968, after a run of disasters due both to bad luck and faulty judgement, I joined the Bron Organization, a management agency and publishing complex. I was a fish in someone else's pond but had no regrets. A measure of security in an expanding organization was better than having my name on the notepaper (which it was, in the minutest of print). But after a year or so I was making useless comparisons between the seemingly ugly present and a generally enjoyable past.

The artistes managed by Gerry Bron were mostly pleasant people, but the business generally had a fair proportion of monsters, many of whom we booked on behalf of our clients. We booked a much publicized group to play a ball for a fee of £750, a quite handsome figure for a one-hour spot. The group's management laid down a variety of contractual stipulations, one of them a lengthy clause obliging the sponsors to provide full security arrangements to safeguard the group from being mobbed by fans and their equipment from being burgled or damaged.

It was a reasonable enough stipulation, albeit one couched in terms more appropriate to the announcement of the Second Advent, but on the night of the engagement a security guard apprehended a drunk, dishevelled and ranting figure in the grounds round the venue. It was the leader of the group.

Inside the hall the group leader abused the guard and the organizing officials, threatened the guard with a fire axe and demanded that unless he were instantly dismissed the group would not play the engagement. He further insisted that one of the girl employees strip off, and ordered everyone else out of the room.

Denied this extra-contractual stipulation – I am sure his office had the omission of such a provision rectified in subsequent contracts – he demanded to be told the whereabouts of the lavatory. Advised of this, he decided it was too far for him to walk – he had had a tiring day – and urinated out of the window over passers-by.

The promoter could have justifiably cancelled the engagement but not with two thousand people in the hall who had paid to see the group and were unaware of back-stage dramas. Such extreme behaviour wasn't that common, but more frequent than was good for business and, as my share was a percentage of gross turnover, I was particularly unhappy if these misdemeanours resulted in less commisson or, when the group was sent back, none at all. My moral indignation about unprofessional behaviour became a fire of rage if I lost out financially.

I have a strong antipathy to the overwhelming volume at which most pop is played. When I had to listen to the groups, I lacked the physical and nervous stamina to withstand the impact for any length of time. Never before had any kind of music been played at such sustained volume. Musicologists and psychologists may ponder the reasons for this phenomenon; I can only record that I had to retreat when the decibel levels took me to the threshold of pain.

One of Bron's more famous groups was Uriah Heep. Typically, they carried an incredible amount of equipment. In 1971 their inventory comprised:

MAKE	ITEM
4 Dave Martin	bass bins
4 Dave Martin	double horn units
3 Dave Martin	single horn units
4 Dave Martin	monitor cabinets
2 Phase Linear	power amps
2 Allen & Heath	8 way mixer
1 Altec	biamplifier
1 WEM	19 way multicore
2 Quad	power amps
1 Hammond (B74142)	B3 organ and stool
2 Leslie	PRO 900 cabinets
1 Moog (D1392E)	mini synthesizer
1 Simms-Watt	200 watt amp
2 Simms-Watt	4 x 12 cabinets
5 Marshall	100 watt amps
2 Marshall	4 x 12 lead cabinets

MAKE	ITEM
2 Marshall	4 x 12 bass cabinets
2 Acoustic	370 amps GA 1009/1279
2 Acoustic	370 speakers GB 1006/1019
2 Acoustic	271 amps HA 1056/1062
2 Acoustic	271 speakers HB 1001/1069
1 Acoustic	amps GA 1280
2 Acoustic	speakers GB 1091/1207
2 Fender	champ amps A31630/31672
1 Slingerland	drum kit (chrome): bass drum 24 x 14, tom-toms 20 x 18, 15 x 10, 14 x 10 + Hayman snare drums
3 Avedjis Zildian	cymbals and stands (22 inch, 18 inch 15 inch)
10 AKG	D1000 microphones
2 AKG	D12 microphones
8 Electrovoice	microphones
1 Ludwig	drum kit (silver glitter): bass drum 22 x 14, tom-toms 12 x 8, 13 x 9, 16 x 16
1 Levin Acoustic	guitar
1 Acoustic 'Black Widow'	"
1 Gibson Les Paul	"
1 Gibson SG (Cherry)	"
1 Epiphone Custom (Sunburst)	"
1 Martin Acoustic (Natural)	"
1 Fender Jazz Bass (Natural)	"
1 Yahama Acoustic Bass Fg300	"
1 Gibson SG (black)	"
1 Fender Telecaster	"
1 14 x 5 Hatman (gold lacquer)	snare
1 Pr 15" Avedis Zildian	cymbal
1 Premier	snare drum stand
1 Ludwig Speed King	hi-hat pedal
1 Slingerland	tom-tom holder
2 Ludwig	cymbal stands

MAKE	ITEM
4 Slingerland	spurs
2 Premier	bass drum pedals
1 Premier	stool
1 Ludwig	anchor

4 tuning keys, 2 lengths of rope, 3 toolboxes.

Only the technically informed can fully grasp the significance of a list of gadgetry that cost £15,000, weighed five tons, took two 3-ton vans to transport, five 'roadies' six hours to set up and another six hours to dismantle.

Uriah Heep comprised five musicians. On the road they had a team of seven to support them. Without these workhorses and this assembly of equipment, the group couldn't play a note.

Moreover, this gargantuan equipment and the roadies were idle if one of the group was afflicted with a sore throat. Engagements worth up to a thousand pounds in this country and up to ten thousand in America (in vast stadiums and the like) had to be summarily cancelled because of the indisposition of the indispensable, another booking hazard in the pop scene.

Sheer volume was in itself an attraction to young people. 'My kids like to feel the noise,' claimed one promoter. Not all promoters could indulge their patrons in what some acoustic experts regard as a highly dangerous absorption of abnormal noise level. Some had to consider residential neighbours and include a clause in their contracts – the right to limit volume.

As a booker I used to reject offers that carried this stipulation. I knew that groups were psychologically as well as mechanically reliant upon electrical power and would resist entreaties from promoters to reduce the volume. They were incapable of performing without the surge of decibels to which they had grown accustomed.

Rightly or wrongly, I was highly critical of the influence of the rock and roll star, an influence often quite terrifying and out of proportion to intrinsic talents. When I tried rationally to assess my hostile reactions to certain musical and social trends, I was acutely aware that with the stiffening of the arteries comes a rigidity of attitude to things beyond one's understanding. The generation gap was a yawning artistic as well as social chasm. Like many other middle-aged people, I saw rock and roll as a deafening symptom of an increasingly unsettled and tormented era.

A group's manager called to see me. He outlined the group's act, a feature of which was the slitting of a live chicken's throat during a 'composition' where the lyrics related to the Black Mass. I earnestly assured this wretch that if I ever heard of this obscenity actually occurring I would see to it personally that he and the group would be prosecuted for unnecessary cruelty to animals.

On a more hilarious note, there was a group where the highlight of the act was the drummer leaving the stand and returning through the audience completely naked *and* with a roll of newspaper stuck up his anus. If this wasn't enough of a novelty, the end of the newspaper was alight. Leaving aside the grave dangers of a wider conflagration in a crowded hall this was indeed something different.

I thought of my heroes when I read of these extraordinary antics: Duke Ellington, for instance. If, say, the audience had been apathetic one night at the Cotton Club in New York, where he was resident for years, would he have called saxophonist Johnny Hodges aside and said, 'Look, John, we're not getting much of a reaction tonight. Here's a copy of *Tribune* and a box of matches. Would you mind stripping off and. . . ?'

Is this where the jazzmen of my acquaintance went wrong? Would features as arresting as this have helped make their fortunes, or retain their popularity when the rock and roll bombshell hit the profession? Too late now, but I wouldn't have put it past George Melly, and I had an intriguing image of Acker quite naked except for his bowler.

Musing about this drummer exhibitionist, I thought how much I would have liked to be near when he was preparing for his big moment, and surreptitiously dash some highly inflammable spirit to the paper to accelerate his act of nether incendiarism.

As a result of this bold drummer the promoter (who had the act sprung on him as an additonal attraction and with no extra charge) insisted on yet another stipulation in his contracts: a 'No Stripping' clause, heaven help us. To have seen Humphrey Lyttelton's expression reading that proviso in one of his contracts would have been worth a king's ransom.

We received some intriguing literature advertising another novel presentation that included a dog and a cockerel. The group obviously knew they couldn't go wrong with a dog in the act. A canine looking up pathetically would have moved even an audience of anti-establishment hippies. At a given signal, the dog peed against the microphone stand and the cockerel had been trained to eat corn off the top of the guitarist's head. No mention was made of what sort of music the group played. With such novel features in their act, music was obviously a minor consideration. The cockerel was dressed in red drawers.

A necessary part of my duties at Bron's was to listen in the evening to our groups, and to others who were prospects for representation. One night I went to hear a group at the Marquee Club in Wardour Street. Also present was a young propagandist for 'heavy rock', Nick Jones, Max's son. Nick wasn't interested in jazz, despite (or perhaps because of) intensive jazz conditioning from birth. When we began our conversation the room was quiet, but then the bass guitarist began to tune his instrument with his amplifier fully turned up. I involuntarily jumped, and hastily sought comparative shelter behind a brick wall, which for all the sturdiness of its construction, trembled under the decibel impact. Nick hadn't noticed anything untoward, except my hasty movement and pained expression, both of which caused him considerable amusement. I was genuinely shaken, almost as if I had been shot at, and railed against the insensate volume.

'The trouble with you, Godbolt,' said Nick, 'is that you've still got the musty smell of 78s about you.'

How true, how very pleasurably true! How happy I am to acknowledge the fact. How very pleased that I've long enjoyed Duke Ellington, Louis Armstrong, Bix Beiderbecke, Coleman Hawkins, Jack Teagarden, Sidney Bechet and Ed Hall and their fellow giants, whose music came to me on the 78 rpm record.

Even with the financial security at Bron's, I was becoming increasingly tetchy about the aggravation, disliking more and more the overall atmosphere of the business, ever more reluctant to listen to the music I was selling. An old anxiety neurosis returned. At the end of the day the inside of my mouth was raw from compulsive biting.

As I was on commission and, I like to think, a conscientious person, I hoped that my personal feelings didn't affect my booking approach, but perhaps these innermost thoughts showed through the surface enthusiasm. In any case, this play-acting was becoming wearisome, even for money. Money speaks all languages, opens most doors, and soothes most pains, but it can't obliterate truths and one of these was that I was something of an anachronism in the rock and roll scene. The musty smell of 78s didn't blend too well with some of the more malodorous aspects of the business.

During one lunch break I bumped into my former dentist in Soho Square, off Oxford Street. I asked him where he was practising. 'I'm not, old boy. Finished with dentistry. Got fed up with peering down people's horrible mouths – er, excepting yours, of course, old boy.'

This reply helped to crystallize my feelings. I was fed up with peering at horrible date sheets. After long years of darting from one sheet to another, from this query to that problem, I had developed the mind of a grasshopper. I couldn't even read a newspaper without jumping paragraphs and to read a book involved a massive application of willpower. I was weary of the monosyllabic grunts that passed for conversation among so many performers and their representatives. I was sick of having my ear drums rattled, having to scream hard to make a simple comment at rock clubs. I was tired of the posturing and unreliability of egocentric idols.

I realized it was time to quit. Then (1971) I was nudging fifty, a middle-aged jazz buff in a business where I had seen many changes and helped to ring some of them. I can claim to have been a hard-working, reasonably honest agent, even though I have been involved in deals I'm hardly proud of. I had kept my head above water for twenty years, but I had been without the driving ambition and financial acumen really to succeed as a business man. I realized that my energies had often been misdirected, my funds dribbled away on useless projects. And – no humbug – had I been making a fortune, no doubt I would have stayed in the business, whatever the irritations. That's what belonging to the rat race means.

I'd had my moments and a lot of laughs. I had met an incredible variety of people and made some highly valued friends.

I had long wanted to try my hand at writing, having no illusions about the fact that this could be as frustrating as the agency business and certainly worse paid; but I hoped I might find it more fulfilling. At least when a piece of writing is finished there is a sense of *completion*, a feeling I never had as an agent/booker dealing with forever open-ended date sheets.

I had moved into a flat near Hampstead Heath, itself a sweet heritage, a little pocket of almost rural peace in the frightening conurbation of Greater London. The flat, five floors up, has a sun balcony with a southern aspect and overlooks peaceful gardens. To work from here, especially during the summer, seemed infinitely preferable to the din and pollution of the West End and the machinations of commerce.

This prospect struck me with particular force after I left the dentist and walked back to the Bron Organization in Oxford Street. This litter-strewn thoroughfare is a vision of hell on earth to come. Thousands of people, many with tense expressions, were jostling for space. Dense traffic jerking forward in fits and starts was emitting a clearly visible purple haze of poisonous carbon monoxide.

The October sun was still summer-warm and above the canyon of shops and offices, I could see a strip of blue sky. I decided to get out of the business as soon as possible. It was a Thursday and I went to see Gerry to ask if I could leave the following day. We were still in the summer recess and my sudden departure would cause no inconvenience. Gerry, an understanding person, accepted my immediate resignation.

On the following night I went to hear Jon Hiseman's Coloseum – a group I had booked at Bron's. They played under a vast screen on which stroboscopes projected dazzling, sometimes eerily beautiful images. Jon, a very nice person, announced my retirement from the business to a palpably uninterested audience. I suspect they thought he was announcing a new number with a weird title, but it signalled the end of my involvement with pop music, and the entertainment business generally.

The next day I played cricket with the Ravers in our country-house fixture at Great Martins, Waltham St Lawrence, Berkshire. I made sixteen runs, not out, took a good catch in the deep, and for the first time in twenty years felt as free as the song birds flitting around this lovely ground.

That night I went to the 100 Club where, by sheer coincidence, Humphrey Lyttelton was guesting with a Manchester trad band and blowing as he did those twenty-three years earlier with George Webb's Dixielanders. George Webb was himself present and sat in on a few numbers. Beryl Bryden sang. This, I thought, is almost where I came in. The following week the *Melody Maker* had a few lines in their gossip column, 'The Raver', reporting that I had quit the business and would have 'more time to devote to my Miff Mole LPs'.

Miff Mole! Now, that's really where I came in, at the 161 Rhythm Club, Sidcup, Kent, thirty years previously, and I wondered whatever happened to that young lady who had fled during Frank Teschemacher's solo on Miff's record of 'Shim-Me-Sha-Wobble' when she saw the spider crawling down the wall. It was an odd thought on which to end thirty years' association with the music business.

PART TWO

Reading meters in 1974 watched by Flo Brown, Sandy Brown's widow, at her flat in London NW6. Not all meters were so accessible. (Photo: *LEB News*)

1

What is There to Learn, Migawd?

I was soon to realize that my expectations of making an income from writing were, at best, optimistic. I had a few small pieces accepted by the *Melody Maker*, these for a fiver or so, enough to keep only the smallest wolf from the door. Otherwise, my efforts, accompanied by rejection slips, hit the front door mat with the regularity of bills for gas and electricity, the postal certainties of life. Lying half awake at 8.30, or thereabouts, in the morning, I would hear the thud that told me, without my having to get up, that another typescript had returned to its author.

Some of the rejection slips had a few words written on them, some of which were complimentary. Miles Kington, then assistant editor of *Punch*, gave me advice, which was nice of him. But these little scribbles, although mildly comforting, were not negotiable. Not a patch on payment for articles, or a publisher's advance on royalties.

My savings soon ran out. I should have been moderately well off. As manager of George Webb's Dixielanders I had been in at the beginning of the traditional jazz boom, but I had failed to capitalize on this. It didn't bother me at the time – such was my attitude to money – but as I glumly read the rejection slips I wished I had money in the bank.

An inveterate hoarder of memorabilia, if not of money, I have since looked at some of the manuscripts that were returned and fully realize why they were rejected, but at the time I was as much puzzled as disappointed. It was obvious that I had an enormous amount to learn.

I went on Social Security. After a lifetime of contributions I was fully entitled to handouts from the state but – and this is a throwback to attitudes to the dole in the thirties – I felt some shame about it and kept the fact to myself. There was no reason why I should have felt any stigma, but nevertheless I did.

This shame soon withered and after a year I was called into the Employment Exchange manager's office for a 'little chat'. I could probably have continued to draw the fourteen or fifteen pounds a week for a further period but that 'little chat' jolted me into action. In the same way, cork-like, as I had drifted into becoming a magazine editor and agent I became a painter and decorator, working for a very amiable young man. Unfortunately we brought out the worst in each other. The tensions, more my fault than his, were simply because neither of us liked what we were doing. He came from a wealthy family in a one-time colony but had fallen out with his parents. I came from a poor family, but had previously enjoyed a limited status with my own business and staff.

It was a *rotten* job: tedious, messy, repetitive. I had no enthusiasm for stripping five layers of paint and becoming entangled in pasted-up wallpaper. My employer had an infuriating habit of standing over me as I worked and one morning when I was on bended knee, filling the cracks round a skirting board, I could feel his eyes boring into the back of my neck and with a few sharp words, I stormed out. He returned to the bosom of his affluent family, but I had no such recourse.

I had saved a little money during these five or six months and managed to stay away from the DHSS. Fortunately – at least in this respect – I was single, paid a low rent and, except for daily trips to the off-licence, lived frugally. Apart from playing cricket on Sundays with the Ravers I was virtually a recluse. More time with myself than is good for anyone: time to ponder over past stupidity. I frequently dwelt upon the maxim that a fool and his money are easily parted.

I took a course to become a GPO telephone operator but failed that, too. Periods of black depression led me more and more to the false solace of the bottle with inevitably debilitating effects. My low state of mind was aggravated by rejections of a book I had written about the Ravers. This is another manuscript I have since re-read and I am *thankful* it was turned down. Indeed I had a hefty capacity for self-deception in submitting this and other efforts to publishers.

During those bleak days I cursed both my luck and my self-pity. The only bright spots in my life were telephone conversations with my closest friend, Robin Rathborne, a fellow record collector and the best cricketer the Ravers ever had. Robin has a sunny personality and a ready wit, and a few laughs over the telephone with him always lifted my depression.

Some time in 1973 trumpeter/author John Chilton suggested that I write about my experiences as an agent. Having received so many rejections, I viewed the prospect with little enthusiasm, but I sold a few possessions, mostly treasured 78s, and set about putting down my recollections. One memory led to another and I was sufficiently spurred on to do the necessary research in the area I had been operating in. There was much I had forgotten. On and off I spent two years writing these memoirs and constantly redrafting them. I called the book *All This and 10%*.

It was rejected several times over. Cash ran desperately low and I needed work in a hurry. One of the new members of the Ravers told me about casual employment where he worked – the Savoy Hotel in the Strand. He said the work was highly paid and the hours short. As a trainee manager, straight from public school, he was rather misinformed about the rates of pay and the length of hours for those employed in the grey areas of this institution.

The money was derisory – twenty pounds a week – and the hours were from 8.30 to 5.00. My job was to hoover the corridors, replace light bulbs and dust the pictures adorning the corridor walls. Looking at these was my only pleasure. My duties could be completed within a couple of hours, but a flat-chested, sharp-tongued virago of a 'housekeeper' saw to it that I was ostensibly employed throughout the day.

My 'foreman', although he did not have such a formal title, was Tommy, a little, sad, man who had spent all his life in hotel work. He was about sixty, a bachelor who lived in digs in Lambeth over the river. He wasn't exactly crushed, but he was servile and mortally afraid of the virago. To tell the truth, so was I. Conspiratorially, he led me to a cubby-hole under the stairs and whispered: 'You's can keep all yers gear here. Nobody will find it.' Tommy had a dread that our cleaning equipment would be stolen. Brush and Brasso bandits – a sinister dimension to my new job.

One morning he gave me the task of dusting the picture rails in the opulent suites. 'When yers doing that they can't give you anything else to do, can they?' he inquired with friendly earnestness and irresistible logic. Tommy was Irish. He was one of Nature's meek and mild, but he and his kind will never inherit the earth. Its riches and the power they bring go to the occupants of the luxury suites in that hotel. I was in exactly the same position as Tommy at that moment, but I felt an overwhelming compassion for him. Later I wondered whether my attitude towards him was really a reflection of self-pity at my being in the same situation. A bit of both, perhaps.

There were several gradations of dining-room for the staff at the Savoy, depending on your place in the hierarchy. One of these was obviously for the upper echelons, but grand enough, I would have thought, for state banquets. The long tables were dressed in shiny best-quality tablecloths with clusters of gleaming wine glasses and silver cutlery for several courses. Not that I wanted to be sitting there, but its grandeur intrigued me. The staff dining-room in which I and others of my grade ate was in a dingy basement where we queued for cheap stodge, our nostrils assailed by stale odours from nearby kitchens. In the corner of this dungeon was a small bar run by a gaunt and sallow-faced fellow with greasy hair and, it appeared, an all-consuming hatred of humanity, particularly cleaning staff. Foreign waiters babbled noisily and threw bread at each other. Having to eat in that babel was no great hardship, but I was aware that its smelliness and grubbiness in the bowels of an establishment catering for the rich reflected the inequalities rampant in our society, the import of which hit me with great force when I was virtually at the bottom end of that society.

I preferred to eat a sandwich among the greenery of the Victoria Embankment and observe the passing show. Sometimes in the evening I would wander around the nearby City where I had spent four years as a stockbroker's office-boy, stamping the letters, making the tea, running errands, delivering stock and share transfers and fiddling the petty cash. I had never even achieved the position of junior clerk. I did not recall these years with pleasure, but I felt a strange compulsion to wander around an area which despite the ravages of Hitler's bombers and philistinism of post-war planners and architects still held a certain magic for me.

After four weeks I gave notice to the Savoy and belatedly joined a 'Professional Register'. I was interviewed by a pleasant man sporting a handlebar moustache and RAF tie who kindly but firmly told me that there were literally thousands of my age and qualifications looking for work, and in a young man's world I was as unlikely to be wanted as anyone else from this army of elderly unemployed. As I left it occurred to me that it was probably only by the grace of his erstwhile rank in the RAF that *he* had a job.

I registered with an organization called 'The Over Sixties Bureau'. I didn't really qualify, being a mere fifty-three; but fifty-three,

sixty-three, eighty-three – in this situation, one's antiquity was
academic.

I was called for an interview at a long-established firm of jam and
preserve bottlers in the City. The man who interviewed me was
intrigued by my jazz background. He eventually explained that the
vacancy was in stock control, and that the company preferred an
older, more 'responsible' person to a younger man. As I walked
home from the City I had a suspicion that I had got the job. I called
in at Collet's Jazz and Folk Record Shop (now Ray's Jazz Shop) in
Shaftesbury Avenue and mentioned to manager Ray Smith that I
might shortly be involved in jam and preserves. Ray didn't think it
was me.

At that time I had been hearing about certain jazz musicians
working as electricity meter readers and 'manipulating' their hours
to fit in with their musical activities. Still, perversely, wishing to
write, I reckoned this might also suit me and through John
Armatage, the drummer I had known when he played with Bruce
Turner's Jump Band, I obtained an interview at the headquarters of
the Regency area of the LEB, Lithos Road, off Finchley Road.

John warned me to play down the jazz association as he, then
playing with the Alan Elsdon Band, had proved a little wayward in
attendance. On one occasion a mix-up in travel arrangements had
found him in East Germany when he should have been reading
meters in West Hampstead. The meter-reading foreman, Ted
Batchelor, interviewed me and warily enquired if I were a musician,
warning that the job was 'no doddle'.

A week later I received a letter to say I had been accepted as a
meter reader and the very next morning came acceptance from the
jam and preserves bottling company. Not exactly an embarrassment
of riches, but at least an option. I apologetically wrote to the latter
explaining that I had found other employment – this no doubt
inhibiting them from further kindly consideration of an 'older
person' when a vacancy occurred in their stock control department. I
felt a little bad about this, but after weighing up the options, I
decided that a nine to five job would leave me insufficient time at my
typewriter. In any case I preferred to be out in the open.

I started my training on a wet May morning in 1975 with a little
bow-legged Welshman called Bob Lee, his features leathered by over
twenty years on the meter-reading beat. For a man so small, barely
five feet four and rising sixty-three, he moved with astonishing
rapidity. As he darted from door to door I, some ten years younger,

reasonably fit and still playing cricket, had trouble in keeping up
with him. Nor did he waste much time in his formal address.
'Electricity!' he cried when the door opened. He had got the
mechanics of the job down to a fine art, moving from one address to
another with the maximum of speed and the minimum of words at
each call. I think he was paid extra for instructing me and this
tuition impeded his normal rate of progress, but on our first morning
we made a good start despite my presence. At the bottom of Holborn
at about noon he gave his 'book' a quick glance, snapped it shut, and
thrust it into one of the capacious 'poacher's' pockets of his uniform.

'Where are we off to now?' I inquired.

' 'Ome, bhoyo, 'ome. I'll see you outside the depot at four-thirty
sharp. Don't be late, bhoyo. I don't want to hang about.' I was at the
depot at the time instructed and once inside the foreman's office Bob
promptly handed in his book and was away in a flash to catch the
train to Kensal Green, to spend the best part of the evening tending
his allotment.

I was out with Bob for a fortnight and at the end of my
'apprenticeship' we were in a part of Willesden with a large Jewish
population. Calling at one house Bob knocked sharply on the door
and over a minute later, a very fidgety minute for Bob, a female voice
from inside cried, 'Who is*itt*?'

'Electricity!' chanted Bob. The door opened slightly, still latched
on a chain. A Jewish lady peered apprehensively at us.

'Why two of you?' Her tone was laden with deep suspicion.

'He's learning,' said Bob.

'What is there to learn, migawd?!' she cried.

On production of Bob's identity card she grudgingly admitted us
and Bob read the meter without, in this instance, any 'tuition'.
Valuable time had already slipped by waiting for the door to open.
But before he could mark down the entry the lady asked, with
anxious expression and splayed hands, a question which was to
become familiar to me in Jewish households: 'Issit*alott*?'

Quite accidentally her earlier question had touched on a sore
point. I was having great difficulty in reading meters. Not the newer
models with the dials clearly arranged in little squares, but the older
type where the pointers between the dials often rested in an
intermediate position. A mistake in reading them could mean ten or
a hundred or a thousand units too many or too little. Having failed
to impress editors, walked out of painting and decorating and
muffed the GPO telephone operator course, I was alarmed that I

would also fail as a meter reader. For my forty-five pounds a week, less deductions, it was imperative that I *did* learn. I later discovered that I had been near to the sack, Bob rightly making an unfavourable report to Ted Batchelor.

The lady's question, again unwittingly, had other implications. For during the next four years I was to learn much about the society in which I lived by calling on so many addresses. The 'Regency' beat covered an area of $15\frac{1}{2}$ square miles, extending as far as posh Highgate in the north, the throb of Cambridge Circus in the south, the fringes of the affluent City in the east and the industrial hinterland of Park Royal in the west. It embraced every conceivable kind of building: houses, flats, schools, factories, hospitals, offices, railway stations, signal boxes and public lavatories. The 'books', rotated daily among a team of readers twenty strong, had over two hundred addresses per day to be called on.

I was to enter the homes of thousands: of the high, mighty and wealthy, of the lowly born and impoverished, and of all gradations in between. I discovered that I had to be contortionistic to read meters placed in every sort of inaccessible position, high up walls, tucked away in lofts, behind hot water pipes or buried under domestic lumber in cupboards under stairs . . . and stranger places.

I was also to become an expert on dogs.

There are an estimated six million dogs in this country, depositing daily about 10,000 gallons of urine and 1,000 tons of excrement. Sickening evidence of the latter was an everyday, all-day occurrence on the Regency beat.

Not that pollution by dogs was new to me. Municipal gardens adjoin the estate where I live. Maintained at considerable cost by Camden Council, they are virtually an excretoria for the inordinate number of dogs on the estate, 'exercised' by anti-social owners indifferent to the gross spectacle of turds dropped by their charges. No children play there; the Council should erect signs proclaiming the area a health hazard.

In my roaming brief with the LEB it was essential for my wellbeing to learn which species to beware of, and I encountered them all: Beagles, Boizots, Chows, Danes, Dalmatians, Deerhounds, Mastiffs, Pointers, Retrievers, Samoyeds, Settlers and Spaniels; gulping Pugs, snotty-nosed Poodles, snivelling Pomeranians and Bulldogs with drools of mucus hanging from slobbery lips;

shrieking, squeaking and barking dogs; baying, howling and snarling dogs. The old adage that a person eventually looks like his or her dog I found to be true.

My first encounter came as I walked up the path of a Hampstead mansion and spotted a huge Alsatian almost camouflaged as it lay stretched out before the brown front door. Catching sight of me it pricked up its ears, rose quivering to its haunches, and charged. Stark terror lent me wings. With an athleticism that in retrospect astounds me I turned tail and vaulted over the gate. I made it in the nick of time.

It also followed that I became an expert on the extraordinary foibles of dog-owners – the 'dogolatrous' – a strange breed in themselves, characterized by an irrational conviction of the intelligence and usefulness of their pets. I met many who seriously attributed human qualities to Prince, Buster and Rover, and who took strong exception to any complaint about their activities, such as clawing at my legs, sniffing up my rear or attempts to attack me.

Some dog-lovers' attitudes defied belief. 'Say friend,' demanded a lady in Finchley Road as a wet-nosed, squeaking Pekingese snapped at my heels. I looked bemused. 'Say friend,' she repeated. Things have come to a pretty pass, I thought. Here am I, trying to make an honest living, and being solemnly directed to address a toy dog. But having nothing to lose, I said 'friend', and indeed, the animal ceased its attention to me. 'There you are!' cried the lady triumphantly. 'Now you're friends, aren't you? Now, Popsie, you musn't be naughty with the nice man who's come to read the meter . . .'

A few days later I rang the bell of a house in Gospel Oak and immediately a fiercely barking dog hurled itself against the door. It was evidently a large animal and I speedily took refuge behind the gate. The door was opened by a man restraining a ferocious labrador. He expressed surprise to find me standing behind his gate and showed some irritation when I politely, if icily, asked him to put the dog away. When I was reading his meter he solemnly assured me that I would have come to no harm as his dog *knew* I was a meter reader. The animal's name, by the way, was Nigger, as offensive when attached to a dog as a human, but considering this dogolator's mentality, his choice of a name didn't surprise me. These years later my mind boggles at Nigger's extraordinary perception. Not that it had any effect on its behaviour. The dog may have known I was a meter reader but it was still obviously intent on doing me a mortal injury.

Many revelled in the terror their beasts could inspire. In a Hampstead villa an enormous Great Dane appeared without warning. I stood petrified with fright but the owner, a breezy Hooray Henry, chirped: 'Don't worry old boy. Not enough meat on you for our Caesar!' His three children simpered at my alarm. At that moment I would have had no compunction in slaying the Hooray and his dog, sparing the children only for the pleasure of seeing the little horrors weep over the prostrate bodies of their father and former pet. I was reminded of W.C. Fields's classic dictum: 'A man who hates children and dogs can't be all bad.'

In a Kentish Town basement a man opened the door and beside him, unleashed, stood a large and ominously silent dog which didn't take its eyes off me for a second. The man was pleasant enough and asked me to wait while he put the dog away. I nodded in full agreement. More out of nervousness than interest I enquired what breed the animal was and commented on its uncanny silence. 'Oh yes, mate,' he said. 'That's a Rottweiler. I've got another one in the back yard. They're German-trained you know. They're quiet, all right, but they'll go for your crown jewels if I give the word. Well, it's the logic of the Huns, ain't it? They worked it out; if you come to nick summink and suddenly you get sixty pounds of dog like that hangin' on to your goolies you'll have tears in your eyes and you won't see where you're running, will ya?'

I was still relatively well known in the small world of jazz and naturally, many of my former associates became aware of my new occupation. It was illuminating to note the reactions of certain acquaintances, and the comment of a Ravers CC team-mate, ex-minor public school and university, made me blink. When I told him that Johnny Armatage and I were in the same team of 'readers' at the Lithos Road depot he remarked: 'Really! I think his case is worse than yours, even.' I looked surprised. Noting this, he added, 'After all, he's a musician, isn't he . . . ? Not that I am a job snob.'

The most astonishing comment came from someone I barely knew. To get to and from Lithos Road and to many starting points I made frequent use of the North London Line, running from Richmond to Broad Street. One morning, dashing to catch a train to Willesden Junction I overtook another running figure and sprinted up the stairs only to see the train moving out. I was alone on the platform but for the person I had overtaken. I had dimly unpleasant recollections of him from my very early days in the jazz world. Not the most sociable of people, I have a vigilant eye in public places for unwanted company and had, up to now, been successful in keeping out of his way. Not so on this platform.

I strode purposefully to the farthest end and sat on an abandoned railway sleeper, pretending to examine my 'book' with a thorough-ness that would have made Ted Batchelor very proud of me. The ruse was a failure. I heard him approaching and a grating voice came from over my shoulder.

'You're Jim Godbolt, are you not?'

I glumly nodded. There have been many occasions when I wished I were not Jim Godbolt, but rarely with the intensity I felt at that moment. I knew I was in for a long twenty minutes before the next train.

DG, as I shall call him, inquired about Mick Mulligan and George Melly and immediately made his first offensive observation. 'Melly; second-rate singer and writer. OK, his singing is a bit niggerish but that's about all.'

This was to be the tenor of his asinine remarks. I wished I had the moral courage to get up and walk to the other end of the platform. Instead I just grunted. It was characteristic of him not to take the hint.

'You were a very good agent,' he said.

'Thank you,' I murmured, but hardly cheered by a compliment from this source. It was merely a launching pad for further questions and observations.

'What are you doing now?'

Since I was wearing the chocolate brown LEB uniform and peaked cap both with the initials LEB clearly visible the query was patently gratuitous.

'I work for the LEB.'

'Oh, an inspector or something?'

'No, I'm a meter reader.'

'Ah-hah! So that uniform's not a bit of *camp!*'

I'm not often stuck for words but just then I was rendered speechless, capable only of an agitated gurgle. It was not until I was safely in the train that I recalled that DG had told me that he, too, had a new occupation: he was editor of a porn magazine.

A young Irish woman whom I had engaged to type yet another draft of my memoirs told me that she thought my new job was infinitely superior to my parasitical existence as an agent. I had become so used to this misconception of an artiste's predatory representative that I didn't reply, but when she produced a pipe from her holdall, filled it with cheap shag tobacco, lit up and filled my room with a choking fug, I must have registered a little surprise. She was a militant feminist and extremely left-wing but I rather think she was over-doing her identification with the proletariat by puffing at a *clay* pipe.

Sadly, a few people avoided me in the street, perhaps out of deference to what they imagined my feelings would be. In a society where 'position' counts for so much it may have been thought that this one-time business man had slipped and I would wish to conceal the fact. Not so; but there was one particular occasion when I fervently hoped I would not be observed.

I was in a run-down part of Harlesden reading the meter in a draper's shop window. To avoid enveloping myself in the merchandise I had to wriggle carefully on hands and knees, and although it was unlikely that anyone I knew would be in this part of the world at nine o'clock in the morning, I read the meter with one eye on the dials and the other on the street, ready to duck under a swathe of purple organdie if necessary. Had I been observed, what would have been said of this new addition to the draper's display? What sort of tag? 'Job lot going cheap'? 'Must reduce to clear'? 'Not to be repeated'? 'Seconds'?

Going out into the street was a moment for reflective introspection. Here I was: fifty-three, broke – not 'middle-class broke', but really impoverished, despite twenty years in business – and now crawling on all fours in a draper's window.

2

Are You Electric?

Never, in all my life, had I been in such demand from the opposite sex. Not, alas, from nubile young ladies, eagerly awaiting the arrival of this stud from the LEB, whose conquests might be boasted of in a sensationalist Sunday newspaper. The come-hither cries were for economic, not sexual, reasons and the demands for my presence mostly from old dears, particularly in working-class areas, with a mistrust of bills estimated by the office staff, even when corrected by an actual reading the following quarter. Too much and the consumer was out of pocket; too little and the next bill a shock. I would enter a street and immediately the bush telegraph would start throbbing. Cries rang out over the back and front gardens: 'Flossie! The electric man's here!' Some would rush out, grab my sleeve and inquire: 'Are you electric?' – often on mornings when I was feeling anything but 'electric'.

These ladies had me darting, like a stickleback in a jam jar, from one end of the street to the other. One scheming old luv, bedecked in a floral bonnet, called me to read her meter *immediately*. She was going out that *very* minute to visit her ailing sister. Half an hour later, at one sweaty stage of my zig-zag reverse-forward course, I was at her neighbour's door when she appeared, minus bonnet, to put out the empty milk bottles. I jocularly inquired after her sister's health and she looked a little shamefaced. The older people would go to any lengths to ensure a reading, their fear of estimates an echo of hard times past. The young housewife brought up in comparative affluence wasn't that bothered.

I was also in demand as a perambulating information centre, from those who imagined that anyone in uniform was automatically at their beck and call. I was frequently tooted on a motor horn, the tooters crooking and twitching their forefingers to beckon me across the road and attend to their queries. In return I gave an admonitory wag of my forefinger. They always looked surprised.

I was in Tottenham Court Road one morning when a bowler-hatted, pin-striped-suited and military-moustachioed Hooray Henry carrying a briefcase spotted LEB on my jacket lapels and barked: 'Fitzroy Square'. I was well aware that this seemingly gratuitous comment was a demand for information and I was quick to supply it. Certainly, I would direct him. A pleasure to oblige! He strode away without a word of thanks. Not, as must have soon dawned on him, that he had any reason for gratitude. I had directed him to Gordon Square in Bloomsbury, a long way from his destination and serve him right.

Class characteristics have long fascinated me. My earliest recollection of social status, as a child in a flat with no bathroom but with an inside lavatory, was when my mother – a South Wales miner's daughter brought up in a tiny terraced house with no bathroom and an outside lavatory – used to refer to 'posh' people, but our 'inferiors' were 'as common as ditchwater'. Four years in the rigidly constituted hierachy of the City office and another five years in the Navy accentuated my awareness of class while the rather irreverent brotherhood of the jazz world after the war attracted a mixture of classes in an atmosphere of social change. I do not think it any surprise that I had become very class-conscious, and now, as a meter reader, moving daily at all levels of society, I was able to observe the social structure more closely than ever before.

On one of my early calls, in Frognal, Hampstead, a middle-class lady of about thirty opened her door and looked at me with unconcealed distaste. 'Show me your identity card,' she brusquely demanded. She looked intently at this for some time and then at me, perhaps to see if I were in disguise or had undergone plastic surgery in order to make a nefarious entry into her villa. Without a word she thrust it back at me and retreated, sniffing, into her hallway. Perhaps her sniffiness was an unconscious echo of less hygienic times when the mere sight of a prole would have members of her class twitching their nostrils.

Her two children giggled and used ostentatiously long words no child should even be aware of. They were a pretty odious threesome.

'May I come in?' I asked politely. In these situations, studied civility was the only counter weapon.

'If you must,' she grated. I asked her for a chair to enable me to reach the meter. She snappily refused. All her chairs were antiques, not to be sullied by rough boots. Eventually she thrust a chair towards me, fussily placing a copy of the *Guardian* on the seat of what looked like ordinary Regency reproduction, mass-manufactured in High Wycombe, I guessed.

The literature that lay on her hallstand was out of character with her unpleasantly autocratic manner. It included copies of *Tribune* and the *New Statesman*. Perhaps she was an example of that peculiar phenomenon who speaks 'liberal', acts autocratically and sends his or her children to private school.

Certain phrases are characteristic of the privileged. One morning I had to read the meters in Heal's, Tottenham Court Road, and came out to witness a little impromptu drama. A traffic warden had slipped a parking ticket under the windscreen-wiper of a majestic Bentley. The lady owner came out of the store, snatched the ticket from the windscreen, flung it to the ground and screamed: 'You silly little man!' at the warden, who was completing his entry of the offence in his book. He was of average height, but the rich invariably diminutize those who upset them. I was reminded of the abusive Hetty who had similarly addressed me at the Six Bells several years previously.

The lady pulled at her car door, forgetting that it was locked. Fuming, she fumbled for her keys, unlocked the door, wrenched it open and sat down with a resounding thump. By now her antics had attracted a small crowd, infuriating her even further. She snapped on the ignition key, and still spitting abuse at the impassive warden, thrust at the gear lever, shot forward a mite and came to an abrupt halt. In her anger she had forgotten to release the hand-brake.

Had I been a policeman I would have preferred further charges. One for distributing litter, another for careless driving. In fact, had there been an officer in sight I would have felt it my duty to draw his attention to the misdemeanours of this outraged Hetty. Well, perhaps not, but it was a thought to brighten up the morning.

In a block of luxury flats in Highgate I employed the meter reader's stratagem of ringing both bells of opposite flats to save time. The doors were opened almost simultaneously, one by a cleaning lady (as I discovered), the other by a very grand dame. As the charwoman answered just a second or so before the dame, I walked into that flat first, telling the dame I would not be long. But she followed, ostensibly to advise the cleaner where her neighbour's ladder was kept and meaningfully remarking that this should be used so that the meters could be read 'properly'. As I mounted the ladder she railed against the public services generally, berated the LEB and, in respect of her telephone bill, vilified the Post Office.

'It's *quaite* enormous,' she boomed in a voice that would have carried round Sloane Square, 'quaite enormous, but then a'im always ringing mai son in the *cun*tray' (this last word, with the emphasis on the first syllable, conjuring up feudal estates and servile rustics, and stirrup cups sunk astride handsome chestnut hunters before charging off with the hounds in pursuit of some unfortunate fox).

The cleaner countered this obvious bit of swank by saying that her husband had just settled a bill for 'twenty-five pun'. 'Oeuih,' retorted the dame, 'main was much more than *thet*, I can tell you.' She was not having any one-upwomanship from a mere char.

In Hampstead, I stood suffering while an unpleasantly over-bearing Hooray maintained an emotive commentary on the dire state of the nation. This, he avowed, was wholly attributable to the belligerence and unpatriotism of the unions and it was about time a strong man stepped in to curb their power. He blamed the preposterous cost of electricity on my grossly inflated pay packet. It was evident from his tirade that he considered patriotism the exclusive prerogative of his class.

A question constantly asked of the meterman by middle-class people was: 'Why *doesn't* the same man read both gas and electricity meters?' A variation of this was: '*You people* should read both meters,' sometimes accompanied by the patriotic rider, 'and save the country a lot of money.' Again, patriotic considerations were uppermost in their minds and 'you people' was often emphasized by jabbing a forefinger within an inch of my chest.

It was a classically simple panacea to rectify the balance of payments and usually expounded with the air of someone having hit upon a notion as valuable to the nation's economy as Newton's discovery of the laws of gravity was to science, or the splitting of the atom to the destruction of humanity. Those who solemnly proffered this solution never seemed to realize that it would require the meterman to carry two bulky books, take twice the time seeking out two meters, almost certainly in different parts of the house, and making two separate entries; not to mention the logistics of both books finding their way to the respective accountancy offices of two Boards at addresses far distant from each other, and the awesome confusion of bills and accounts that would assuredly ensue.

Naïvely, I made these points to a lady who proposed this bright idea. Bob Lee would not have bothered nor, as I discovered, would another grizzled veteran of the Regency beat, Bert Harris, whom I came across in a Camden Town pub one lunchtime.

Bert was fond of a drink: four or five pints 'of a midday' and a 'real drink of a night': eight to ten pints. I mentioned my encounter with the lady who would have us reading both meters. He looked utterly shocked. Not because of the idea's impracticability, but because I had tried to discuss the matter.

' 'Ere mate, you don' wanna *talk* to 'em! Don' ever do that! Fuckin' 'ell, no! That's the last thin' you wanna do! Just get in there, mate, read the fuckin' me'er an' get aht as soon as you can. You'll never get fru yer book if yer *talk* to 'em. Yes, I will, thanks. I'll have a pinta IPA with yer.' He accepted the pint with a wink and a leer at the young barmaid and continued his homily: 'Your very best health, mate, and don't forget, when you see 'em, say fuck-all.'

If from the middle class I experienced no more than the occasional snootiness, harangues about the iniquities of the unions and doubts cast upon my patriotism, I met with some verbal abuse and the threat of physical attack at the bottom end of the social scale.

I rang the bell of a derelict house in Willesden and an unshaven young man appeared at the window and threatened to kill me. I didn't hang about and moved quickly to my next address, a basement. He followed me until to my relief he realized that I was only a meter reader. He was a squatter expecting eviction.

In a block nearby a rough-looking youth of about seventeen answered the door of a flat and his eyes narrowed when I asked to read the meter. 'There's nobody in,' he said. Observing the cast of his features, the thickness of his forearms and the size of his hands, I elected not to point out that his own presence contradicted this. Instead I took the hint and departed.

A few minutes later a man in his fifties approached me. 'My boy says you want to read the meter. It's OK now.' I had the feeling that certain items had been put out of sight. His manner was friendly, but his features suggested that he'd been in many a fracas. He was, to use another term of my youth, 'pug ugly'.

The reading was exceptionally low. I checked it again, and looked to see if the seals had been broken, the usual evidence of meter tampering.

'Anything wrong, mate?' he inquired.

'Just checking. It's a very low reading.'

'Oh yes, cock, that's because we've been away.'

'I bet they have,' I thought. 'For a considerable *stretch* of time, no doubt.'

I had another chilling moment in a Harlesden high-rise block. A thug with a scar stretching from mouth to ear opened the door, his eyes glinting with anger, and snarled: 'Don't you ever, *ever*, knock on my door like that again, John, or I'll . . .' He didn't complete what was certainly to be an ugly threat because I quickly, cravenly, sensibly, offered my fervent apologies.

I found car salesmen a very unpleasant breed. Their reputation for sharp practice is matched by their appalling manners. I encountered two of these selachians in a Hampstead car emporium and was immediately met with complaints about the hour – 10 a.m. – I was calling, but I could come the old madam when it suited me. 'I thought it best, sir, to call at this hour rather than later, when you'll maybe have some customers and my call would be inconvenient.' I allowed myself a shade of emphasis on 'maybe'.

To enable me to read the meter a gleaming Silver Ghost Rolls Royce had to moved. The man who reluctantly shifted this expensive piece of status hardware referred to me in the third person to a colleague: 'Get him a ladder, Maurie.' Maurie, sleek with a well-trimmed moustache, spluttered: 'You people are a bloody nuisance.' As I mounted the ladder I had a manic notion. If I were to lean backwards the ladder would fall away from the wall. I could leap for safety and, with a bit of luck, see Maurie's head jammed in between the middle rungs of the ladder and its prongs embedded in the bonnet of the Rolls. Maurie's colleagues would have left him for dead as they anxiously crowded round the dented car. That emporium would have become a vale of tears.

But I abandoned this wild idea. Not on account of Maurie and the Rolls. My physical wellbeing was the overwhelming consideration – I might not have landed safely. I descended the ladder, thanked Maurie for his help and wandered over to the Silver Ghost. 'How much for the mo'er?' I enquired.

'Eleven thousand,' he said, in a reflex response to a question involving money. Had he paused to think, his answer would have assuredly been very different – like telling me to be off, although not in such restrained terms.

'That seems reasonable to me,' I replied. 'Very fair. But I'll have to think it over.' Maurie's jaw dropped. 'Let's be honest. It's going to take me a bit of overtime to get that sort of cash together. If you get a firm offer in the meantime, I think you ought to take it.' He shot me a malevolent glare. 'My, my,' I said, tapping the world-renowned radiator top with my pen, 'that really is a nice-looking mo'er!' Maurie blanched and choked as I cheerily bade him farewell.

One morning I'd had more than the usual quota of problems – digital, human and canine. My expression must have reflected my feelings when I knocked on the basement door of a crumbling house off the Edgware Road. The door was opened by a bedraggled crone well into her eighties. She was bearded, her skin yellowed and crinkled like a relief map. She peered balefully at me as I announced my business. Her meter was high up and covered with grease and dust, in a dark recess of a foul-smelling hallway. All metermen can tell of places where the odour of age is so strong that it can be tasted. A groan slipped out. I shouldn't have let it escape; I was at fault and I got my come-uppance. With surprising ferocity for someone so old she spat through toothless gums: 'What a miserable *fucker* you are! What do you do for bleedin' fun, mate? Watch the fuckin' grass grow? If I were younger I'd smack you round the kisser!'

The combination of her bedraggled appearance, harsh cockney accent and the ferocity of her abuse both frightened and amused me and I broke into uncontrollable laughter. In seconds both of us were chatting away merrily, but that geriatric odour hung about me all day . . .

The older people's anxiety about cost was perfectly under-standable. A very refined old lady in Belsize Park told me her consumption *must* be low. The reading confirmed what is usually a false claim. She told me why. She sat in the dark to save electricity. She was probably living on a fixed income, too old to work, too proud to sponge on relatives or to apply for aid from Social Security. When I told another lady the amount of units she had consumed she sighed and said, 'I suppose it's because I've had the emulsion heater on.'

To many, *any* sort of caller represented a few moments' relief from the ache and tedium of a lonely existence. In a block of flats in Kilburn a frail and bent old woman said, 'I know you're busy and I won't ask you to read it all, but can you tell me who this card is from?' Naturally I read the whole card for her. Her gratitude was touching, if a little disconcerting: 'That's very kind of you, dear. I hope someone does the same for you one day!'

That same week I called at a council block in Somerstown where an old lady told me that her son also worked for the LEB but, she added with great pride, *'He's* one of the higher-ups.' It was rare that I was given the same 'book' for two quarters running, but it happened in this case and she again informed me of her son's status in the LEB and added, 'I'm glad they sent someone decent this time – the last man was a right old scruff.'

If only as a sop to my beleaguered conscience, I was helpful whenever possible: taking in milk, replacing light bulbs, shifting furniture and the like. I prepared breakfast for an old lady with arthritis, captured another's escaped budgie, and cut flowers from the garden of a crippled octogenarian to brighten the room in which she was imprisoned.

In one block of flats I found the door open. The lady was awaiting her lunch from the meals-on-wheels service. In a tone of urgency she called me into her lounge; she wanted me to remove another lady from her bath. While I was prepared to read postcards, replace light bulbs and pursue escaped budgies I cavilled at removing a lady from a bath. But it turned out that the lady in the bath was a figment of the complainant's imagination.

In a run-down Harlesden street with the houses and shops boarded up and awaiting demolition one shop remained open. In the window, next to a pile of tyres and spare car parts, stood a magnificent tomato plant, four feet high or more and heavy with bulbous fruit, not yet ripened but with the glistening sheen of healthy trusses. Inside an elderly man, mid-seventies, I guessed, sat placidly. I complimented him on such a magnificent plant. 'I've got green fingers an' I mate?' he replied, holding up hands with palms, fingers and nails permanently impregnated with black axel grease and the carbon of tyres. I asked him the time. He shrugged. It wasn't a dismissive gesture; he had no watch. Time was not of the essence to him. I don't think he cared if he sold any tyres or not. I got the impression that he cared only for his splendid tomato plant.

In the jazz world we had a name for commissionaires, porters, caretakers and hall managers who went out of their way to obstruct musicians wishing to deposit their gear or make use of the facilities. They were called Jobsworths – stemming from their favourite phrase 'No – I – can't – let – you – do – that – it's – more – than – my – job's – worth!' I came across a multitude of Jobsworths on the meter-reading beat, many of them deliberately, fiercely and exultantly unhelpful.

One of my first was at the entrance to a Holborn office block. As I approached him in his little cubicle he gave me the non-seeing eye, the corollary of which, I well knew, would be the non-hearing ear. He addressed me as I waited for basement keys to be collected from another part of the building. 'A boring job you've got there, mate,' he said with a tact that matched the pleasure he displayed on advising me that he could not find the keys I required. His duties were to sit at that desk all day, accept packages, lock and unlock a few doors and stare into space. I rather thought *I* had the more interesting job.

If the obduracy of Jobsworth was one occupational hazard, the relentless jollity of Mr Jokerman was another. Always ready with a laugh and a quip, he would be the life and soul of the Christmas party, the first to don a funny paper hat and lead the Hi-Hi conga chain around the dining table.

Mr Jokerman's garden told me much about him before our first meeting. It was packed with an assortment of animal figures including reclining fawns, beaming gnomes, cute bunny rabbits, pop-eyed toads, a Scottie dog begging on its hind legs, a stork with a fish in its beak and a grinning black cat sitting on its haunches. Dotted about this plastic menagerie were stone toadstools and in the middle of the garden stood a 'water well', its brickwork two-toned, its porch multi-coloured and complete with handle, rope and bucket. The only thing it lacked was water.

From the front porch hung an oblong piece of oak, highly polished with scalloped edges and 'Chez Nous' incised on it. I pressed the bell and the first few bars of 'Colonel Bogey' chimed from within. The door was opened by a man of about sixty-five. He was lean and cadaverous, with thinning grey hair cut short back and sides. He had a pencil-line moustache and wore brown gaberdine trousers, a pale blue nylon shirt and a Shetland pullover.

'Good morning. Electricity to read the meter.'

'A meterman, eh? You want to meet someone, then? *Ha ha ha ha!*'

I did my best to muster a smile and Mr Jokerman asked to see my identity card. The photograph, I admit, showed a gaunt-featured, wild-eyed fellow. He stared at it, and then at me, and exclaimed, 'Cor! Convict 99!' I am a great fan of the late Will Hay who created the character of Convict 99 but I was hardly flattered by the comparison. Chortling, he bade me enter and repeated his witticism for the benefit of his wife, who after a good look at me exclaimed, 'You're right, Sid! Convict 99!'

I went down on bended knees, not to pray for deliverance from gags like these, but to read a meter hidden away under a trinket-laden thirties sideboard, above which a flock of mallards flew in angled ascent towards the ceiling. This sideboard bore a quite incredible array of nick-nackery. Little glass horses, a miniature platinum dinner gong, a brown bakelite biscuit barrel with brass-plated hoops, a thermometer in the shape of Big Ben, a china Dutch boy and girl in traditional dress, a brass tray with Buckingham Palace in relief, another portraying the Tower of London, two porcelain shire horses hauling a dray, a photograph of Mr and Mrs Jokerman on their wedding-day, circa 1945, in an ornate gilded frame, and innumerable other bits and pieces.

On my way out Mr Jokerman, still chortling, said, 'You've got to have a laugh, haven't you?' and as I neared the door I noticed a wooden plaque on the wall proclaiming 'Home is where you scratch if you itch'. A miniature figure of a seated spaniel on the hall-stand turned its head when Mr Jokerman opened the front door. How this movement was achieved I do not know; by a magnetic device I suppose. I didn't stop to inquire but I pondered on the sublime ingenuity of the gadget's inventor and the crass mentality of its purchasers.

3

A Sturdy Egalitarian

From the time I started working for the LEB I jotted down notes and impressions of my travels and one day I wrote to the *Evening Standard* suggesting that I should contribute a meter reader's notebook. I received a highly enthusiastic reply from David Johnson, the Features Editor: 'A smashing idea . . . the sooner you can let us have an article the better. The idiosyncratic flavour of your outline seems an ideal approach, using your own clearly defined views on people and places . . . Certainly don't pull any punches for the *Standard* . . . An article is invariably stronger when the writer takes a distinct stand.'

I could hardly believe my eyes when I read this letter and I quickly submitted the articles, but nothing was ever printed. I couldn't, despite repeated attempts, get the formula right. Another newspaper editor to whom I had made a similar suggestion wrote back, 'It is evident that nothing of significance happens to a meter reader.'

Meanwhile I continued redrafting *All This and 10%*, which continued to be rejected. I was struck by a term many publishers used in their rejection notes: 'Not for us'. 'Us' seemed the operative word, implying that while the work might be acceptable to another, lesser, publishing house, 'we' had higher standards. Scant knowledge of grammar and difficulty in ordering my often tangled thoughts entailed repeated re-writes. Inner conflicts affected my concentration and after a day's tramping I was physically exhausted. I envied those who are able to visualize their work as a whole, and see it through without tedious re-drafting. Another problem was that my efforts were intended to be funny. It is easier to pontificate on any subject than to write humorously. Serious comment will be accepted or rejected on its merits, but when a joke falls flat it does so with a fearful thud.

In July 1975, again at John Chilton's suggestion, I placed *All This and 10%* with an agent who, to my surprise, reacted favourably. I arrived back at my flat one lunchtime and was steeling myself for a further bout on the typewriter before reporting to Lithos Road, when the phone rang. It was the literary agent who said: 'Robert Hale are interested in publishing your book and would five hundred pounds be acceptable?'

Had he inquired if fifty pounds were acceptable I would probably have agreed, so overcome was I that I was actually going to be published. I did no work that afternoon. I got drunk instead and reported back to Lithos Road with glazed eyes and slurred speech.

On a day off I went to see one of Hale's directors, who was also to be my editor. It was an amicable meeting. I was to rephrase certain passages and make certain cuts, to which I readily agreed. But I was in for a shock when I received a thirteen-page listing of their libel lawyer's objections. It was an astonishing document, whose contents had me gasping in disbelief. I had not written a single lie about anyone, but the contradictory and confusing laws relating to libel and slander can make the truth appear defamatory. Even so, the lawyer's objections were highly absurd and had they been upheld my book would have been denuded of its substance. I had spent long hours slaving over a volume that, whatever its literary merit, was at least a unique record, and I was determined that it should not be bowdlerized. Friction soon developed between myself, the publisher and the lawyer.

The lawyer was unhappy about my comments on press reactions to Riverboat Shuffles, particularly about my use of the word 'lasciviousness'. I had used this word ironically, but the lawyer wrote: 'Description of Riverboat Shuffles apparently based on an account in the magazine *Illustrated*, but "the lasciviousness of it all" seems strong and there must be a possibility, even if remote, that there might be trouble from respectable citizens objecting to being tarred with such a brush.'   .

There were literally hundreds of these shuffles, thousands upon thousands of people attended them and would any one of them, however 'respectable', have sued on this account? After a tussle it was agreed that the 'lasciviousness' could be retained provided it was in quote marks. I eliminated these from the galley-proofs, but my editor restored them; he was at least watchful in this respect. Not, as

I later discovered, that he was meticulous in his editing generally.

The lawyer, a very old man, very establishment-minded, very courteous, made suggestions that verged on the surreal. He was concerned that I had described Bruce Turner as 'a fine musician, but rather low on moral fibre'. He wrote: 'The expression is a bit ambiguous. What about lacking in guts or something like that?', a term which is admittedly unambiguous but would certainly have upset Bruce Turner more than my original comment did when the book was published.

The lawyer's class bias was apparent in his objections to the quotes I had taken from the 'Londoner's Diary' of the *Evening Standard*, which then was devoted almost entirely to the social activities of the gentry. He questioned the reports of the antics of Ladies Jane Wallop and Chetwynd-Talbot and Messrs Richard Tatham and Jeremy Grafftey-Smith, and the story about the Duke of Kent 'having a go on the drums'. 'Suggestion they were tight,' he wrote. 'What corroboration is available?'

He demurred at my description of Jim Bray as 'noticeably scruffy', and added: 'The author is a sturdy egalitarian and does not mind showing his contempt for the upper classes, as also in his remarks about Tatham and Grafftey-Smith.' Jim Bray and I were old friends and once shared a room in Gloucester Place. We were from different backgrounds and jocularly 'fought' the class war; never was there any animosity. Once, returning from the Oslo trip with Bruce Turner's band, I was sitting next to Jim on the airline coach and, travelling along the Great Western Road, we passed St Paul's, his old school. He made great play of pointing this out to me and, somewhat lamely, I remarked that the architecture was the worst sort of Victorian Gothic (which, in fact, I quite admire) and that the cricket outfield looked rough. Bray, fruity-voiced, drawled: 'Not so, *ectually*, it was an excellent wicket and outfield, but then you wouldn't have known about it, would you – except, *possibly*, as a groundsman.' I liked that. The bland, well-read and indisputably scruffy Jim usually won these exchanges.

The lawyer noted my description of Spike Mackintosh's 'wretched' city friends and wrote: 'I have already referred to the author's loathing of the City gent and the establishment in general and I think this reference should be removed.' I'm no egalitarian. I'm well aware that the transmission of genes from generation to generation largely determines intelligence, or lack of it, and in this lottery, some are winners, some losers. I could have told this old man that I bow to my intellectual and moral superiors, but refuse to accept the notion of social betters, but I would have been wasting my breath. It was time-consuming enough fighting to resist his cuts.

It was my description of Mick Mulligan which troubled him most of all. I had tried hard to present a fair picture of this rake-hell, listing his more admirable characteristics as well as his more dubious ones, but I suppose my efforts did result in a rather Rabelaisian portrait. To get his permission to print I visited Mick at his lovely house in the heart of the Sussex countryside. Puffing at the inevitable cigarette and flicking ash on to the deep pile carpet of his sitting-room, he drew breath with quite Jobsworthian emphasis as he scanned the draft. 'Oh no, cock,' he said, 'I can't let this pass. Pam won't like this. I got into a lot of trouble with Melly's book and I don't want that again.'

A moment later his wife Pam appeared, read the draft, and said tartly, 'I don't see anything wrong with this. In fact, I think you've let him off very lightly . . .' Mulligan was cornered, and throwing me a characteristic half-glower, half-grin, he gave his assent. I took his word but the publisher had demanded permission in writing and I quickly proffered a pen. He signed with mock exasperation and a shake of the head. Business over, we visited a few of the rural pubs in the area.

He was then a well-worn forty-eight, but he still had that compelling charm that worked wonders with both sexes, especially women. He has an incredible magnetism which I had tried hard to convey, although I did not entirely succeed. Such a complex character, full of every conceivable contradiction, was beyond my descriptive powers.

To satisfy lawyer and publisher I sought out various others featured in the book, one of whom was Ian Christie, still the *Daily Express*'s film critic. Christie hisses his words, especially in his cups, and on the morning I met him he was at his most assibilative. I mentioned that one or two people seemed reluctant to see me in connection with what I had written about them and that I was getting rather paranoid about this.

'Paranoia, Godbolt,' he hissed, 'is *imagining* people don't want to see you. In your case they obviously *do not* want to see you.'

Conversation over, we went our separate ways, he to a film preview and I to read meters. He lived in NW5 and as this area is part of the Regency district I often saw him on my rounds. On one occasion he introduced me to a friend of his whose name I didn't catch. We shook hands and the man suddenly looked at me as if he'd just touched a leper. 'Godbolt!' he cried. '*Godbolt!* How do you *live* with a name like that?' When I next saw Christie I inquired the name of this chuckle-head. It was John Coleman, film critic of the *New Statesman.*

On another occasion Christie hissed a story he'd heard about Wally Fawkes which kept me chuckling between meters for the rest of the day. An acquaintance of Fawkes, in his late forties, was boasting in Wally's presence that he had left his wife in order to live with a girl half his age. He kept repeating this fact, with many a side reference to the girl's prodigious sexual demands which, he implied, he was amply fulfilling. He went on and on in this vein, obviously hoping for an impressed reaction. Finally Fawkes murmured, '*Mmmm*, I wonder . . . Would it help to *talk* about it?'

I visualized the scene: Fawkes's eyes glinting, that tilting jaw and that mouth tightening as the question formed in his brain. In a way it was reassuring to know that although the era to which I'd devoted my book had vanished, one of its heroes was still capable of that softly delivered thrust which demolishes the pretentious, and with a wince I recalled how often I had been the victim.

Eventually I managed to obtain all but one of the necessary clearances for publication, much to the astonishment of Hale's lawyer. The ethos of the jazz world was something quite beyond his comprehension. He could hardly believe, for instance, that George Melly not only gave me permission to publish my description of him, but subsequently helped me to obtain reviews and mentions on the radio.

The lawyer would probably also have been surprised that Humphrey Lyttelton later devoted the entire hour of one of his 'Best of Jazz' programmes on Radio Two to the book and wrote me a complimentary letter in his elegant script.

But if I managed to win most of the arguments with this bemused and out-of-touch eighty-year-old, there was one particular objection he raised which, had his fear proved correct, would have placed me in a position unique in the whole history of publishing.

The objection was to my reference to Len Bloggs in Wally Fawkes's 'Flook' cartoon. My description of Bloggs as a 'snarling anti-social inverted snob with a chip on his shoulder', was, I like to think, extreme, but not unfaithful to the character as Fawkes and

Melly portrayed him, but the lawyer wrote: 'Page fifty-one: I don't know if this is libel or vulgar abuse, but one doesn't want a libel action to find out. Avoid possibility and omit.' He had completely overlooked the fact that 'Len Bloggs' was myself!

When, with total disbelief, I read this stricture, I realized, with due sense of occasion, that I was the first author ever in a position to sue himself, but the lawyer's instructions could have presented me with a variety of legal, moral and personal problems. First, which of my innumerable selves would sue the other? To sort out these many disparate parts into two clearly defined litigant identities would alone have been a monumental task. I would then have to decide which party would have the better chance of winning and invest that self with my more endearing characteristics. Not that it was of any importance which way the case went. I could always switch sides. As to who paid the costs and/or damages, the question was purely academic as neither party had any money and in any case both would have had to obtain legal aid.

Another tantalizing poser: what if one of my respective lawyers were to suggest that a deal be made out of court? Which of my selves would dig in his heels and elect to take the witness stand? Reading the meters of the proletariat in council estates and the privileged in luxury flats, I let my imagination run riot at the infinite variations of the theme and at the prospect of seeing the judiciary in a state of total chaos arising from the confused thinking of an aged libel lawyer. Surely the self who bought joy to old dears on his meter-reading beat, helping them to catch their budgies and shift their furniture, would seem a likely winner? How could such a patently amiable fellow be described as a disagreeable misanthrope? But would his geniality make him easy prey for a wily counsel? Perhaps egalitarian Godbolt/Bloggs, with his hard-edged tongue who, for fun, watches the grass grow, would be better equipped to counter a lawyer's smooth eloquence.

Another singularity of the case was that both parties read meters. In this regard the judge, in the fashion of his profession, would no doubt indulge in a few witticisms, observing that his meter was never properly read, at which counsel, ingratiating themselves, would hee-hoy in uncontrollable merriment.

The most pleasurable aspect of this fantasy was the discomfort and confusion it would cause the lawyers. They are indeed smart people who belong to a profession in which, whatever the outcome of the case, they can't lose, but they would need all their wits about them with me as both plaintiff and defendant. It was conceivable that my book would sink without trace, but the litigation would make me a household name. I drooled at the prospect of playing Old Harry with the Legal Petes.

In my last meeting with the lawyer I pointed out his oversight and he replied: 'You think I'm an old BF, don't you?' In deference to his age I made no answer, resisting the temptation to nod emphatically, but allowing myself a slight concurring shrug.

The octogenarian man of the law was not the only aggravation for this neophyte author. The galleys were splattered with mistakes of every kind, and the photo captions had been entirely overlooked. Inserted at the last minute, one picture was credited to the *Radto Times* and, apropos the blue film session I had attended with Mick Mulligan and George Melly, the typesetter, in a splendidly Freudian slip, had changed: 'In another epic the casting director had obviously been hard pushed to fill the roles satisfactorily' to 'hard pushed to fill the holes satisfactorily'. Apposite, but not what I had written.

4

It's the Yids, Innit?

There were many days when I was very glad to be a meter reader, not cooped up in an office or factory with only glimpses of sun and sky. I was free from immediate supervision. As long as I got through my 'book' the day was mine. I was especially grateful for this freedom during the long, hot summer of 1976. I was able, for instance, to wander round the Twyford Tip, a twenty-six-acre rubbish dump bounded by the North Circular Road and the Grand Union Canal.

On hillocks of mounting refuse Nature had asserted herself in a profusion of foliage: ragwort, cocksfoot, creeping thistle, stinging-nettles and, threading its way through all this, the convolvulus, marking its progress with its lovely, lily-like white flower. In the heat of summer a myriad of insects buzzed. It had been many years since I had seen so many butterflies, mostly the familiar cabbage white but also the more exotic tortoiseshell, holly blue, peacock and red admiral. Thanks to wanton use of insecticides I doubt if any comparable area in the Home Counties enjoys such an abundance of these lovely creatures.

I was able to amble along the canal bank, cooled by the breeze and gently rippling waters. On other golden days of this remarkable summer I took my lunch-break on the deserted banks of the Brent Reservoir, the Welsh Harp, close to the noisome North Circular, and bathed my sore and aching feet in the cool water lapping through the reeds. The sensation was divine. I watched the swifts weaving and diving for insects, the dabchicks ducking and bobbing and the fractious mallards squabbling. By narrowing my vision on to the trees on the opposite bank, I could create an illusion of being far from the dull suburbia which hemmed in this stretch of water, and tried to think how it all looked just fifty years previously, before the ravages of speculative developers.

I enjoyed wandering through street markets, the stalls and their vendors a colourful alternative to the drab impersonality of the supermarket. I would savour the cries of the market men, deriving vast amusement from their sallies, their impudent brazenness and crudities. 'Now come on girls, how about a nice clean pair of knickers for the weekend?' cried a trader in Queen's Crescent, Gospel Oak, ostentatiously holding up a pair of his wares and especially emphasizing his plea to passing old ladies who giggled in response to the fun of it all.

Also in Queen's Crescent an obese trader with beery features complained that no one was buying his carpet off-cuts. 'I could sell this lot to the darkies in Dalston Lane for a fortune – they like a bit o' colour do the darkies. What's the matter, you bleedin' lot? Don't you like a bit of colour. . . ?'

In Leather Lane market I would often see Little Jimmy, a local character. Jimmy is only four feet tall and whatever the weather, dresses in a long, zippered anorak, peaked cap, baggy trousers and baseball boots. Bright-eyed and cadaverous he stumps around the market, sometimes acting as traffic-master, with a theatrical flourish of commands and signals to ease the congestion. At other times he assumes the role of traffic warden, taking down the numbers of cars parked illegally or otherwise, and shaking his head in moral outrage at this defiance of the law.

I was repeatedly asked with a nudge, a wink and a leer, when I was going to write my 'Confessions of a Meter Reader'. From what I could make of the bill-posters advertising the 'Confessions' films, and reviews I had read of these epics, it would appear that meter readers are not made of the same randy stuff as milkmen, window cleaners, plumbers and postmen.

Certainly, I had no erotic adventures or any real invitation for such on the rounds and only once did I hear a fellow reader boast of sexual conquest on duty. I did not believe him. The only naked woman I ever saw – and I wished I hadn't – was a bearded and sagging geriatric who appeared at the window to refuse me admission. The one remark that could have been construed as a suggestion was from a grubby-looking young woman in a seedy King's Cross tenement: a prostitute – not much of a recommendation for my magnetism.

I could, perhaps, have made something of a comment by a young woman who told me that she had complained about a dog constantly barking in the builder's yard next door, only to be told by the builder that she was neurotic. Touching my arm, she added: 'He said I needed a good man in my bed.'

There were fruity comments from working-class women of elderly vintage but such banter was not to be misconstrued.

'Show me your doings,' said a woman in a tobacco kiosk in Euston Road.

'Madge, you mustn't ask the man to do that!' shrieked her friend. Madge, quickly putting her hand to her mouth, realized she had made a gaffe. My 'doings' was my identity card, often referred to as such. Depending on a quick assessment of the person who phrased the request this way, I would sometimes raise an eyebrow in mock surprise and jocularly decline, perhaps on account of it being too cold.

Unintentionally, I was responsible for 'coitus interruptus' in a large Victorian house in Kilburn, converted into flats. A muscular young Australian complained that I had disturbed him in the moment of sweet truth with a female companion. Actually, what he said was: 'You bugger! I was just on the short strokes with me Sheila!' I was genuinely apologetic; far better he receive an estimate rather than be disturbed on the short strokes. Seeing that I was so contrite he gave me a broad grin, bless him, although he could afford to be magnaminous. He was able to return to his Sheila and consummate. I was to encounter a hundred or so women that day, but only to read their meters.

The job took me into an emporium in Tottenham Court Road, the like of which I'd never before entered – a 'sex shop', selling titillatory manuals, videos, posters, badges, photographs, statuettes, dolls and other 'devices'. Why, in this permissive age and wearing a uniform that clearly denoted that I was on official business, I should have looked furtively around me as I entered I don't know, but I did. Perhaps I had some irrationally puritanical objection. If so, it was hypocritical, as I found the merchandise of great interest and if any of it makes people's sex lives any happier I feel it is a good reason for its manufacture.

A fresh-complexioned young woman, who wouldn't have looked out of character in a Salvation Army uniform, rolled up a strip of carpeting and opened a trap door to a ladder where the meters were. As I descended my eye fell on a poster illustrating a number of copulatory positions, some of them requiring a contortionist's rubber-limbed flexibility. These positions have been practised by the more pliable since Adam and Eve, but only in this age are posters depicting them as easily available as *Woman's Own* and *Radio Times*. I managed to take my eye off the intriguing poster, descended to read a prosaic meter, and when I returned felt sufficiently emboldened to browse round the merchandise.

I goggled at an enormous rubber penis, well above the length and circumference of an erect organ of average size. In the course of five years in the Navy, three of them in Africa, and twenty seasons in a succession of cricket dressing-rooms, I had observed, often with envy, the male reproductive organ of many an ethnic group and discovered that some groups are indisputably better endowed than others, but I had never seen a cock of these awesome proportions. It cost five pounds and was available in pinky-purple, light chocolate and dark tan, enabling women of different nationalities to choose an organ the colour of their skin, or indeed the very contrary.

A spectacle quite extraordinary to me was a family group of impassive Arabs gathered round the young assistant as she showed them three doll figures with movable parts, consisting of two men and a woman in a three-way sex romp. The customers were mother and father, fiftyish, and a young couple who could have been brother and sister or man and wife. They listened intently and without any display of emotion as the young lady explained how each 'toy' operated. It was as though she were explaining the workings of a domestic appliance at the LEB showrooms. How attitudes have changed in my lifetime!

This particular street is also known for cinemas showing sex films. I read the meter at one of the latter. A cheery young projectionist showed me round, commenting that the film was 'a load of horsecrap'. I had a peep at the production he had described so uncomplimentarily. A nude, fat and ugly man bounced up and down on the back of a fairly attractive naked girl, in colour. Again, the girl's willingness to appear nude and bounced upon by this obese leading man before the cameras was a far cry from the films of my youth, with virginal heroines like Mary Pickford, Mary Brian, Anne Shirley, Olivia de Havilland and Janet Gaynor, whose handsome leading men, the likes of Ronald Colman, Patrick Knowles, John Payne and Walter Pidgeon, behaved like gentlemen!

If it was enlightening to visit these palaces of the permissive age, it was intriguing to chance upon reminders of London's past, sometimes representing a standard of living and a way of life wholly unacceptable nowadays; like a dark and satanic tenement block, the wall of which bore a plaque that proclaimed: 'Improved Dwellings for the Industrious Classes'; or a wall sign advertising a cider bar in which the industrious occupants could get as drunk as lords on scrumpy for a pittance. The cider bar itself had long gone, a casualty of affluence.

I would pause at drinking troughs for horses, benevolently provided by the Metropolitan Drinking and Cattle Trough Association, an example of Victorian philanthropy, still with offices in London. I admired the rococo ornamentation on the façade of many Victorian buildings, even those as prosaic as the public washrooms in Grafton Road, Kentish Town, built in the days when it was unthinkable that bathrooms should be installed in improved dwellings for the industrious classes. The signs advertising 'Men First Class' and 'Men Second Class' still exist. The washrooms' function is proclaimed in chunky block serif letters on the fascia panel, and at the bottom of the Doric pillars set into the brickwork are classical nudes, their 'private parts' decorously hidden from view by a tangle of foliage, as befitted the morality of the time.

Echoes of the vanished 'Upstairs Downstairs' society remained in elegant Downshire Hill where a sign outside a front door announced that the tradesmen's entrance was at the rear, and in York Rise, NW5, I was intrigued by still clearly visible sign-lettering on a wall abutting a one-time draper's shop, listing the draper's wares, including maids' caps, gowns and dresses.

Outside a Euston tobacconist's a delightful glass sign displayed all the old signwriter's skills in ornate lettering, acid-engraved with gilded and blended shade, advertising 'Mitchell's Compos Flake', circa 1900. A waggish consumer had pinned to the brickwork next to his front door another Victorian advertisement on an enamelled sign. It read:

Dr Drake's Universal Pill cures:
bad blood, early decay, scrofula, aggravated pores,
underdevelopment, internal complaints, smarting loins,
lowness of spirit, abdominal griping, flat feet, weakness of the
knees and diseases of all descriptions.
CONTAINS NOTHING INJURIOUS

There was many a morning when I would have been grateful for a few samples of Dr Drake's panacea in my poacher's pocket: to ease my smarting loins after being chased by Prince, Buster or Rover, my lowness of spirit before facing an afternoon in Neasden, my abdominal griping after a glass too many the night before, the weakness of my knees and flat feet after trudging up and down the North Circular.

On the front door of a squat in King's Cross I was riveted by the following proclamation:

Hear Ye Our Royal Edict
by virtue of our Royal Prerogative we Joseph do Hereby Decree
the Acquisition of this here Deserted Domicile to Serve
Together with a Frugal Personal Need in the Execution of the
Most Vital Role on Earth. We herewith duly verify any
Adversaries cum whatever Ambitions that Conspiracy to
Intrude upon our Sacred Precincts will beget the Direst
Consequences.
Signed, JOSEPH, DEFENDER OF THE FAITH
Hear Ye: Our Decree of Acquisition is NOT a tourists'
souvenir.

I loved calling upon craftsmen's little shops, often tucked away in alleys or mews, like the firm of wheelwrights still making steel-bound barrow wheels in Neal St, Covent Garden. In this age of mass production such havens of craftsmanship should be cherished, but time and time again I was aware that they were threatened by developers whose talent for applied ugliness has earned them their wretched reputation.

Frequently I saw attractive rows of houses or shops replaced by hideous constructions, designed to accommodate the maximum number of bodies. If I needed any convincing that the civic authorities are hell-bent on the uglification of our environment, I have only to look from the balcony of my North London flat, from which the majestic dome of St Paul's, erected to the glory of God, once dominated the skyline. Now it is hemmed in by gross concrete and glass, monuments to Mammon, a desecration of a once splendid vista.

There were many, many high-rise blocks of flats I had to visit and I had only to approach these gaunt constructions to feel my spirits swiftly dipping. Concrete, unlike stone, will not be washed clean by the rain; unlike brick it will not mellow with age; it turns into a streaky yellow-grey, as unappealing as the main body of the structure. Invariably these high-rise blocks were council flats for working-class occupants. In the main they were well kept, but sometimes the appearance of a reasonable standard of living – the colour TV, the spin dryer, the hi-fi centre and furniture – was set in conditions of squalor: filthy, litter-ridden floors, dust-choked curtains and messy, malodorous kitchens. Often, too, the stairs and corridors were litter-ridden, the walls scarred with crude graffiti: 'Maisy is a Tramp'; 'Gus is fucking Tracy'; 'Jason's a Wanker'; 'Karen loves Fred'; 'Chelsea Rules OK'; and vicious, racist slogans: 'Wogs Out'; 'If They're Black, Send 'Em Back.'

In a barely completed block in Harlesden most of the flats were already inhabited. Outside the block were squares of levelled soil where grass had been sown and tree saplings planted. Little spears of grass competed with the dross of litter, much of it embedded in the soil by tramping feet. To open a cupboard of meters I put my book down on the floor. When I picked it up my hands felt sticky; the book was smeared with a large dottle of green spit. Other affronts to common decency were wrenched-out railings and smashed staircase windows. I was witnessing the collapse of an environment before the paint was dry. I returned the cupboard key to a friendly caretaker, making some comment about the vandalism. 'If I made any fuss here, mate, they'd shove dog shit through my letter box. That's if I was lucky. Some of the bastards would set fire to my front door.'

It was a familiar cry in my childhood, even at the social level in which I was raised, that there was little point in installing bathrooms in council flats as the former slum dwellers would 'only put coal in them'. That allegation, mostly unfounded, echoed uneasily in my ears as I left the block.

The degree of vandalism changed from area to area – Harlesden and Stonebridge Park were the worst – but it was evident even in a pleasant area like Adelaide Road. Walking down the stairs of a high-rise block I came across a woman cleaning up faeces.

'We had a right dirty bastard here,' she said.

'A dog?'

'If it was it used arse-paper!'

Most of the music I heard on my rounds was raucous pop, often played at an obscene and punishing volume. During one exhaustingly hot day in 1976, a raging thirst to be slaked only by a cool bitter found me in a Gower Street pub which, on my arrival, was quiet except for the buzz of conversation.

The barmaid gave me a cursory glance. She was being chatted up by a young man. I would have to wait until his blandishments were completed. A polite 'excuse me' produced a reluctant move in my direction. The merest inclination of her head indicated that she was prepared to take my order. Not a word passed her lips. Maybe she found it difficult to speak with a cigarette in her mouth. I ordered my pint. She took a noisy drag on her fag and stubbed it out in an ashtray already choked with butts. With fingertips now the colour of the tray's contents she drew the pint, having, of necessity, to hold the handle. The glass filled, she gratuitously transferred it to her other hand, placing her dirty fingers round the rim and pushing the glass before me. 'Thirty-five,' she said. Nothing more. She didn't believe in wasting words, like 'please'.

Suddenly the jukebox was started up by some wretched fellow who, in the patent barrenness of his existence, required the junk that issues from these contraptions, even though he was in conversation. It was untypically remiss of me not to have noticed this jukebox. Had I done so, the pub would have done without my custom. Without much pleasure I drank in the relative peace of the roaring traffic outside.

I suppose that had this machine contained records by Duke Ellington, Louis Armstrong, Jack Teagarden or Benny Goodman I would have been draped round it, absorbing every note. But jazz records are rarely found in jukeboxes, any more than people who walk through the streets carrying transistor sets playing at monstrous volume are ever tuned into anything but pop.

I took my glass back to the bar. 'Any charge for the music?' I icily inquired of the barmaid.

'No,' she coolly replied, 'it's free, if someone else puts the money in.' Touché!

Very rarely did I hear any jazz on my rounds, but one morning as I approached a house in Primrose Hill, familiar strains delighted my ears. To my surprise I found myself listening to a record by Luis Russell and his band, a great gutsy black orchestra of the late twenties and early thirties. I rang the doorbell of the house from which this divine sound was issuing and a pleasant young man led me to the room in which the record was being played. In typical jazz buff's fashion I had to declare my knowledge of the disc, and that the trombonist whose solo coincided with my entry into the room was J.C. Higginbotham, one of my favourite players. The American critic Whitney Balliett once described jazz as the 'sound of surprise' and here the surprise was mutual. Records of Luis Russell, very much a 'collector' band, I would never have expected to hear, any more than the consumer expected his meter reader to know the band and its personnel.

At a junk shop off Queen's Crescent market I often looked in to see if there were any 78s for sale. After all these years of collecting jazz records I still feel a thrill of excitement in spotting a pile of old shellac discs, with perhaps a long deleted jazz item to be salvaged from the inevitable dross. I was in this tat emporium one morning when a customer came in and inquired of the owner, 'Have you seen Alf lately?'

'Nah! Oi doan deal with the schmuck no more, do oi? 'E was diddlin' me, wan'e? I doan mind being diddled as long as oi know, do oi?'

This combination of denial, assertion and question had a succinct unity transcending errors of grammar and pronunciation, but catching a glimpse of the speaker out of the corner of my eye as I quickly flipped through the records, I fancied the chances of diddling him were very remote. A hopeful with that intention would, to use a term of my youth, 'have to get up very early in the morning'.

Meter reading increased my awareness of race as well as class, and not always happily. The white man in the LEB uniform was redolent of colonial authority, sometimes insulted by West Indians, solemnly regarded by Asiatics, and fair game for Jews to haggle with.

I own up: my heart used to sink when I was working in parts of Willesden and Brondesbury and I saw the names Finklestein, Goldberg and Levy in my book. I knew I could expect fervent claims that their electricity consumption was low or virtually non-existent, and heated assertions that I was out to ruin them, migawd, and that it was all right for me, as I got my electricity free – which was not the case.

The ancient tradition of bargaining in the ghettos and markets of Europe and the Middle East was maintained, perhaps by force of ingrained habit, in the Willesden and Brondesbury hinterlands, even though, in the electricity trade, the meterman had no part in determining the current tariff and was merely there to record what he saw on the dials. It was of no consequence to me if the reading was astronomical or minimal. But having had a Jewish girlfriend (whose mother was appalled that her Dulcie was going out with a 'goy'), a Jewish employer, and having dealt with several Jewish people in the entertainment business I was well acquainted with their humour and would often respond in like fashion: 'Do me a favour! Does the LEB consult *me* about prices? For *you*, I'd let you have it cheaper, but the man that calls next quarter might be a schmuck . . .'

No such banter was possible with a lady in a Bloomsbury block of luxury flats, and it was a confrontation that made me very sad, not just because her attitude was peevish and hostile. The meter was ceiling-high and politely, as always, I asked for a chair. 'No, you cannot use any of my chairs! They're antiques! Why don't you carry a ladder?' she snapped. More antiques! Did rude bums ever sully these priceless seats?

I adopted my haughty pose and delivered a homily: 'Madam, I can't possibly carry a ladder about all day and I can't read the meter from here. *They* will send you an estimate.'

The dreaded estimate jolted her into action and with much clucking she thrust a chair towards me. It was not, I observed, an antique. I read her meter to the accompaniment of a sustained whine. Such lamentations over a meter reader doing his job!

'Why doesn't the stupid LEB send the same man round each time?'

'To ensure, madam, that mistakes are not perpetuated. Meter readers, like everyone else, are prey to human error. The LEB management are most concerned with accuracy and it is in your interests that the quarterly calls are made by different readers. Also, from the Electricity Board's point of view, it avoids the possibility of corruption.'

I delivered this intentionally verbose riposte with, I like to think, a certain aplomb, but my audience was unimpressed.

'Corruption! That would never happen in *my* country!'

She was unmistakeably Jewish and with a thick German accent and I found it utterly astonishing that someone who had almost assuredly suffered at the hands of the Nazi regime should still hold this esteem for the country which had spawned it.

'And what country was that, madam?'

She had no reply. There was none she could make. Instead, she countered with the familiar enquiry: 'Issitt*alott*?'

In my childhood anti-semitism of a mild but incipiently dangerous sort was commonplace and with it phrases like 'sheeny' and 'ikeymo' were freely bandied about. Had there been any danger of it being rekindled by confrontations such as this I needed a corrective to restore the balance. I had such a few days later in a crumbling three-storeyed house in Euston.

It was about eight-thirty in the morning. After the third or fourth ring, a spectacle of human decay presented himself at the door. His heavily jowled features sprouted three or four days' stubble; as many days had passed since these had received the application of soap and water. He wore a soiled, collarless shirt; his paunch spilled over the top of greasy cord trousers held up with string and open at the flies revealing grubby pyjamas; his eyes were bloodshot and rheumy, and a self-rolled shag-fag hung from his tarred lips. He eyed me suspiciously as I made my formal address: 'Good morning, sir. Electricity Board. Can I read your meter, please?'

'What fucking meter?'

'Electricity meter, sir.'

'Ain't got no meter.'

'This is number seventy-two, sir?'

'Nah, it's seventy-three, ainit?'

'It says seventy-two on the numberplate.'

He stepped out to stare at the numerals on the door. 'Well, so it fucking well does! Well I'm buggered! But I ain't got no meter!'

'My book says it's in the cellar.'

He pondered for a moment: 'All right mate, you can come in but . . .' he leaned forward in an emphatic manner . . . 'I wanna see yore identity card. With so many bleedin' villains abaht, you've gotter be careful, 'aven't yer?'

He coughed and spluttered over my card and handed it back well moistened. The cellar was an evil-smelling rubbish dump, particularly under the pavement grille where passers-by and dogs had contributed to the morass. The meter was hidden under a stained and rotting mattress. Fearing that I would be contaminated by fleas, at the very least, I hastily made my reading and returned to the doorway. I own to the feeling that at that moment I, in more senses than one, had gone down in the world.

The consumer was waiting in the hallway having a violent cough-up, the fag miraculously sticking to his lower lip as he heaved, retched and spluttered.

'It could do with a coat of paint down there!' I remarked, my jokiness more an expression of relief at having safely emerged from such a foetid pit than a desire for banter.

'Nah! No chance! It's owned by the bleeding Yids, innit? All the 'ouses rahnd 'ere are owned by the bastards, ain't they? Bleedin' Yids! Would'n do a thing for yer. 'Ate 'em, I do. *'Ate* em. 'Itler 'ad the right idea . . .'

He abruptly ceased this tirade to peer closely at my features, particularly, I thought, at my rather long nose. '*Eyah*! You're not a Yid, are yer? If you are mate, no offence meant . . .'

With the greatest regret I gave up playing cricket in September 1976, one month before *All This and 10%* was published. I could still make a contribution in the field, although I was beginning to creak audibly on Monday mornings as I strained to reach a meter placed high up on the wall or hidden away under the stairs. But the old spirit of the Ravers had gone. Most of the originals had left for one reason or another and their replacements were alien to the ethos of the eleven.

I had never been much good – I started too late in life – but for twenty years it had proved a marvellous way of spending Sundays. I missed the excitement of crouching in the slips, the thrill of holding a difficult catch and the supreme joy of a properly executed stroke which had the ball cauterizing the turf.

This didn't happen too often in my case but when it did it gave me a feeling which had no price. I still think of those golden days out on the field, and wistfully recall my highest score – forty-seven, including seven fours and a six, each stroke permanently engraved on this indifferent cricketer's memory. My last scoring shot was the glorious six and, going for another that would take me to the fifty – it was beyond my wildest expectations that I would ever make the ton – I was clean bowled.

5

Meter Reader/Author

In the weeks prior to publication of *All This and 10%* I had strange dreams in which the book appeared as a musty and dog-eared volume entitled *Hikes Through the Heather*. On 9 October 1976, four days after my fifty-fourth birthday, my 'author's copies' arrived. I felt no elation as I opened the parcel, removed a copy, opened it at the dedication that had special significance to me, scanned the index listing so many people who had figured in my post-war life, flipped through the photo-pages and shuddered at the badly set captions. I didn't read a word of the text for fear of the errors I would spot. When I did get round to reading it throughout there was a discomforting number of these.

I phoned my octogenarian father to tell him that his eldest son's first book had been published, and set off to work. He bought a copy and never read a single word.

It was widely reviewed. Generally the notices were favourable, reviewers kindly foregoing mention of the many 'literals'. One of the first was headed 'Waiting for Godbolt', written by Peter Clayton in the *Sunday Telegraph*, a heading appropriate in view of the enormous amount of time which had elapsed between my first putting pen to paper and the book's eventual publication. George Melly, reviewing it in the *New Statesman*, commented on the help he had given me after reading an early draft which he found 'stiff, facetious and "literary" ', and added that I had overcome these faults by stubborn application. If this were true, at least in part, I was pleased.

I was flattered that Philip Larkin gave it qualified praise in the *Guardian*, but he insisted that it was the 'revulsion' that came over most. This surprised me, but another reviewer, Richard Boston in

Punch, concluded: 'He can't make it [the jazz scene] sound anything other than an unattractive world, inhabited by people who are clearly more entertaining to read about at a distance than to cope with at first hand.' I had not intended to convey any 'revulsion', but perhaps the less savoury aspects and occupational hazards of an agent's life permeated the narrative more than I had intended.

It was instructive, if not always flattering, to learn how I was regarded as an individual by people reading the book. According to Chris Welsh in the *Melody Maker* '. . . throughout it all emerges a picture of a man bordering on paranoia yet armed with an impish sense of humour . . . older readers will find much in common with a man embattled against the changing world.'

Anybody who writes honestly about himself, or at least as honestly as he dares, is bound to come under uncomfortable scrutiny, and I had to remember that I too had scrutinized many people in my book. Humphrey Lyttelton, in his letter to me, responded to some of my observations:

> I read [*All This and 10%*] with a glee that was only slightly tinged with masochism . . . Can I put forward one other inheritance of the Eton education which might round out the picture? That is, believe it or not, an excruciating shyness, largely outgrown now, but still liable to stir uneasily when I am thrown among strangers without a trumpet in hand . . . But as a fifty-six-year-old man-of-the-people, mild, avuncular and, in my own eyes, unbent to the point of total collapse, I musn't appear to disown the combative aristo of your book. With children teetering on the brink of punk, it's handy to be able to recall arrogant confrontations with the BBC, the press, local councils, etc.
>
> If the book does no more than immortalize Kingswell it will have performed a great service to English literature.

I was delighted to receive such a friendly note from someone with whom I had not got on well, but I had a few wry thoughts about Humph's claim to have 'unbent to the point of total collapse'. I still wouldn't care to cross him. Old leopards don't change their spots.

My local paper, the *Hampstead and Highgate Express*, published an interview with me entitled 'Meter Reader's Blues', and I even made the *Home and Freezer Digest*. The review looked a little out of place among recipes for baps, mousse, choc crunchies, meatballs and quiches, but it was still a notice and I was grateful for every mention.

On account of my novelty value as a meter reader/author I appeared on Radio Four's 'Start the Week'. This programme is broadcast live and I arrived at Broadcasting House in a highly agitated state. I had hardly slept the night before on account of the butterflies fluttering inside my stomach. On arrival at the studio these had been replaced by squirming serpents and burrowing badgers. Taking the coward's way out, I sneaked into the lavatory to anaesthetize these beasts with a hefty slug of whisky from a hip flask.

Others on the programme were educationalist Professor A. H. Halsey; Oliver Giddings, medical correspondent for the *Sunday Times*; Eric Lyons, President of the Royal Society of British Architects; Dr David Owen, then Minister of State at the DHSS; and broadcasters Mavis Nicholson and Steve Bradshaw. Producer Sally Thompson and presenters Frank Bough and Kenneth Robinson went out of their way to put me at ease and I was grateful for their solicitude. It was such a stark contrast to my everyday job that I felt I was dreaming. I had to remind myself that I had written and published a book.

The programme opened with a record by Humphrey Lyttelton's first band and the initial discussion was of Giddings's book, *Who Do You Think You are?*, an examination of the interaction of our genetic inheritance and social conditioning. This was followed by a discussion about the effects of living in high-rise flats, some of which had been designed by Mr Lyons. I had been in more of these constructions than he had and had certainly observed their social consequences more closely than anyone else on the panel, but it was such a struggle to get a word in edgeways that I only just managed to ask Mr Lyons if he would like to live in one of these places himself. I got no answer to that and I soon realized that on a programme of this kind a degree of ruthlessness and determination to be heard are prerequisites.

My spot was introduced by Bradshaw. I had formed a strong dislike of him from our first conversation. Knowing he was going to 'introduce' me, and wanting to establish a common ground for discussion, I had made him several phone calls which he didn't return. When I eventually established contact he was very offhand, dismissing 'Start the Week' as a programme of no consequence. He obviously had the same view of my book.

Plainly, he had given it only the most cursory reading. He seized upon what he thought it was about – trad jazz – and belaboured it from the standpoint of this misconception. Like many other young

men with determinedly 'up-to-date' tastes, he speciously and
mistakenly labelled all jazz that came before his time as trad, and
glibly compared the playing of it to the citizens of Rutland dressing
up as cowboys and shooting it out with toy guns over the weekend.
He cited the objections I had made about rock and roll and played a
particularly horrendous multi-tracked 'heavy metal' cacophony
which, at least, reminded me why I had left the entertainment
business. Bradshaw brusquely suggested that I brought myself up to
date and remarked that I seemed bent on appearing a loser, the very
idea anathema to a person of his considerable ego.

I had begun to answer when I was interrupted by Miss Nicholson
who, desperately eager to identify herself with the tastes and mores
of the young, defended their choice of music. Vainly, I tried to keep
going but the redoubtable lady won hands down. Should I ever
appear on such a programme again I will gird myself up and not be
so easily vanquished, even in the daunting presence of Mavis
Nicholson.

I found Dr Owen, soon to have the most fearsome responsibilities
as Foreign Secretary, extremely pleasant. During the programme
he had jocularly remarked that his claim to fame as Permanent
Under-Secretary for Defence, with responsibility for the Navy, had
been to abolish the lower decks' rum ration. I later talked to him
about the effect the demon rum had upon the crews of the scruffy
trawlers I served on during the war, an intoxication unthinkable in
today's floating arsenals packed with sophisticated electrical
equipment.

Had there been a photographer present I would have had no
compunction in trying to get a shot of Dr Owen and myself for
publicity purposes. I would however have foregone the pleasure of
being snapped in the company of Miss Nicholson and Mr Bradshaw;
they were not Cabinet Ministers. Small fry, of little use to a meter
reader/author.

Heady as this experience was, and I was paid £20 for it, I had been
around too long to think that such isolated publicity was going
to make me famous overnight, or increase the sales of my book to
any marked extent. I had no option but to continue peering at
meters.

I had decided to keep quiet at Lithos Road about my being an
author, but someone there must have half-heard the 'Start the Week'
broadcast and the reference to jazz and mentioned it to Ted
Batchelor. One afternoon I was queueing in the office behind John

Armatage when Ted asked if it was he who had been on the radio. As I was in earshot it would have seemed coy not to own up. Ted looked at me in astonishment. I think he was amazed that someone so slow at learning to read meters should have managed to write a book.

In the following weeks I was struck by the number of people in jazz clubs who came up to me and announced, 'I haven't read your book.' Fair enough; they had no obligation to do so – but why tell me? Very few musicians read it, not even those it mentioned. Jazz musicians generally do not read books about jazz. One exception was Bruce Turner, a self-proclaimed and unabashed skinflint. 'The best book I ever borrowed, Dad,' he told me.

With that perversity of spirit which must be the activating force of so many writers at every level, I was sufficiently encouraged by the publication of my book to begin writing another one.

By this time I had been a jazz enthusiast for nearly forty years, and I was fascinated by the way in which this 'alien' form of music had come to establish itself – albeit as a minority interest – in this country. So I set about researching the introduction, reception and development of jazz in Britain. I spent all my spare time and leave days in the newspaper section of the British Museum at Colindale and the main library in Great Russell Street, making prodigious notes.

I sometimes wrote before I did my rounds, but more often on my return from work. After a tiring tramp around the Regency beat I had to summon up every ounce of my meagre willpower to sit at the typewriter. If my concentration and will to work flagged, which was often, I would open a bottle of wine, slump in my armchair and gape at the television. But writing is a demanding mistress; I felt guilty if I left her even for an hour or so. Why the compulsion to attend her? There was little pleasure in the association and the rewards from it were minimal. At times I felt like a man trying to crunch boulders with his teeth.

I leaned heavily on the suspect crutch of drink more often than was good for my health, my pocket or the intelligibility of my handwriting. After a glass too many my typing became a hiero-glyphic tangle which I had to try to make sense of the following day. One morning I wondered what I had meant by 'two good grinds of mine'. Two! One would have been a triumph of spirit over weak flesh. But two! – surely alcoholic fantasizing on a grand scale! It was some time before I realized that I had tried to type 'two good friends of mine'.

It was some consolation to read that other infinitely more successful and talented practitioners such as George Orwell and Alan Ayckborne had expressed similar comments about the tedium of writing, but if writers are notorious for protesting the agonies of their calling, rarely does anybody twist their arms to pursue it; certainly not editors and publishers, most of whom would apparently have been happier if I, for one, had kept away from the typewriter.

There were no 'spin-offs' from *All This and 10%*. On the contrary; nearly all the articles, TV ideas, and suggestions for Sunday supplements were rejected. It was remaindered without my being told, the unsold copies reaching, I believe, Australia. Like so many other volumes of this kind, some of them will inevitably filter to those who are interested and become a sort of collector's item, but with no financial benefit to me.

Following publication of *All This and 10%* I got to know Keith Stewart, a BBC producer in charge of, among other programmes, Humphrey Lyttelton's 'Best of Jazz'. I was in his office one day when I noticed on his desk a publication called *Jazz Circle News*, which was quite new to me. I was surprised to see that its publishers were Barry Ancill and Jack Gregory, two people with whom I had done business in my early days as a jazz agent, when they used to promote clubs and concerts in the Manchester area.

That evening, more out of curiosity than anything else, I rang Jack Gregory and in his broad Lancashire accent came the rejoinder: 'Bloody 'ell, they're all coming out of t' woodwork!' Jack told me to get in touch with the editor, Clarrie Henley, who had read my book and welcomed contributions to his magazine.

There was no payment for these articles, but I didn't mind. It was a pleasure to write for Clarrie, whose occasionally complimentary remarks did wonders for my ego. It was further boosted by the inclusion of my photograph next to my by-line. But my contributions displeased at least one reader, author Eric Townley. In a letter pleading for coverage of certain labels, he ended with the trenchant comment, 'Should you suggest that there is not enough space, I recommend that you scrap the vapid rubbish by Jim Godbolt, which is a disgrace to your interesting magazine.'

I got to know Clarrie very well, and much admired this

extraordinarily industrious man who ran a guest house in Blackpool with his wife Alice, drove daily to Manchester to work as a sub-editor on the *Star*, played guitar in local jazz bands and single-handedly produced *Jazz Circle News*.

Later my association with the magazine was strengthened by my becoming its advertising agent. In this endeavour I was reasonably successful, but it was difficult to chase up potential advertisers during normal office hours, when I was out reading meters. I overcame this problem by doing my 'book' during the day as usual, picking up the following day's work in the afternoon and completing it that same evening. I was amazed that no one ever questioned the sight of a man in the LEB chocolate-brown uniform presenting himself as late as eight o'clock at night to read the meter, but no one did. The next day was clear for me to sell space.

Eventually, a few small commissions came my way. One was to write the album notes for a compilation of old 78s made by Graeme Bell's Australian Jazz Band and the Christie Brother Stompers with Ken Colyer, for the Esquire label. I was rather pleased with my combination of critical appraisal and personal reminiscence, and when I heard Humphrey Lyttelton on 'Best of Jazz' announce that he was going to play a track or two from the album I was hopeful that my liner note would get a mention, perhaps inducing other record companies to seek my services. Indeed, it was alluded to. Lyttelton said: 'I will forbear to mention the sleeve-writer's notes as he contrived to misspell my name three times.' Once again, typesetters were bedevilling my life, earning me a Lyttelton side-swipe.

Had anybody asked me at this time what I did for my living, I could perhaps have claimed that I was an author/journalist. If pressed, I might have added that I did a spot of meter reading on the side, primarily for the purpose of sociological observation, and an overwhelming wish to treat with my fellow men and the canine breeds. But the truth is that I had to continue tramping the Regency beat in order to pay my way.

Increasingly irritated with myself for being in a position from which I could see no escape, I had to fight hard to conceal my annoyance with the fractious, and above all, my objections to Prince, Buster and Rover. In the latter I can't have been too successful and I became more and more familiar with the question,

'Don't you like animals, then?' I am passionately fond of animals and genuinely mourn their destruction at the vicious hand of man, but I make a very sharp distinction between animals of the wild and domestic pets, many of which have my sympathy for being so heartlessly confined in small flats.

If I ever wondered whether my objections to the dogolatrous were misplaced I had only to read advertisements such as this, which appeared in the *Evening Standard*:

> Lost. Staffordshire Bull Terrier. Brown with black face, eight
> months old. Small and fat with only one testicle, but much
> loved. Substantial Reward.

The conclusion I drew from this advertisement was that had the animal had its full complement of balls it would have been even more doted on by its dotty owner.

Only twice in my time with the LEB was a complaint lodged against me, and on both occasions dogs were concerned. Descending a very narrow basement staircase one day I suddenly became aware of an Alsatian charging towards me. I frantically turned tail. It transpired that the beast merely wanted to get out, its 'animal lover' owner evidently not giving it enough exercise. But I was not to know this, and far from getting an apology from its owner, the amused look on her face revealed how much she had enjoyed my discomfort. I held my temper and enquired as to the whereabouts of her meter.

'Where it's always been,' she curtly replied.

'Bollocks!' I retorted, and stalked out.

The very next day, in Primrose Hill, I politely asked a lady to put away her baying Doberman. She exploded in fury. 'You people! You think you're running the *cun*tray, telling people like *me* what to do.' I denied I had been impolite. 'Oh, yes you were,' she replied, 'you're an ill-mannered pig! I know good manners. I know a lot of titled people!' This aristocratically-connected lady increased her tirade to such a pitch that, fearing she might physically attack me, and with the dog no doubt on her side, I walked away.

Both these women reported me.

I often used to see plaques in hallways, in wood or brass, which read: 'The more I see of humanity the more I love my dog.' The more I saw of the dogolatrous the more I loathed them. I was now convinced that otherwise rational people became unbalanced with the ownership of a dog.

In a well-appointed block in Gospel Oak I walked up a flight of stairs to see a man in his early twenties crouching to speak through a letter-box. 'Hello Winston, is Mummy in?' he inquired. By the time I presented myself for entry the door had been opened. Once in the flat I discovered that Winston was an enormous sheepdog. As it made the usual grunts and snuffles when kissed by the young man, I was at least satisfied that I had not encountered my first talking dog.

Ironically, I was never actually attacked by a dog, but by a tabby cat called Katy in the cellar of a Holborn pub. I went to stroke her when a paw with extended talons shot out and lacerated my wrist. Frightened and shocked, I backed away with Katy pursuing me, hissing and spitting. I had to beat her away with a broom. I insisted that she be locked away before I ventured below again, a request which was loudly echoed by a scornful barmaid to a packed bar which included workmen from a local building site, who hooted with laughter at the spectacle of a grown man frightened of a cat.

This particular meter was one described as 'maximum duty' which I had to read monthly, and the regulars became accustomed to my shame-faced enquiry as to the whereabouts of Katy.

By the winter of 1978 I had been with the LEB for over three years, and I kept on telling myself that I was better off than many confined within the four walls of a factory or office. 'Better than being chained to date sheets,' I would say to myself, and although much of this thinking was self-persuasion, it was, in its relative way, quite true.

I had been out and about under the sun during summers; I had enjoyed the sweet melancholy of autumn, the sensual pleasure of shuffling through piles of russet leaves – nature's litter that pleases the eye and refurbishes the soil – relishing their smell as they burned in park and garden pyres, the blue smoke mingling with the evening mists. I never ceased to wonder at the relentless cycle of the seasons; a mysterious and immutable phenomenon of a magnitude no human agency can boast.

I even enjoyed the bitter winter, revelling in the keen air and the bleak symmetry of gaunt, leafless trees silhouetted against a sullen sky. Even the charmless North Circular looked dramatic when hostile winds howled across the grey expanse of the Welsh Harp, whipping up waves with foaming crests a foot high, the bleakness of the scene heightened by hundreds of shrieking and swooping gulls. Here, only a few months earlier, I had bathed my burning feet.

I had quite a few spills on the frozen tiles of garden paths, on one occasion describing a series of arabesques rather like Mr Pickwick on Manor Farm pond, before thudding against the front door. Shaken, I rang the bell and noticed a cluster of brightly coloured flowers peeping through the snow. They had an unhealthy translucence. I soon discovered why. They were made of plastic; factory-produced flora stuck in the garden soil. Durable, though. Unlike the feeble creations of nature, they would not wither and die, nor suffer the attentions of the suckling bee.

But the cold did nothing to subdue Mr Jokerman. 'Breee! Freeze the balls off a brass monkey, eh? Got mine tucked away in me long johns, I can tell you. Got to keep *them* warm, eh? *Ha ha ha ha ha!*'

Again I did my best to muster a smile. At least Mr Jokerman didn't complain, as some people did, that the snow on my boots was spoiling his carpet.

On another particularly Arctic morning I encountered a railway worker in a Camden Town basement. A Welshman, he whined his objections to being called upon at 7.45 a.m. I would have thought that he, in his job, would appreciate that others too had to work unsociable hours, but not so.

'Start early in the morning, don't you, bhoyo?' he said, a gratuitous question which heavily emphasized his displeasure at the fact. Perhaps he was a ticket collector, one of those unhappy species doing a really boring job whose only pleasure, it seems to me, is misdirecting passengers and shouting at them for excess fares. His meter was high up and I asked if I could use the ladder already in his hallway. He huffed and puffed a reluctant assent and gave me firm instructions to tell the LEB to move his meter to eye-level; he wasn't having his ladder worn out (yes!) by bloody meter readers. 'Why the hell don't you carry one, bhoyo?' he asked.

Indeed, why not a whole battery of equipment to see me through the day? Such as a shovel to clear away the snow; climbing tackle to scale outside walls; dynamite sticks to disperse piles of rubbish blocking my way; a net to ensnare Prince, Buster and Rover; an oxyacetylene flame to burn through jammed steel doors; air-fresheners for meters installed in lavatories; a gas-mask to protect my eyes and lungs from paint sprays in workshops; a crash-helmet for burrowing into litter-packed cellars with low cross-beams; an oil-can for stiff and rusted bolts; first-aid equipment to treat bruises, cuts and abrasions – a daily occurrence.

Would this be all? It would not! I would require ear-plugs to protect me from rock and roll and reggae blasted from radio and hi-fi sets; a pocket calculator to compute 1,456 units of electricity at 3.257p normal rate, plus standing charge; rubber gloves to seize and safely tuck away bare wires that may or may not be live; spring heels to elevate me a dozen feet or so when the lady of the house forbade me to use her antique chairs or lean a ladder against her William Morris hand-blocked wallpaper; a scythe to mow my way through the dense foliage of neglected gardens. Finally, a car (which I didn't have) being out of the question, because of the door-to-door nature of the job and parking restrictions, I would need a pack mule to carry all this equipment and I could well imagine the comments of this miserable prole if he were to notice such a beast tethered to his front gate when I came to depreciate the value of his ladder at 7.45 a.m.

Most people I met on my rounds were friendly and co-operative and I recall many kindnesses: offers of cold drinks on hot days, hot drinks in the winter and friendly banter about the cost of electricity and occasional discussions of decor, gardens, music and cricket. In the house of musicologist Jerrold Northrop Moore I found myself discussing Edward German, having recently heard Mr Moore presenting a programme on the radio about this composer. In the house of the then England cricket captain, Mike Brearley, I asked his wife (Mr Brearley being on Test duty) to convey the best wishes of this admirer of his captaincy. A pleasant surprise was a consumer recognizing me from Wally Fawkes's drawing on the front cover of *All This and 10%*.

One of the pleasures of my roaming brief was amusement at the comments of very young children, most of them curious about my activities. One little girl, about three years old, pert and pretty, watched me crawling under a stairway and gravely enquired: 'Are you looking for mice?' Another, about the same age, stood near to see me struggling with a mass of impedimenta under another stairway, and when I emerged, dusty, sweaty and ruffled, considerably softened my mood by saying, 'Sorry my mum had all that stuff in the cupboard – it must have been an awful nuisance for you.' As I left, much mollified by this charmer, she lisped: 'Nice to have met you – see you later.' At another address a tot lifted her dress and enquired: 'Do you like my new knickers? My mum put them in the airing cupboard and they're nice and warm.' I erupted into laughter, but her mother looked away, red-faced with embarrassment.

I was astonished and alarmed that very young children were left to answer the door and roam the streets alone, in a society where so many depraved individuals commit ghastly crimes against the young. On a public bench in Kentish Town a huddle of derelicts were swigging at bottles and cans – cider and Carlsberg Special Brew apparently their favourite tipples. Animatedly chatting to them was a neatly dressed little girl of about five or six. Charmingly, she made no distinction between the well-scrubbed 'respectable' and these grubby vagrants.

While, happily, it was the case that the majority of people were friendly, it is one of the facts of life that the obnoxious loom larger in the memory and by the end of 1978 I had had my fill of these, the repetitiveness of the job and – dogs. My hopes of earning a living by writing were ebbing further and further away. One literary swallow was not going to make a summer, and that, and the articles for *Jazz Circle News* were about all I had to show for the long, long hours spent stabbing at the typewriter.

6

Loser/Pessimist Editor

The escape route from an unending vista of meters came, in a flash of inspiration, when I was sitting on the lavatory seat on a February morning in 1979.

I was idly glancing at the 100 Club Newsletter, a single A5 sheet which listed the month's attractions and carried the occasional advertisement. The one advertisement in this case had been placed by a travel agency conducting a trip to New Orleans. It occurred to me: why not a proper 100 Club house magazine? I knew where to go for advertising; I knew the club's background and the bands who played there; and I thought I knew how to put a magazine together. I was quickly off the pan and on to the telephone to Roger Horton, co-proprietor of the 100 Club. I put it to him that a house magazine for the 100 Club would not cost the management much more than their existing newssheet, and the advertising revenue would make up the difference in the production costs. I did a rough 'mock-up', showed it to Horton and we agreed terms. I was also to receive payment as the club's publicist.

So, for the first time since 1950, I was editor of a jazz magazine, albeit that my production was only a four-page 'giveaway'. I had no problem writing it, but in the search for a printer my first issue suffered a painful birth.

An ex-Ravers team-mate who had given the impression in the dressing· room and bar that he was 'running' a West End branch of a well-known printing office accepted the job, but failed to keep our appointment early one morning at his office. A girl employee sniffily indicated that his appearances were unpunctual and sporadic. It transpired that he was a friend of the boss, owed his position to the old boy network and chose his hours accordingly. He let me down badly, with my deadline imminent.

A friend gave me the address of a printer in the East End who proved to be a rogue, albeit a most likeable one. I had moved from poseur to wide-boy. Like all who lived by their wits, Larry, as I shall call him, nurtured the fond belief that a mug crosses London Bridge every day, and it was his profound hope that a reasonable percentage of them came his way. He must have congratulated himself that I had wandered over the span that March morning in 1979. He wasn't really a printer at all but sub-contracted and I was to prove a 'nice little earner' before I discovered he was grossly overcharging me.

He could have been the inspiration for the character of Arthur Daley in the TV series 'Minder'. The street language of the fly-boy was quite natural to him. He was very funny; he had the most winning ways – an engaging and generous man. I bear him no malice, even though he took me for a ride. He illumined many a day, raising my spirits with his perky humour and picturesque phraseology as often as he depressed my finances.

On the morning I first met him he obligingly rang up a typesetting firm and I heard the man at the other end of the line inquiring about my financial credibility. Larry replied: 'No trouble at all. As good as gold!' He had known me for all of fifteen minutes. He drove me to the typesetters in his gleaming white Mercedes Benz (proudly referred to, of course, as 'the Merc') and two days later I picked up my first galley proofs.

Mistakes abounded. In one paragraph I had written the word 'painstakingly' which by some typesetter's transmutation became 'hainstralized'. *Hainstralized!* What a lovely word! I have often used it since, in a variety of contexts. 'Get the hainstralizing hell out of here!' or 'He was hainstralized out of his skull', but it was not to appear in my first *100 Club News*.

I pointed this out to the young lady typesetter. In a strident cockney accent she inquired, 'Did you writ it yourself?'

I thought I'd heard incorrectly and looked askance. She repeated the question, 'Did you writ it yourself?'

'Er – yes,' I replied, realizing with horror that I had heard her correctly the first time. What with my ill-ordered typescript and her illiteracy no wonder my galleys were riddled with mistakes.

'Then it doan' ma'er, do it?' she retorted.

I'm not exactly certain what she meant by this question/assertion. I suppose she was implying that had the mistake appeared in the writing of a contributor I could have expected a complaint, but as I was the author it was of no consequence. However, she did put me right about certain other matters.

I mentioned to her that I intended to glue the galleys on to the 'grids'. Amazed, she told me to use cow-gum – never glue – and a scalpel, not scissors. My appalling ignorance of the mechanics of a project which I had talked another party into was confirmed when I attempted to do my first paste-up. I got no further than one single column of type, and even that I could not properly align. Whatever I had learned from producing *Jazz Illustrated* all those years previously I had completely forgotten.

Desperate again, I phoned to plead help from Glaswegian Bob Houston, who had worked on the *Melody Maker* and was now an independent magazine publisher. 'Are ye finding it no easy? Are ye covered in blood and cow-gum yet?' he enquired with relish. A seasoned professional, he took pleasure from the vision of a hapless amateur in a mess, and indeed I had gum all over my hands and I had nicked my thumb with the scalpel. Houston laid it on thick that this was a job for 'professionals' only, and gave me the name of a layout artist, Sue Dransfield.

Sue, mercifully, got me out of trouble; Larry printed the paste-up, and the first 100 Club house magazine appeared in May 1979. On receiving delivery Horton's first act was hastily to insert a copy into an envelope and weigh it, obviously concerned that the postage might be more than for his previous newssheet. Horton was a great believer in the dictum that if you look after the pennies, the pounds will look after themselves.

There were several misspellings in the text and a mistake in one of the advertisements. It was not the most auspicious début, but a start, and subsequent issues improved in appearance. Sadly, *Jazz Circle News* folded and I was able to concentrate wholly on Horton's magazine. By obtaining more advertising I soon increased the number of pages to twelve. It was just a giveaway, but it entailed a degree of creativity in the writing, researching and preparing the layout. I loathed having to sell space – it was going back to those pleading, cajoling, imploring days as an agent – but advertising revenue was my profit.

Editing *100 Club News* was only the smallest of toe-holds in my climb back into the jazz world. I had no firm contract and was well aware that if business sagged the house magazine would be the first thing to go. Nevertheless I decided to take a chance and, rising fifty-eight, gave notice to the LEB.

In my last days as a meter reader Ted Batchelor firmly instructed all the readers to assemble for a lecture on the many types of meter in service. Ted's enthusiasm for these was quite genuine. 'Do you know,' he said, 'there are some types which *I* haven't seen before, and I've been with the board for thirty years!'

It was not an enthusiasm I shared. At a rough calculation I had read two hundred thousand in four years and the old cliché, 'if you've seen one, you've seen them all' certainly applied to meters. Looking back I have no recollection of the last one I read, but I do remember Harold, whom I met in my last week with the LEB.

I was admitted to a house in Brondesbury by a pleasant lady who called to Harold to vacate the bathroom, as one of the meters was installed there. I was reading the meter in the hallway when Harold emerged from the bathroom in his towel. He sniffed at me investigatively and said, 'A meterman, did you say Doris? A *meter*man? Good heavens! I haven't seen one of those in *years!*' He peered at me as though I were a rare piece of Victoriana, an ornate chamber-pot perhaps, and shook his head in wonderment as he changed position to observe the phenomenon from various angles.

Farewell Messrs Jobsworth and Jokerman, farewell Mrs Finklestein, Goldberg and Levy, farewell Prince, Buster and Rover and Popsie, Caesar, Nigger and all the other noisy, pollutant and accident-precipitating beasts. The nature of the job meant only scant contact in the evenings with fellow readers and I formed no close associations, but I remember Ted Batchelor with affection, if only because he didn't give me the sack when he was fully entitled to.

Shortly after I had produced my first *100 Club News*, a posthumous miscellany of writings by Sandy Brown, *The McJazz Manuscripts*, was published.

When Sandy died in April 1975 I had taken part in a multi-tribute on the BBC's 'Sounds of Jazz' programme, presented by Peter Clayton. My recollections of the man were both warm and critical. Had I been wholly eulogistic, in the fashion of most obituaries, it would have been more than celestial life is worth to confront Sandy again. He would have gone on interminably about what a fraud I had been. Sandy was a very honest man; he would not tolerate dissembling. I mentioned in the broadcast that our relationship was highly charged, and this was reflected in a chapter in *The McJazz Manuscripts* devoted to our correspondence and entitled 'Gentleman Jim'.

Jazz at the 100 front cover, November/December issue 1979, featuring clarinettist Monty Sunshine's impression of himself.

Jazz at Ronnie Scott's

the house magazine of ronnie scott's club
published bi-monthly

MEMBER OF
LONDON TOURIST
BOARD

47 FRITH STREET, LONDON, W1V 5TE
Open Monday to Saturday 8.30 p.m. to 3.00 a.m.
Telephone 01-439 0747—Cables: Jazzco, London, W1

AN internationally acclaimed and sophisticated night club right in the heart of London's night life and theatre land but with a surprisingly casual atmosphere. Patrons can dress as they wish; casual wear is the general practice. Patrons can sit at tables (with no obligation whatsoever to eat or drink) or stand at the bar. There are no hypes.

Our primary aim is to provide music for the soul and mind, but eating and drinking requirements are well catered for at our bars and by the *a la carte* cuisine Prices are average for the West End (see details on page 2).

The club is three-tiered; the main room; 'Upstairs' for Disco dancing; downstairs bar where you can meet and drink with the artistes.

The club presents the very finest of American, British and European jazz talent and playing a significant part in the reputation London has as one of the most flourishing jazz capitals in the world.

It isn't necessary to become a member to gain admission, but membership carries certain distinct advantages and is only £5.00 per year. We are pleased to give reduced admission rates, on production of their cards, to students and members of the Musicians Union.

We welcome visitors from abroad. To these our multi-lingual staff will give every assistance.

Nearest tube stations — Tottenham Court Road, Oxford Circus and, the nearest, Leicester Square.

—— plus ——

EARL HINES
Giant of the jazz piano, a living legend.

Illustration by STEVEN NEMETHY

CONTENTS

Club information, advertiser's announcements, reviews and articles by Brian Davis, Jim Godbolt and Alun Morgan. Illustrations by Richard Cole and Monty Sunshine.

Photos by David Redfern

☆☆☆☆☆☆☆☆☆☆☆☆☆
☆ **Attractions for** ☆
☆ **APRIL/MAY** ☆
☆☆☆☆☆☆☆☆☆☆☆☆☆
(Programme subject to alteration)

Mon 31st—Sat 12th Apr
DEXTER GORDON Quartet
Tony Lee Trio

Mon 14th—Sat 26th Apr
EARL HINES Quartet
with Marva Josie
Bobby Wellins Quartet

Mon 28th—Sat 10th May
HORACE SILVER Quintet
Tommy Whittle Quartet

Mon 12th May
KANSAS STATE UNIVERSITY
JAZZ ENSEMBLE
(20 pieces)

*Tues 13th and Wed 14th only
WOODY HERMAN
and his Orchestra
*Two shows nightly; 8—11 and 12 to 3 a.m.
Admission by ticket only
(early booking recommended)

Thu 15th Fri 16th Sat 17th
ZOOT MONEY
and the Big Roll Band

Mon 19th—Sat 31st May
L A FOUR
Bud Shank, Laurindo Almeido,
Ray Brown, Jeff Hamilton

MARK MURPHY

☆☆☆☆☆☆☆☆☆☆☆☆☆
☆ **FUTURE** ☆
☆ **ATTRACTIONS** ☆
☆ Buddy de Franco ☆
☆ Art Pepper ☆
☆ Zoot Sims ☆
☆☆☆☆☆☆☆☆☆☆☆☆☆

JARS front page, issue number 5, 1980. Drawing of Earl Hines by Stephen Nemethy.

Peter Clayton reviewed the book in the *Sunday Telegraph*. He rightfully praised Brown's incisive wit, but referring to the Brown/Godbolt correspondence, he observed:

> Most of his carelessly witty correspondence with friends and adversaries is here also, including a long series of acrimonious exchanges with agent/manager/loser/pessimist Jim Godbolt. Very few people have actually maintained written contact with Jim because he starts his letters stating how unlikely it is you'll ever reply and you try and cheer him up by proving him right. But Sandy was merciless enough to write back.

I have no idea what I could have done to Clayton to warrant the opprobrium in this piece. At the time I was struggling to get back into the business and the – wholly false – allegation that I habitually wrote letters presupposing that the recipient would not reply was hardly likely to encourage potential advertisers in *100 Club News*. Perhaps it was the 'winner' in him mocking the 'loser'. One thing is certain: the cut-and-thrust relationship enjoyed by Brown and myself was quite beyond the comprehension of one so bland.

I wondered how he *knew* that so few people 'actually' (which the *Oxford English Dictionary* defines as 'in actual fact') maintained written contact with me? He had no access to my files. Did he think he was clairvoyant? If so, he needed to get his psychic emanations realigned. I have extensive correspondence with people from the UK, France, Germany, the US, Czechoslovakia, Australia, Holland and Switzerland.

I wrote a letter along these lines to the *Sunday Telegraph*. They printed it in part, but showed the original to Clayton. That was fine by me, although I wished their readers could have seen exactly what I said about him. I found it very difficult to be civil to him subsequently. I am not good at dissembling; I often wish I were. Prior to this we had been quite friendly, and he had written a favourable notice of *All This and 10%*, although he compared me with Eeyore, the donkey in the Winnie the Pooh stories. We subsequently exchanged tart correspondence, he signing off with 'Yours wearily' and me with 'Yours brayingly'.

In May 1979 the idea hit me, quite out of the blue, that Ronnie Scott's club in Frith Street, Soho, should also have a house magazine, produced and edited by me.

I had known Pete King, co-director at Ronnie's, slightly in my agency days and went to see him in his dimly-lit and windowless office to make my suggestion. He looked at me in total astonishment. A man of few expletives, his reply was: 'Fuck off.' The reason for this abrupt rejection, typical of his deceptively brusque manner, was that he regarded me as the quintessential mouldye fygge.

Although my interest in jazz has never been limited to the traditional kind, it is true that the bands and musicians before the advent of bebop, those surviving it, and some emulating the music of a past tradition, are more to my taste. I have always, however, had a great respect for the modernists' musicianship and integrity. When editing *Jazz Illustrated* I gave considerable space to the (then) new jazz when other magazines were savaging it. Booking the Johnny Dankworth Seven and Kenny Graham's Afro-Cubists at the Wilcox office gave me my initial insight into the music's qualities and by listening since I am anything but ignorant of its history and particular ethos.

I didn't 'fuck off'. Although a more experienced journalist, Mike Hennessey, had previously mooted the idea, my trump card was my willingness to seek the necessary advertising, a chore that Hennessey's other commitments, even had he been willing, precluded. I got the job on account of the one aspect of my new livelihood that I loathed – selling space. Such a commission going to a mouldye fygge caused many an eyebrow to be raised, among them, I suspect, Peter Clayton's.

For a music with a patently joyful spring in its step, much writing about jazz has been solemnly ponderous, and in both the *100 Club News* and *Jazz at Ronnie Scott's* (*JARS* for short) I tried to maintain a steady level of humour. In Scott, famed almost as much as a humourist as a saxophonist and club proprietor, I had a sympathetic eye for my efforts. Not that he ever laughed at my jokes when I showed him the typescripts before going to press. On the few occasions his features registered a glimmer of a smile, he quickly suppressed it and was probably ashamed of himself for such an uncharacteristic lapse.

Seeking information about him and his associates was utterly frustrating. Invariably he shook his head, protesting that his memory was gone. I ran a series of 'interviews' with him and each one was a brick fashioned out of the merest wisps of straw. It was hard to convey the character of this essentially rather private man, although he has been a bandleader for over thirty-five years and has run a nightclub for twenty-seven of these. He has kept hardly any memorabilia – records, photographs, press cuttings – connected with his career and seemed genuinely unwilling to talk about himself.

Not that he is without an ego. *Quite* the contrary, but then I've never met a musician without one, especially, as in Scott's case, a musician who has been long accustomed to giving orders, and to seeing people jump when he does. He can be very autocratic; peremptory in his demands; and has no qualms about butting in on a conversation if he wants action.

The club has an agency division, in an office above the premises, run by Brian Theobald and on one occasion Scott rapped an instruction to his secretary, Bonnie Blair: 'Get Brian.' Bonnie rang the number but Theobald's secretary told her that Theobald was 'engrossed'. Given this information Scott took the phone from Bonnie and barked, 'Then bloody well *disengross* him!'

But apart from these autocratic outbursts he is generally amiable, if somewhat moody, and a very relaxed character. Relaxed, some would say, almost to the point of inertia, but being so laid-back has undoubtedly seen him through a succession of crises in his history. Like his counterpart on the other side of Oxford Street, Roger Horton, he is practised in what, euphemistically, could be described as 'delegation'. Both remind me of a thirties Mae West film in which the curvaceous Miss West, dressed in a revealing nightgown, glides across a luxurious carpet in her sumptuous lounge and languidly addresses her coloured maid: 'Beulah, peel me a grape.'

Scott and Horton, running two entirely different kinds of jazz club, had at least one thing in common. Both were well versed in the art of getting others to peel their grapes.

Tours apart, when he is compelled, unwillingly, to move further afield, Scott rarely strays from a patch bounded by his bookmaker in Frith Street to the north, Bill Lewington's instrument shop in Cambridge Circus to the east, and Mama's Cafe in Old Compton Street to the west. If he moved from one to the other and back to the club in one go, the distance would amount to no more than six hundred daunting yards. Sometimes he is booked to appear with his quintet at the Pizza Express, Dean Street, two hundred and fifty yards from his own club. On one such occasion, he enquired of Theobald: 'Is it far? Have you fixed transport?'

Tongue in cheek, of course, but his answer to a question of mine was made in deadly earnest. In May 1986 I told him that a film, *George in Civvy Street*, made in 1946, and starring the Lancashire comedian George Formby, was showing at the National Film Theatre for one night. As Ronnie was a sixteen-year-old member of the Johnny Claes band in the film, I naively enquired if he would be going to see it.

Without blinking an eyelid he asked solemnly, 'Where is the National Film Theatre?'

'On the South Bank, near Waterloo Station.'

He looked at me as if I had said Murmansk, or Montevideo. 'But that's a *hell* of a long way away.'

It was fifteen minutes by cab, but too far, even to see this memento of his youth on celluloid.

I put many such stories about him in *JARS* and people were amazed that he passed them for publication, but he is always honest about himself. In June 1986 author John Fordham (who achieved miracles in prising so much out of his subject) published a biography of Scott called *Let's Join Hands and Contact the Living* (taken from one of Scott's many oblique insults to his audience). During the book's preparation, Scott referred Fordham to Brian Theobald for details of an incident when Scott was in a state of acute depression and had taken an excess of pills and alcohol. Theobald and Henry Cohen, then the club's bouncer, tried to gain access to Scott's flat. Ringing the bell and hammering at the door to no avail, Cohen, eighteen stone, smashed the door down to find Scott unconscious on the floor.

Theobald demurred at Fordham's questions and asked Ronnie what he should say. 'Tell him the truth,' Scott replied.

It was also typical of him that, when praised for his feat of keeping a nightclub with a jazz policy for over a quarter of a century, he immediately paid warm tribute to Pete King as the major force in this extraordinary achievement.

In the gossip column I often listed, in a variety of contexts, some odd names (after all, my own is odd enough) culled from the personnels of pre-war American bands, and among the more outlandish I listed were Ducky Yonce, Tino Isgrow, Yaneg Hobespan, Rupe Biggadike, Ponzi Crunz, Johnny Nadlinger, Joe 'Google Eyes' August, Dyke Bittenburger, Ernie Intlehouse and Merrit Kenworthy. As many of these names are Jewish, a fractious correspondent sniffed anti-semitism in quoting them, rather over-looking the fact that Ronnie is Jewish and hardly likely to

Ronnie Scott, Jim Godbolt and chauffeur: Stephen Nemethy's impression of an imaginary ride from Buckingham Palace after Scott had received his OBE, 1981.

Scott anxiously consults his watch as the author labours a point. (Photo: Jody Boulting).

Club 11 alumni in London's West End, c.1951. *Rear*: bass player Lennie Bush, fan Albert 'Ace' Rockwell, saxophonist Ronnie Scott. *Front*: drummer, pianist and writer Cecil 'Flash' Winston, drummer Jeff Ellison and drummer, pianist and composer Tony Crombie. A reunion at Ronnie Scott's Club in 1985, organised by the author, was filmed and shown on BBC television's *Arena* programme.

countenance anti-semitic comments in his own house magazine.

He could be very waggish about his race. An inveterate watcher of television on the set in his office, he and some of the staff were viewing a thirties film starring a young, swashbuckling Errol Flynn. 'You know,' said Scott gravely, 'in my youth I was often mistaken for Flynn.' Mocking laughter from all present. 'Not Errol Flynn – *Abie* Flynn.'

In 1981 Ronnie was awarded the OBE. At the investiture the Queen asked, 'And what are you involved in, Mr Scott?' I would dearly have loved to be a fly on the palace wall to witness perhaps the merest quiver of the Scott eyebrows when Her Majesty made that polite enquiry.

My financial dealings were with Pete King. Built like an ox and with a square jaw that juts alarmingly when aroused, he can be very abrasive, but much of this is an act, and behind it I found a very kind and generous man.

Ronnie and Pete: it sounds like the title of a pre-war music-hall double act, but a double act is what they are. Two totally different but complementary temperaments who have played an important role in the history of jazz in Britain. It was one of my better ideas, however seemingly outlandish, to approach them to start their first ever house mag. I've had what Larry would call a 'result'.

In both magazines I was extremely fortunate to have regular contributions from Alun Morgan, an architect by profession, but a highly knowledgeable author of three books and some two thousand record sleeve-notes. In having him as an associate I also gained a valued friend. I was also very lucky to draw upon the illustrative talents of Monty Sunshine, Barney Bates, Richard Coles, Hedley Picton, Jack Pennington, Stephen Nemethy and Wally Fawkes for cartoons and column-breakers and photographer David Redfern.

I was truly enjoying my new career, the happiest I have ever had, but it was not without its problems. The biggest hazard was typesetting, aggravated by the fact that all the typesetters I initially encountered were militant feminists. Seeking operators who would not transform words like 'painstaking' into 'hainstralized' I was recommended a firm in Camden Town. Among the leftist and feminist posters adorning their walls was one urging castration of rapists, with an uncomfortably graphic illustration of a pair of slashed testicles. I, too, deplore the vicious crime of rape, but that illustration was distinctly unnerving. I felt it in my water I was in for trouble and, tackling the problem at source, I timidly inquired if they censored material not to their liking, but I was assured that only rarely did they cut.

They set one issue of *100 Club News* and the work was of a high standard, but copy for the following issue was returned to me with the information that I had offended their feminist susceptibilities and they no longer wanted my business. Their explanation had me reeling in astonishment.

I was running a series called 'On the Road' in which musicians related their touring experiences – with Jobsworths, landladies, other musicians, and the public. The contributors, intelligent and literate people, were George Melly, trumpeters Digby Fairweather and Alan Elsdon and trombonist Campbell Burnap. It was part of Burnap's story that offended the collective. He wrote:

> One night at a gig in Walsall, the bandleader spotted from our stage a girl he fancied. He brought the tune and the set to an abrupt premature end and beetled off into the crowd to chat her up. A little later he appeared back in the dressing-room looking fed-up. He told us that the girl had accepted the offer of a drink with alacrity, specifying at the same time that she would prefer a *double* gin and tonic.
>
> He queued up, got the drinks and pushed his way back, three quid lighter but comforted and excited by the fact that the ice had at least been broken. After a few tentative sips and some small talk he ventured . . . 'It's hot in here . . . do you fancy a walk outside or we could even go and sit for a while in my bandcoach?'
>
> 'Oh, ah'd love to, duck,' she chirped in her West Midlands twang, 'but me boyfriend's outside 'avin' a shit.'

Burnap told a story that, in essence, was as old as time and while the sexes remain physically and mentally different, it will be told until the end of time, but a spokeswoman for the collective said, 'We object to buying drinks for women as an investment.' I could not grasp their logic; the scheming male had got his come-uppance and at the cost of a double gin. Surely it was as much a tale of female duplicity as male sexism.

Eventually, I found a typesetter, female, liberated, sharp of tongue, but who did not presume to act as censor: Gill Hooper. Moreover, through her husband Ian, I landed yet another commission. Ian told me that he was starting a magazine for bookmakers and asked whether I would like to edit it.

I owned that I had never been to a racetrack in my life and that the only time I had entered a betting shop was to look for Ronnie Scott. But the mechanics of magazine production are the same whatever the subject-matter and, by commissioning writers knowledgeable in the field to write the specialist articles, while I contributed features on well-known personalities of the track, I edited *Bookmakers' Office Supplies* for its first five issues, but it wasn't really my scene.

Afterwards I continued to write features on such people as tipster Prince Monolulu, boxer Freddie Mills, jockey Steve Donaghue and boxing promoter Jack Solomons. I permitted myself a little self-congratulation on receiving a phone call from Jack's brother Maxie, asking when and where it was that I had met Jack. I had never met him, nor even caught sight of him, but I had researched carefully and apparently my pen portrait was accurate.

Until I dispensed with his services, Larry was a constant visitor, usually to ask if I had any 'readies' to meet his recurring emergencies, the amount(s) to be knocked off his printing bill. As a result our accounts were in an unending tangle and he had a poor memory for fivers and tenners he had borrowed. Like all big spenders, he considered his creditor's recollection of such trifles as niggardly. He put me in mind of one of Groucho Marx's classic remarks – 'Don't lend people money, it gives them amnesia.' Unfortunately for Larry many of his creditors were of a kind to take punitive action if he didn't pay up.

One morning he went to answer the door of his little mews house in Hampstead, which he had rented at great expense. Peeping through the letter box he recognized a 'heavy' who had been sent to collect a debt. Larry took to the fire escape. It was a route he had carefully noted on taking up residence. He appeared at my door a little later, frightened and dishevelled, to see if I had any readies available.

If he was going my way (or, being an obliging chap, even if he wasn't) he would give me a lift in the 'Merc'. I had never been in a motor car of this kind before and I was utterly amazed by the long, blatant stares that we received from the loveliest of ladies, women whom one might expect to be stared at, but not to return the compliment. Envious males, too, gaped longingly, no doubt thinking that the ownership of such a motor was the gateway to sexual conquests.

In his sharp suit, dark glasses, and with his hair flowing in the wind, he was Larry the Lad. He had a girlfriend who was a model – the obligatory accessory to the Merc. He was extremely vain – constantly peeking into mirrors to see how spruce he looked, checking his receding hairline ('my rising brow', he called it). Later he took to wearing a dashing but concealing wide-brimmed sombrero. I was with him one morning when he stopped at a traffic light and a sleek maroon Rolls Cornische drew up alongside. Larry gave the car and its owner a disparaging glance. 'I wouldn't 'ave one of *them* as a gift,' he told me. 'They're *common*.'

In one of his many crises he was so desperate for cash – another party had threatened him with a serious injury – that I came into possession of his beloved Merc against a loan hardly commensurate with the value of such a vehicle, but he was that desperate. When the transaction took place – I was genuinely scared that he would be roughed up – I naïvely accepted his assurance that the car would be garaged until the debt was repaid. One evening I was struggling up Haverstock Hill on my bike when I was passed by a familiar Mercedes Benz, the driver and his lady companion known to me. It was, of course, Larry, no doubt making for one of the chic brasseries in Hampstead High Street where a splendid meal and a bottle or two of Châteauneuf du Pape would cost him a 'long 'un' which, I had discovered, was a hundred pounds. He was a hopeless spendthrift. After that I took the keys off him but he probably had a spare pair.

He was a compulsive talker, an inveterate storyteller. I gave little credence to half his tales, but one had the ring of truth. It concerned a bizarre episode of his childhood in Hackney. His father had been a buyer of animals for circuses and zoos and one evening he brought home a small bear in a cage, prior to delivering it to a customer. The bear escaped from the cage and Larry, then only five years old but sensing danger and typically quick-thinking, picked up his baby brother and offered him to the bear.

He had a succession of acolytes – not exactly minders, although he could have done with a few of these – more like runners, fetchers and carriers. Sitting with Larry in the Merc, they basked in reflected glory. One was a pustular, adenoidal, Dickensian youth who a century earlier might have been one of Fagin's prize pupils, but another was an intelligent, 'well-spoken' young man of about twenty-five who seemed out of place in Larry's set-up. I asked Larry about him.

'Alistair. Oh, he was training to be a priest, won'e? But he realized it wasn't an earner.'

Alistair had indeed been to theological college, but had suffered a crisis of faith. He was soon to undergo another one concerning Larry, and they parted company.

When I too dispensed with his services, I ceased to be a 'personal friend' (one of his oft-used phrases about me) and I lost one of my perks of the association. A very natty dresser, Larry could not bear to be seen in the Hampstead and Covent Garden pubs and restaurants he patronized wearing the same clothes for long and he used to give me his hand-me-downs; all, needless to say, good quality bespoke. We were about the same size and shape and I didn't look a gift-horse in the mouth, although now when I wear one of his discards, I ponder ruefully on just how expensive a gift it really was.

In November 1983 *100 Club News* folded in acrimony; a dispute over content which culminated in my giving Roger Horton my notice. It was a matter of a split second as to who put the phone down first. I missed being part of the scene in which I had moved for so long but did not miss him, any more, I suspect, than he missed me.

7

You Can't Emasculate a Harlot

In my reluctant but imperative pursuit of advertising, one of my regular clients was Quartet Books, a major publisher of jazz titles by such renowned authors as Ian Carr, John Chilton, Leonard Feather, Brian Priestley, Ross Russell and Val Wilmer. I had previously submitted my *History of Jazz in Britain* to them, but their rejection slip was duly added to the rest of these bleak notices.

After this, and the uninterest shown by two or three literary agents, I was persuaded that my book was of no value. Shrugging my shoulders over the time, effort and typing expense, I consigned it to the spare room, where it gathered a symbolically appropriate layer of dust. I didn't even consider it worth the cost of postage to other publishers, and, if it was the quality of the writing which damned it, the business of earning a living took precedence over further revisions.

The publicity director at Quartet was Juliette Foy, one of the seraglio of well-connected young ladies Quartet boss Naim Attallah had a penchant for employing, this recruitment enthralling the gossip-columnists and their readers. The roll-call of these blue-blooded young ladies over the years reads like a page from *Debrett's* – Nigella Lawson, Sophia Waugh, Sabrina Guinness, Bridget Heathcote-Amory, Lady Cosima Vane-Tempest-Stewart, Baroness Andrea von Stumm, and many more. Phoning Quartet, one's ears were greeted by the clipped accents of the shires. I visualized these ladies in Sloane Ranger headscarves, pictured them dashing 'orf' to the *cun*tray at weekends, and I often used to see their photographs in *Country Life* or the *Tatler* at the dentist's.

When they answered the telephone they all used a sort of verbal shorthand: 'Qut' for 'Quartet' and 'p' you thru' for 'put you through'. They never inquired as to the caller's identity; that was someone else's problem.

Talking to Juliette one day I mentioned that my *History* had been rejected by Quartet and jocularly added that I thought it as good as some of the other jazz books they had published. Juliette suggested that I should get in touch with their jazz editor, Chris Parker. I made a note of the name, but gave it scant thought. I entertained no more hopes of this Chris Parker than of any other editor.

However, a week or so later I did ring him and his first question was whether I knew Bruce Turner, who had just sent him a manuscript. I replied that I most certainly did know Bruce Turner. Living in the adjacent bedsitter for some years and working for several more years as agent of his Jump Band had given me quite an insight into this vegetarian, non-drinking, non-smoking confectionery addict.

Chris Parker, a donnish young man with a Byronic mop of curly hair, took me out to lunch at an Indian restaurant; a delightful change from the usual editor's instructions to submit one's manuscript and wait for the work to be considered in due course. Would I care for wine? he asked. Heavens! My cup was full and overflowing! An editor showing interest in my work, inviting me to eat *and* drink with him! A grave Indian took the order, returned with the bottle and poured a little of its contents into my glass.

I have never been one for this tasting ritual. Even if I had a connoisseur's knowledge I wouldn't have the neck to wave the bottle away peremptorily if I judged it unsatisfactory. Besides, my knowledge of the grape is restricted to off-licence plonk, and that more for its becalming effect on my nerves than for my palate. But I was puzzled as to why I had been accorded the tasting instead of Chris, who had made the order. I was soon to discover the reason: Indians venerate age. 'Is he your father?' the waiter inquired of Chris as he filled up both our glasses. It was a dimly-lit restaurant.

About a month later Chris rang to tell me in a somewhat casual manner that my book had been accepted. Of course, there was no reason for him to sound excited – he had made many such calls – nor indeed did I feel much elation, probably because the news took some time to sink in. It had been eight years since I experienced a similar state of disbelief when *All This and 10%* was accepted.

The manuscript was given to an 'out of house' editor who had recently acquired a degree in English as a mature student at Cambridge, and while I shall be eternally grateful to him for the Trojan work he did on my sprawling text, it was not long before we were in heated disagreement over the extent and nature of his cuts, some of which I immediately restored.

This editor was having no truck with a tetchy author. He took his complaints straight to Chris, who, I imagine, reacted like a schoolmaster having to sort out the squabbles of two fractious schoolboys, albeit that in this case the combined age of the two boys was well over a hundred years. I had a sharp telephone call from Chris one Saturday morning, informing me in the strongest terms that his company did not employ editors at considerable cost for authors to restore their cuts.

At Hale's my adversary had been an aged libel lawyer totally out of sympathy with *All This and 10%*. Now it was a ruthless editor with, in my admittedly subjective view, an unduly high-handed approach to my work, granted that having been sent the manuscript for his opinion he had recommended its publication. He had considerable strength of character and I answered his strictures with trembling lip, but in one conversation I did find the courage to say, 'Look, mate, this is *my* bloody book.'

I had included snippets of history of a more social than musical interest, not absolutely vital to the text, but redolent of the period I covered. The editor arbitrarily deleted these, but in one conversation wearily relented: 'OK, I'll give you that.' 'Thanks a lot, thanks *very* much,' I muttered to myself, but I kept my peace.

In one paragraph I had written about the 'prettification' of jazz in the twenties by commercial bandleaders, and in a burst of misapplied imagery I fetched up with the sentence, 'The harlot jazz had been emasculated.' The editor made a sharp rejoinder in a margin note, 'You can't emasculate a harlot!' Point taken and with a blush, but I was in a constant state of apprehension as he scored his blue pencil through my prose, slicing out parts which I thought to be essential.

There were disagreements regarding racial terminology. As my book was in part concerned with many American jazzmen of African ancestry (and this circumlocution I use to indicate the problems I had), I employed the terms 'coloured' and 'Negro'. But by now my typist was casting censorious eyes on racial references and advising me against this usage. 'Black', she told me, was more appropriate. 'Negro is hopelessly outdated and consigned to pre-civil rights terminology. Haven't we all got a colour?' she inquired, with a shake of her blonde hair twirled in 'dreadlock' plaits. The editor, however took a different view. He wrote:

> Re. 'Negro' and 'Negrophile'. I can't understand your concern here. The word 'Negrophile' is no more unacceptable than Anglophile, Russophile or whatever. And . . . as far as I'm concerned 'Negro' remains either neutral or positively dignified. To test this I brought the matter up gingerly with a Kenyan friend of mine in the local pub and he laughed his cock off. (If you'll excuse an expression which really is unacceptable to many people.)

The book had been accepted for only a matter of weeks, but already noses had been put out of joint, harsh words exchanged and feelings were running high; the notion of a Kenyan losing his vital member, laughing the while, added a macabre touch to the saga.

As if this wasn't enough to bedevil a poor scribe, Chris, on feminist grounds, changed the word 'girls' to 'women' in several parts of the text. My reference was to the immediate post-war years when *girls* were taught the intricacies of jitterbugging or jiving by US servicemen stationed in Britain. And *girls* they were, teenagers, the same age as the *girls* with whom I, too, jived when I had the vigour of youth.

It seemed to me that my book had become a battlefield for the triumph of 'isms': anti-racism, pro-feminism, and so on. Of course, it was protested by all parties that their advice was for my benefit. I believed them, but I began to feel like some beleaguered neutral country becoming a proving ground for the superpowers, when they protest that it is all for the good of the country they are razing to the ground. Like many a hapless nation caught up in such struggles, I too would be a total wreck by the time the main contestants had fought their ideological battles.

Then came another assault on my equilibrium: sight of the first galley proofs from the typesetters.

In *Jazz Circle News* I once wrote a full page 'obituary' of one Chauncey Blutmore, the quintessential jazz buff. Passionately fond of the music, Chauncey was maniacally punctilious about personnels, dates of recordings, catalogue and matrix numbers, and specialized in spotting mistakes in print.

I was already acutely aware that on publication of my history the Blutmores would swoop like vultures upon factual mistakes, but I was unprepared for the thousands of 'literal' errors spattered throughout the galley proofs which the Blutmores would seize upon just as joyfully.

It had been the luck of my unfortunate manuscript to receive the attention of what, in the printing trade, is called a 'monkey' – someone who can't read or spell; unfortunate limitations in a typesetter and a chilling echo of the errors in *All This and 10%* and of the young lady typesetter who asked me if I had 'writ it myself' when I was about to launch the first *100 Club News*.

This typesetter had misapplied the 'i' before 'e' rule and the simple word 'their' was misspelt throughout. In the early part of the book I had deliberately included a misspelling of a musician's name, taken from a contemporary press account. The musician was the great Creole saxophonist and clarinettist Sidney Bechet. By the grace of my editors and typist I had been allowed the racial designation 'Creole', but the typesetter, as if to counter indulgence on the part of the 'ismists', used the misspelling of the press account throughout the entire book.

The transfer from typescript to galleys also revealed many imperfections in my own construction, which I rewrote in a mixture of my hieroglyphic handwriting and inaccurate two-fingered typing, the mistakes in both blotted out with Tippex. Chris, understandably, looked askance at these chaotic revisions and muttered, 'This is a pig's breakfast. God knows what the studio will make of it.'

Of all the intricate relationships in the production of a book, one of the most fraught is that between the editor and the production department, with many a harsh word between the two coming as a result of last-minute revisions. Almost every day I phoned Chris about some point or other and I soon realized that his voice had progressively hardened since I first spoke to him, that pain and apprehension registered on his face when, without appointment, I poked my head around his door. 'I hope you realize that I have other books to edit,' he snapped. Chris, a cricketer, was batting on a sticky wicket here. I should have thought that as an editor of several years' standing he would know that the last, the very last, of any author's worries is *other* authors' books. It's a hard fight to get published, to get one's work through the editorial and production processes as effectively as possible, and it's everyone for himself in the struggle.

One morning when I dropped another pig's breakfast on his desk Chris picked up a manuscript and told me it was Bruce Turner's. 'Look at this,' he said. 'Cleanly typed, regular margins, no corrections. But then, *he's* a biddable author. Most biddable.' He sighed heavily, and it was obvious that he wished I were equally 'biddable'. Authors can be a dreadful occupational hazard for editors.

It is also an occupational characteristic of editors to think and act like schoolmasters. Some authors' papers are clean and correct; others are grubby and mistake-ridden and the miscreants have to be slapped over the wrist. There was more than a touch of the schoolmaster in Chris, although I shall be forever indebted to him for the attention he gave to my work.

In gathering up photographs and other illustrations for the book I was moved by the kindness of a great many people who provided me with assorted memorabilia. One of these was George Penniket, seventy-five years old, one of the founder members of the No 1 Rhythm Club in 1933. He lent me a photograph of club members posing on a Thames steamer prior to one of their 'Riverboat Shuffles'. It was clearly a respectable middle-class gathering which, jocularly, I wanted to describe in the caption as 'Early Jazz Fiends' (the sobriquet invariably applied to jazz enthusiasts), but sadly it was too late for inclusion.

In the photograph I recognized George, Bill Elliott, co-founder and secretary of the No 1 Rhythm Club, and a face which was certainly that of the cook in the ship's company of the *St Zeno*. We had occasionally talked about jazz in his tiny galley and he may have mentioned the No 1 Club, although I cannot remember his doing so any more than I can remember his name. Another face which intrigued me was that of a plump lady who, I'm almost certain, was Miss Mason, my first teacher at Belleville Road Infants School, Wandsworth, in 1927. This is feasible; one of the entrances to the school was in Wakehurst Road, where another of the founder members of the club, Eric Ballard, used to live. I would dearly like to think that my beloved Miss Mason, of whom one of my first recollections is staring up from the palliasses of the schoolroom floor to see her ample, pea-green bloomers, was a 'jazz fiend'.

As the date of publication drew near the hundreds of errors which remained in the text and index nagged at me like an aching molar. Chris was reassuring but it was made clear to me that I would not be allowed to see the 'camera-ready' pages, the last chance to make corrections before the book finally goes to the printer. The production manager was brusquely adamant: 'No, you are NOT seeing the camera-ready!' I'll give him this: there was no false bonhomie about the fellow.

Apprehensions tormented me. My only hope was Chris, but tensions between myself and this highly likeable young man were mounting towards an explosion. I was ready to renounce the book if it came out as I feared, and one morning I had half a mind to storm out of his office in an authorial huff. Instead, sensibly, I asked him out for a drink. Over pints of Ruddle's County we exchanged apologies.

'It's an aggro business,' he said. 'There are constant disputes with all concerned; sometimes with the printer, sometimes with pro-duction, and inevitably with the author. I reckon on at least three good fights a book. Yours will be all right in the end.' Yet up to the very last moment I was uncertain how many mistakes remained out of the hundred or so I had listed in the page proofs.

I made one final approach to the production manager. Plainly he was not enamoured of authors. He abruptly advised me that the company had made a considerable investment in my advance, editor's fees, typesetting and studio time. The book had to be 'got out of the way' and I was taking an unduly emotional approach. Since I could not trust myself to speak to him without losing my already well-frayed temper, I wrote to him saying that I too had invested in the book by dint of three years' hard work, by paying for typing and index fees, by obtaining advance publicity as much for the benefit of Quartet as myself, and it was me the Blutmores would dismember if a flawed book were published. I delivered the letter to him on the day the camera-ready was due to be despatched to the printers.

After a sleepless night I set about cleaning my flat, long neglected owing to my utter preoccupation with the book. Glancing out of my balcony window, I could almost see the Blutmores perched on the plane tree in the garden below, poised for the take-off, their eyes glinting, beaks slavering and claws twitching. The telephone rang. It was Chris to say that he and the production manager, with some previous proofs, a bottle of Tippex and a scalpel, had worked late into the night to rectify all but a few of the errors.

While not wholly convinced, I felt an enormous surge of relief and, to the accompaniment of a Duke Ellington LP, did a little buck and wing as I dusted. My euphoria was soon shattered by an outraged woman from the flat below leaning on my doorbell and abusively demanding that I 'turn off that wretched jazz'. But even this termagant could not dispel the delight I felt on that fateful Saturday morning. I had been saved at the eleventh hour, although it was brinkmanship I wish never to experience again.

A month or so later the book arrived, handsomely produced and with an attractive cover. In the event, I had every reason to be thankful to all concerned for a fine job, but, as with my first book, the previous months had been too long and harrowing a gestation period for me to derive much pleasure from the finished product. Instead I anxiously searched for the 'literals', but mercifully, there were very few, as Chris had promised. The overall feeling was more of relief than satisfaction.

I was soon to get my shamefaced come-uppance in the form of a number of factual errors attributable entirely to me. The Blutmores did indeed swoop, but before they did so I enjoyed a most heart-warming experience, one that I shall always remember.

Naim Attallah had agreed to hold a party, an expensive operation, to launch the book. This information took almost as much time to sink in as the news that the book had been accepted. I drew up a list of those I wished to attend, representing every facet of the jazz world, some of whom I had known for over forty years. I spent a long time tracking down certain veterans and fixing a date that was mutually convenient.

I was particularly anxious that Spike Hughes, composer, author, critic, arranger and bandleader, should be present. I admired him for being one of the first in the early thirties to fly the jazz flag in this country. I had many of his two hundred British records and all of his Negro Orchestra recordings, made in New York in 1933, one of which, 'Donegal Cradle Song', is in my personal top ten. Several of the musicians who played with him had accepted my invitation and if Hughes were to attend, the party would be the first ever reunion of the surving members of his Decca-Dents and Dance Orchestra. I wrote to him enclosing a drawing of himself which I had used in the book, by a black cartoonist, Charles 'Spinky' Alston, which first appeared in the *Melody Maker* in 1933, and which Hughes may well not have seen since then. I also enclosed a copy of his entry in the index. Back came my letter with these curt annotations:

I am afraid I am too old and busy to do any of the things you ask.
The punctuation of your index is appalling . . . Spinky (Charles)
Alston is more than 'a black cartoonist'. His paintings are in the
Museum of Modern Art in New York. My bibliography will be
found in the new *Groves*. Under my entry you will also find how
to spell the title of my ballet.

I felt sick at heart. It was a mistake to send him an uncorrected
galley, but the keen disappointment I felt was tempered by my
objection to his unnecessarily harsh tone, affecting my view of him
as a person.

After the tensions of the previous months, the night of the party was
a joyous occasion. Held on 25 July 1984, it proved to be one of the
most representative gatherings ever of the jazz movement in Britain –
musicians, critics, discographers, record producers and retailers,
radio presenters and critics. Steve Race, then sixty-three, remarked
on arrival, 'Half my boyhood heroes are here!', a sentiment I
immediately echoed. Among the hundred or so guests were my dear
friends Robin Rathborne and Alun Morgan, and the lady who has
meant more to me than any other in my life.

Throughout the evening I was suffused with a warm glow shot
through with a sense of unreality. To all intents and purposes I knew
where I was, and the hundred or so people present, but although it
was four years since I had read my last meter, and nine since I had
dusted and cleaned at the Savoy, I could not believe that so many
people, some quite famous, had gathered to help launch a book of
mine which had originally been rejected by the publishers now
holding this party.

This feeling of unreality suddenly vanished when I caught sight of
Fallabout Fred framed in the doorway, standing rigidly erect to
pretend a sobriety his glazed and popping eyes belied. The toper who
had been such an ardent fan of Mick Mulligan's band some thirty
years before had been drinking in the pub opposite, and seeing
familiar faces through the open windows, decided to stumble up the
stairs to join us. I was suddenly back in the real world.

Another familiar face was the forever smiling Peter Clayton's. As
I watched him bustling about the room I recalled a story of Bing
Crosby doing a screen test and getting turned down because the
producer thought his ears too big. Years later, when Crosby had

become world-famous, they attended a service at the same church. Walking up the aisle after the service Crosby fixed the producer with a stare, and then ostentatiously waggled his ears at him.

I hadn't become world-famous, but I was sorely tempted, metaphorically speaking, to waggle my donkey's ears at Clayton. But it was too enjoyable an evening for any recriminations.

8

A Flock of Blutmores

Quickly following publication the Blutmores, red in tooth and claw, swooped. The long-standing tradition of discographical and factual pedantry was energetically upheld. Fair enough; as a fully paid-up Blutmore myself I would have put in my ten cents' worth had it been someone else's book. I haven't paid my dues for nothing; and ludicrous as this obsessive concern for facts, some quite pettifogging, may seem, from it has emerged a wealth of accurate data about a music once dismissed as a mere novelty. Blutmores are essential to jazz scholarship.

Discographer supreme, Brian Rust, was one of the first to pitch in:

> Crown Records cost sixpence, not a shilling; it was Tiny Winters and his Bogey Seven, not his Bogeymen; 'Kalua' (not 'Kaula') was written by Jerome Kern and not by Spike Hughes; you gave Monday 24 June 1933 as the opening date of the No 1 Rhythm Club. This can't be – 24 June was a Sunday that year.

I am very fond of Brian and have an enormous admiration for his scholarship. He was one – Alun Morgan and Robin Rathborne the others – to whom I dedicated the book, but his last thrust had me gasping. I queried 'How do you know that?' thinking that he might have had a pocket calculator to hand. 'I've got that sort of brain,' he replied. In a vain attempt at retaliation I asked, 'What was the day of my birth, 5 October 1922, then?' Without a moment's hesitation came the answer, 'A Thursday.' I didn't know this myself, but I checked, and of course he was right. Rust didn't produce a massive discography involving ten thousand bandleaders, musicians and singers and twenty thousand titles without having an eye for facts and figures.

I received various corrections in the mail from people I didn't know and in each case the phrase 'I have read'/'I have obtained your book' told me that I had gained a critic but not a royalty. The exception was a man who had had the book given him as a present and in a lengthy plaint, suffused with quintessential Blutmoreish ire, he avowed that a work with such a large number of elementary errors was, at £14.95, a 'take on'.

Considering the vast number of facts in the book the goofs were relatively few, but still inexcusable. I had relied too much upon my memory, had not cross-checked and had perpetuated the mistakes of others. I deserved the brickbats. As for the price being iniquitous, in terms of my blood, sweat and tears, it should have retailed at a hundred pounds, but as bestseller author Gordon M. Williams once growled to me in his strong Glaswegian accent, 'There are no bloody prizes for hard work.'

Critic/radio presenter Brian Priestley discovered a mistake in a Hot Club of London programme reproduced in the book, which I had made thirty-seven years previously – a mistake of a digit in a catalogue number – but one which no self-respecting Blutmore would let pass! Steve Race pointed to a topographical goof.

The critique that particularly delighted me was from poet Philip Larkin in the *Observer*. A thousand words from a highly literate Blutmore that got to the heart of the book, but in enumerating its errors he hoist himself with his own petard. The following week the *Observer* published a counter correction in rhyme from 'Ken Bull' of Colchester. Mr 'Bull', I discovered, was Ken Bell, with whom I had corresponded for over thirty years but whom I had never met:

> Philip Larkin must learn the terrors
> Of correcting an author's errors.
> He must not make
> His own mistake
> As he did when, misbegotten,
> He said that Jim Godbolt had forgotten,
> In his jazz history
> To nineteen fifty,
> The concert in the Festival Hall.
> This couldn't have happened then at all
> As that place was built to fit in

With next year's Festival of Britain.
(Excuse the rhyme,
There is no time . . .)

I intended to write to Mr Larkin thanking him for the review and
explaining (though not excusing) some of the errors, but he died
before I got round to it. I deeply regret being so tardy and was moved
to see part of his memorial service at Westminster Abbey filmed on
TV with some of my contemporaries from the traditional field –
trumpeter Alan Elsdon, trombonist Pete Strange and saxophonist
Johnny Barnes – paying musical tribute to someone whose elegant
writing contributed so much to jazz criticism.

Considering that about 55,000 titles were published in 1984 and
how few of these get reviewed I was very fortunate in receiving over
fifty press notices and almost as many radio mentions, including
interviews. Most of the comments were favourable, but of course
there were exceptions.

Peter Clayton's review in the *Sunday Telegraph* was airily
dismissive on the one hand and damning with faint praise on the
other. He referred to 'factual errors' which I suspect he'd read in
other reviews, for he didn't specify one of them; I learned that I
suffered from 'incurable galloping nostalgia', but he acknowledged
that my examination of the 'once evangelical traditonal [*sic*!]
movement in this country would come in handy'.

I felt as if I'd written a DIY handbook that would assist Clayton
in his chores about the house and added 'traditonal' to 'hainstralizing' as a superb literal. It has a nice onomatopoeic ring about
it. As for my galloping nostalgia – since the history of jazz in Britain
started in 1919 I had, perforce, to look back and I fully explained in
my foreword and closing summary the good reasons why I ended my
narrative in 1950, but it would appear that Clayton hadn't read this,
or indeed, other parts of the book.

I wrote to him answering a few of his points, expressed the hope
that my lengthier examination of the beginnings of British bebop
would also come in handy and waggled my ears in a postscript:
'Quite a large, star-studded and representative turn-out at Kettner's
on 25 July to launch this loser/pessimist's book, but perhaps they
were there for the beer . . .'

My real reason for writing was to ask for an appearance on
'Sounds of Jazz', to talk about my book, the practice with many
authors of newly published jazz books. I reminded myself, as I

swallowed my pride, that the programme was the BBC's, not PC's. It took three months, two last-ditch cancellations from Clayton and the intervention of producer Keith Stewart, kindly disposed towards the book, to get on 'Sounds of Jazz'.

One afternoon I walked into Ronnie Scott's office and the moment I entered alarm-bells rang, for I spotted the light of joy dancing in his normally expressionless eyes. There was even a hint of animation in his torpid figure. 'Liked your book, Jim,' he said. There was a significant pause and in a perfectly matched unison of pitch, tone and emphasis, both of us exclaimed the crucial '*But!*' and Scott continued, 'you put "pianist unknown" in one of the captions. You should have asked me. I could have told you that the pianist was Ronnie Selby.' I recalled how many hundreds of questions I had asked Ronnie about himself or his contemporaries and received only a shake of the head, or, if he were feeling particularly energetic, a twitch of the shoulder to indicate the negative.

If I had ever bothered to keep a dated graph that represented the highs and lows of my life from the time my business folded in 1969, the year 1984 would have shown an uncharacteristically high reading. Publication of my history and the launch party represented the peak, but a look at the previous undulations, or rather lack of them, at the bottom end of the chart should have been a warning of what could so easily happen again.

Despite my firm resolve never ever again to embark upon so punishing an exercise, I must have got a little carried away by the steady sales and number of press notices, for I decided to write a follow-up to my history, covering 1950–70. The unfamiliar intoxication of praise had obviously made me over-optimistic in my expectations and I was forgetting the ups and downs on my graph as I contemplated Chris Parker's reaction when I gave him the good news. It would be another feather in his cap; glad tidings for the company; the prospect of another good seller; another lunch at the Indian restaurant, the waiter again acknowledging my years as he poured out the wine for my tasting; a pleasant hour discussing the new volume's outline.

Vain, vainly optimistic author! Chris immediately rejected the proposal. And no invitation to lunch, either.

I suspected he couldn't face another succession of pigs' breakfasts, but this, it transpired, was not the reason for him turning me down.

He too saw me as the mouldye fygge suffering from incurable galloping nostalgia and unqualified to cover later developments. He didn't put his rejection in so many words, but his meaning was clear.

At that moment the graph would have registered a sharp drop; an unexpected dip at that, but with the perversity now ingrained in my temperament I persisted. I think I could have approached another publisher with some confidence, but better the devil you know than the one you don't, and despite our disagreements Chris and I had got on very well.

Eventually he agreed, but gave me the news with the air of a man who had been cajoled into the manufacture of the rope that would hang him. 'I haven't told the studio yet,' he said. 'I'll have to choose the right moment to let them know.'

In the event, further hassles with me were to be deferred. I had come up with another suggestion for Quartet: this book. It fell to another editor, Julian Bourne, to stare mournfully at a succession of pigs' breakfasts.

During my meetings with Julian I sometimes popped in to see Chris in the adjacent office, once to show him a critique of my *History* in *Jazz Express* by the veteran critic Max Jones, expressing the view that a 'firm editorial hand had tightened up Jim's prose and punctuation', which was perfectly true. Chris was not displeased with this bow to his work, but not so charmed when I admitted to restoring a few cuts in the confused comings and goings of the galleys, and that one of them had been picked up by Barry Fox in the *Hampstead and Highgate Express* and Paul Vaughan in the BBC's 'Kaleidoscope' programme. I said, very gently, 'Sometimes, Chris, the author knows best.' He looked at me as if I had not played the game – like a batsman who knew he had got an 'edge' and been caught behind, but hadn't 'walked' like a true sportsman should.

Writing this book and the second instalment of my *History*, I was often hunched over the typewriter for fifteen hours a day, with a bottle of red plonk to sustain me in the evenings.

One night in February 1985 an idea occurred to me which I hastily scribbled down on a piece of paper and thrust amid a pile of illegible notes similarly produced. A couple of weeks later I chanced upon it and peered, utterly puzzled, at my own hieroglyphics. Eventually I deciphered it: 'Ring Phil Speight re Club Eleven Reunion TV'. Phil Speight was the producer of the BBC TV's 'Jazz on a Summer's Day'

Friends at the launch of the author's *A History of Jazz in Britain 1919-50*: Robin Rathborne, Joan Biggs, the author and Alun Morgan, at Kettners, Restaurant, Soho, 24 July 1984.

Veteran British jazz musicians at Kettners on 24 July 1984. *Left to right*: saxophonist Harry Hayes, trombonist Lew Davis, saxophonist and tap dancer Philip Buchel, pianist Gerry Moore and violinist George Hurley.

Jazz writers and broadcasters gathered at Kettners, 24 July 1984. *Left to right, standing*: Steve Race, Humphrey Lyttelton, Brian Priestley, Keith Howell; *seated*: Leslie Perowne, Charles Chilton, Roy Plomley, Rex Harris, Brian Rust.

the previous year. Certain members of the Club Eleven, Britain's first bebop venue, whose founder players included Ronnie Scott and John Dankworth, had been discussing a reunion, ideally to be held at Ronnie Scott's. That the reunion should be televised was my idea, with the aid of Torino Vino Siciliano.

I had little expectation that it would be accepted – every suggestion I had made before to the BBC had been turned down – but it was, and the reunion took place on 1 September 1985 and was shown in the BBC's 'Jazz Week' in December. I was engaged as programme consultant and got a credit as these rolled up at the end of the film.

The episode represented a little upward movement on my graph and I couldn't resist telling Chris that this mouldye fygge had been the instigator of, and programme consultant for, a BBC TV film about the beginnings of modern jazz in this country. He took the point; indeed, he had little choice, as I lingered on it to make certain the irony sank home.

That same year Grafton Books accepted *A History of Jazz in Britain* as a paperback, the extra income from this welcome, as was the opportunity to correct the errors to which countless Blutmores had obligingly drawn my attention.

With the hardback and paperback out, this book, another in preparation, and continuing with Ronnie Scott's magazine, I feel at last that I can reasonably describe myself as a writer, but still with the feeling of insecurity that goes with freelance status. Not that I have much alternative. Even if I could face Prince, Buster and Rover again I am too old to be accepted as a meter reader. I am so completely out of touch with contemporary pop music that I could never be considered as a booker in an agency, and anyway the very thought of it fills me with revulsion.

It's the typewriter or the dole, but in writing I have more satisfaction than in any job I've had before, even though its financial rewards, for me at least, are hardly commensurate with the labour and anxieties involved. As the one-time amateur-turned-professional traditional jazz musicians of the fifties used to say, 'It's better than working.'

A month or two after the publication of my *History*, and after a few reviews had been published, I walked into a pub I don't normally use and failed to spot a certain person already there.

As I ordered my drink a figure suddenly loomed near. 'Put your money away,' he rapped, 'I'm buying that. Now, I hear you've been up to something! Come on, what is it?'

Oh my God, it was DG – eight years since he had me trapped on Gospel Oak Station! As he was not one of my favourite conversationalists I refused his barked offer and, rapidly sinking my pint, I just as rapidly departed, leaving him for dead.

If he really wants to know what I've been 'up to' he can buy this book but, I fear, there will be no royalty from that quarter. He, for sure, will be one of the I-have-obtained or I-have-read your book brigade. Rather like Bruce Turner, who wrote, in a letter, sent second-class: 'Confined to my bed with back trouble I read *Jazz in Britain* from cover to cover. May I say I found it to be very fine. I nearly went out and bought a copy, but the spinal twinges precluded any such rash behaviour.'

Index

Join the Northway Books mailing list to receive details of new books about jazz, as well as events and special offers. Write to Northway at 39 Tytherton Road, London N19 4PZ, email info@northwaybooks.com

We do not pass information from our mailing list to other organisations.

www.northwaybooks.com

Other books about jazz published by Northway

John Chilton,
Hot Jazz, Warm Feet

Vic Ash
I Blew It My Way

Alan Plater
Doggin' Around

Ronnie Scott with Mike Hennessey
Some of My Best Friends Are Blues

Ron Brown with Digby Fairweather
Nat Gonella – A Life in Jazz

Peter Vacher
Soloists and Sidemen: American Jazz Stories

Alan Robertson
Joe Harriott – Fire in His Soul

Coleridge Goode and Roger Cotterrell
Bass Lines: A Life in Jazz

Digby Fairweather
Notes from a Jazz Life

Harry Gold
Gold, Doubloons and Pieces of Eight

Forthcoming books about jazz
from Northway

Chris Searle
*Forward Groove: Jazz and the Real World
from Louis Armstrong to Gilad Atzmon*

Derek Ansell's
biography of Hank Mobley

Mike Hennessey's
biography of Johnny Griffin

Peter King's
autobiography

Ron Rubin's
musical limericks

A History of Jazz in Britain 1919–50
Jim Godbolt

revised edition with new illustrations

2005   hardback, £16.99

This book covers the visits of American trail-blazing artists of
the twenties and thirties, their influence on British musicians,
the emergence of specialist magazines, rhythm clubs, discographers and pundits, and the fascinating cloak-and-dagger
plots to defy the Musicians' Union ban.

'As breezy as a riverboat shuffle, ever on the lookout for the
preposterous detail and the opportunity for raffish reminiscence,' *Times Literary Supplement.*

'Enlivened throughout by the author's passion for the music
itself and his sharp eye for human failings,' George Melly.

'If you have not bought this book, I urge you to do so – now!'
Humphrey Lyttelton, BBC *Sounds of Jazz.*

285 pages
ISBN 978-0953704057

www.northwaybooks.com